A Force to Be Reckoned With

A History of the Women's Institute

JANE ROBINSON

virago

VIRAGO

First published in Great Britain in 2011 by Virago Press
This paperback edition published in 2012 by Virago Press

A CIP catalogue record for this book
is available from the British Library.

ISBN 978-1-84408-660-3

Typeset in Dante by M Rules
Printed and bound in Great Britain by
Clays Ltd, St Ives plc

Papers used by Virago are from well-managed forests
and other responsible sources.

MIX
Paper from
responsible sources
FSC® C104740

Virago Press
An imprint of
Little, Brown Book Group
100 Victoria Embankment
London EC4Y 0DY

An Hachette UK Company
www.hachette.co.uk

www.virago.co.uk

For Kathleen James
with love

Contents

A Force to Be
Reckoned With

Introduction

This is a book about defying expectation. The Women's Institute has been described as the most important body formed in the UK during the twentieth century – of men *or* women. It's part of the fabric of our lives; few appreciate just how far its members have been responsible, over the decades, for moulding modern Britain. The WI was the original social network. Politically and religiously it was entirely non-sectarian, entirely inclusive. It also looked beyond its own community, pioneering campaigns to raise awareness of others' needs.

Despite all this, no figure has suffered more grievously from stereotyping than the lady from the WI. There are many Institutes these days in metropolitan areas, professional workplaces or university campuses, yet the image of a violet-scented matron of decided maturity, a bit like a dim Miss Marple, sensibly rather than smartly dressed, favouring harmless (useless?) pursuits like beetle-drives and découpage, lives on. She's right-wing, naturally, and Anglican. The kitchen is her natural domain, in a neat little home in the country. Apart from venturing on mystery coach trips or to national meetings (where she tends towards hot flushes), her compass is comfortingly small, and her life serene. Nothing more is expected of her than to busy herself inoffensively in the background of rural life.

Recently, it's true, the media have sensationalised a fleshly new image, involving naked middle-aged ladies, pole-dancing classes and sex therapy sessions. Thanks to the well-publicised Tony Blair incident, the WI has acquired a reputation among certain journalists for battleaxing and handbagging too. But these are merely different caricatures, just variations on a depressingly frumpy theme. In fact the slow handclap delivered to Mr Blair at the WI's 2000 AGM at Wembley Arena should not have surprised anyone. It was the latest episode in a long tradition of activism, credited in hindsight with marking the turning-point in his premiership: the first sign of Middle England's disillusionment with New Labour.

The Women's Institute Movement in Britain was founded in 1915 by the feistiest women in the country, including suffragettes, academics and passionate social crusaders. Its purpose was to give village women a voice, and the courage to use it in speaking to one another and to the world beyond. Politically – at a time when women still couldn't vote – this was considered unfeasibly radical, but suspicious critics were soothed by an apparent emphasis on domestic and rural accomplishments and a comfortable preoccupation with 'home and country'. Its founders weren't daft: they knew the value of camouflage.

The structure of the WI, involving secret ballots in which everyone took part, gave British women their first practical experience of democracy. Right from the very beginning, as well as being an organisation to encourage creativity and practical skills, it was expressly designed to dissolve the solid hierarchies of class and seniority and to create a level, far-reaching network in which women were educated and given the confidence to speak their minds – just as they would eighty-five years later at Wembley Arena.

The characters involved in the WI's development ranged from shy and isolated young wives to gloriously bossy organisers, inspirational speakers, educational pioneers (several of whom I met when writing my book *Bluestockings*), royals, political agitators, pains in the neck, and some of the most influential – if backstage – players in the establishment of the Welfare State in Britain. Never before has such a disparate group of people come together, worked together, supported one another and got so much done.

All that sounds rather serious, and I must admit that when I first conceived the idea of *A Force to Be Reckoned With* I wasn't expecting to discover (as I later did) a story about the invention of feminism in this country. The personal significance of the WI attracted me initially, and still plays a vital part in the book: the camaraderie of its members, its heritage in art and music, crafts and the spoken word, and a very healthy appetite for silliness (my mother was in the WI – often she came home from meetings with her sides still sore from laughing).

As the Movement approaches its centenary, I wanted to explore its longevity, find out what gave its astonishingly diverse and genial membership such confidence, and how far its progress reflected that of the whole country. I knew it had done great things with evacuees and jam during the Second World War, but wasn't sure what happened in the early years – during the Great Depression, the frugal 1950s, the permissive 60s, the restless 70s, the hard-hearted 80s and so on, up to our own new age of austerity, when we're all being asked to make do and mend once again.

Most of all, being a dedicated shatterer of stereotypes, I wanted to know the truth about a movement described by the writer Edna Healey – with a certain amount of inside knowledge – as possessing 'more combined wisdom, experience and knowledge than exists in all the corridors of power'. I can add to that list: the WI members I've come across – past as well as present – have had more humour, spirit, courage, eccentricity and common sense than any other individuals I've ever written about. And that's saying something.

I

The Beginnings: 1897–1913

*It won't last long without
a man to run it.*[1]

The traffic around Wembley Arena Conference Centre on 7 June 2000 was crazy. The streets of north London wheezed with coaches from all over the country, each one packed with well dressed women fanning themselves in the heat. There were ten thousand in all: a horde of biblical proportions. Those of them who had been to the Annual General Meeting of the Women's Institute before were used to a certain amount of chaos, but things were different this year. There was even more traffic than usual; more policemen; lots of unfeasibly broad-shouldered, twitchy-looking young men in suits scanning the crowds; and an extra buzz rippling along the queues of delegates waiting to be admitted to the building. Cameramen wandered around looking for good vantage points, and an irrepressible air of excitement was shimmering above the crowd like a heat haze. Someone Really Big, it was rumoured, was to be this year's guest speaker.

Annual General Meetings of the Women's Institute are always high-profile affairs. The Movement has earned itself a reputation for forward thinking and for addressing issues which haven't yet become fashionable, but soon will. The year 2000 was no different: the Board of Trustees decided the meeting should concentrate on a 'green agenda'.

Planning had started well in advance. In early 1999 an unexpected phone call was put through to WI headquarters from 10 Downing Street. It was Tessa Jowell, Minister for Women, with a message to the Board of Trustees that the Prime Minister would like to come and address the WI. The Board was a little bewildered at his sudden enthusiasm, but agreed to pencil him in for the 2000 AGM. When nothing more was heard from Downing Street over the next year, the Board assumed the idea had been forgotten; and with a certain sense of relief, given the soapbox tendencies of other politicians who have addressed past AGMs, they got on with other things. But in February 2000 Ms Jowell rang again, checking that all was still well for Mr Blair's visit in June.

With admirable sangfroid the Chairman of the WI, Helen Carey, replied that actually plans had already been made, speakers booked, and agendas fixed for the meeting; she had frankly forgotten all about that initial phone call ages ago, and if it was all the same to Mr Blair she would rather he came another time. There was to be no arguing, however, and Mrs Carey was quickly summoned to No. 10 to discuss with ministerial advisers what Mr Blair intended to say.

The WI always makes clear to its speakers that theirs is not a party-political organisation. It wasn't when it was first established, and it isn't now. Its (ideal) members have a duty to themselves to be politically aware and committed to public affairs, but both individually and collectively, political affiliation is not relevant. Party politics are too divisive, too distracting – and in the early days were thought too taxing. Anyone expecting to address the WI at any level – including the Prime Minister – is explicitly warned to avoid them altogether. The Board agreed to Tony Blair's request to speak on the clear understanding that he would do so in his capacity as the elected leader of the country's government, not as a party leader. Fine, said Downing Street; no problem.

Mr Blair had just returned from paternity leave after the birth of his son Leo. This would be his first public speech. Helen Carey explained to his office the ecological theme of the AGM, and assumed he'd be pleased to be associated with such a progressive topic. Ask him to speak on the sort of world he would like for baby Leo, she suggested, and to let us know how the WI can help sustain that world. And remember, she added, that we are intelligent women. There will be ten thousand committed members there from constituencies all over England and Wales: don't patronise us. And please, don't be late. We have a full programme on 7 June, and mustn't keep anyone waiting.

Tony Blair had requested an autocue for his speech, which the WI declined to provide on the grounds of expense. Perhaps that's why he looked so nervous, thought Helen Carey, as she welcomed him on to the stage. He was twenty minutes late, which had made the audience fidget and whisper, and irritated the Board of Trustees. Having been told proudly by Tessa Jowell that Mr Blair's speech was 'really good' and that he'd written it himself, Mrs Carey introduced him with a hopeful reminder of what he was supposed to say, and an encouraging smile. Once he had delivered the obligatory jokes about being terrified of massed women and had expressed the hope that he was suitably dressed – the word 'dressed' was appropriate in light of the exploits of the 'Calendar Girls' (the original calendar had been released the previous year) – the Prime Minister launched into his speech.

After ten minutes, it was clear something was awry. The audience was muttering, the Board members were staring at their hands, and Mr Blair himself was beginning – as someone whispered to a neighbour on the platform – to 'lose the plot'. He had not mentioned the green agenda at all; he spoke instead about Labour initiatives, interest rates and National Health Service reform. Lacking his autocue, he kept turning away from the microphone, so that at times the WI's noise levels were louder than his voice. As he continued relentlessly with what was amounting to a party-political broadcast, women began to leave, while others started a slow handclap.

The atmosphere by now was a febrile mixture of embarrassment, anxiety and anger; and still Mr Blair kept going, his voice gradually rising in pitch until he was almost squeaking. His face, projected on big screens around the arena, grew wild-eyed and panicky. He paused occasionally, unable to ride the noise, and once Mrs Carey interrupted him with a desperate plea for courtesy on the part of the WI, but in the end Mr Blair spoke for over forty minutes. 'I'm glad we're having a good debate,' he offered, before sinking to his seat like a stone.

Mrs Carey rose to thank her guest. 'We always like to give our speakers something to take away with them,' she said with the sweetest of smiles. The relief on Mr Blair's face was clear. Something for Leo, crocheted in an obscure Rutland parish, perhaps, or a pot of superior jam for Cherie? Mrs Carey continued, 'So we've planned a petition signed by thousands of our members against the closing of local Post Offices.'

Not since Edith Rigby lobbed a bomb at Winston Churchill had a WI member so rattled a prominent politician.[2] Alastair Campbell's bus-loads of reporters swarmed through the building at lunchtime; the television cameras rolled, the excitement mounted, and by next morning the Women's Institute's collective 'handbagging' of the British Prime Minister had become international front-page news. History is currently of the opinion that the 2000 WI Annual General Meeting marked a turning-point in the fortunes of Tony Blair's premiership. From then on, the Labour message was met with a measure of disillusionment and mistrust; the spin machine engineered by Mr Campbell was brought under scrutiny, and Mr Blair himself, after such a public display of unprofessionalism, trod more warily.

The fortunes of the WI also changed. They swapped one image – the wholesome old 'Jam and Jerusalem' one – for another scarcely more fortunate. Now they were all strident handbaggers, even more frightening en masse than Mr Blair, in his pre-speech quip, had imagined. This bothered the Board of Trustees, but didn't worry two elderly Yorkshire women overheard in the queue for lunch that day. Bristling, one of them said to the other in the broadest of moorland accents, 'Who the hell does he think he is?' 'Aye,' replied her companion proudly. 'You don't mess about with the WI!'

I wasn't in that lunch queue myself. I wasn't even a member of the WI. But I would have recognised those two women easily: they were just the sort of characters who peopled my mother's WI meetings, north of York, in the late 1960s. I used to go with her occasionally, with a bag of peardrops and a book, when there was no one at home to baby-sit. I remember being unimpressed by the fifteen or twenty familiar faces there who talked and drank tea. Why, I wondered, didn't they just do that at home? Or go to a café instead, for a treat?

I was missing the point, of course – as people still do. It wasn't just talking. Sometimes they chatted, as any friends and neighbours will, to catch up; then someone spoke and the others listened; little discussions would break out in an orderly fashion, and then they would do something: act out a scene from a play, perhaps, or work on an embroidery together. Everything stopped for tea, which was served with great aplomb. There was a pattern to the evening, and a sense of purpose and achievement that was somehow invigorating, yet difficult to define.

I didn't appreciate it then, as I turned the increasingly sticky pages of my book, but this is how WI meetings have been since the very beginning. The official record of the first WI meeting in the world described a simple, explicit structure with space for business, education, creativity and debate. It had a sturdy, capacious agenda which encouraged members to express themselves without inhibition, within that structure. They didn't have to worry about procedure (that was firmly in place), about precedence (it didn't exist), or what their husbands might think of them (men weren't allowed). There was no sense of guilt involved, as there might be in a religious organisation; no imposition of opinions or even moral values; no obligation to contribute or proselytise. Just a sense of security, mutual support, and opportunity for everyone there.

That was the ideal.

Astonishingly – given the novelty of the concept of the WI when it was founded, the undeniable dreariness of its name, and the fact that hardly anything about the structure of its meetings has changed over the decades – that ideal has lasted in practice ever since. I suppose it's because the WI as a movement has neither challenged nor threatened received wisdom about women in this country (only subverted it, as we shall see, with a great deal of tact, steely conviction and – when necessary – a smile). Its meetings have always been infinitely accommodating, a haven yet never a refuge, and a place for people and ideas to flourish. That is why it's survived, and constantly renews.

That, and the tea – the best bit of the meeting by far, according to my childhood memory (I loved the shop-bought biscuits). Blood is thicker than water, but a good cup of WI tea is thicker still. The Movement's founders appreciated this unassailable fact of life, stipulating that whatever else an Institute decided to include, or not, in its monthly programme, everyone *must* share a cup of tea. It was sacramental. It bound people together, especially if the officers at the committee table could be persuaded to come down and join the ordinary members for a gossip, as most (but not all) quite easily could.

The women in this book prove how life-changing the opportunities and possibilities created by the WI turned out to be, both personally and for the society in which its members lived. Think of the Calendar Girls, for example, who set out to cheer up a friend and raise money in her husband's name, then became global celebrities responsible for raising over £3 million for medical research. Theirs is perhaps the highest-profile WI success story of all, but there are countless others throughout the history of the organisation, just as moving and empowering.

It was a bereaved mother, aged forty, who first had the modest yet radical idea of setting up regular meetings for ordinary women to get together, with their husbands' permission, in people's front parlours, kitchens, or even the garden shed, to talk about things that mattered – and consequently to change the world. Her name was Adelaide Hoodless. Although it's assumed to be the most British of institutions, the WI was formed not in the tweedy shires of England but in the backwoods of Canada. Its earliest members may have been of British or Irish stock, a generation or two removed from the emigrant pioneers who settled the Dominion, but its nature was influenced entirely by the exigencies of Canadian life.

Addie Hoodless was the ideal WI woman – before the Institute was even invented – being passionate, intelligent, and damned determined to succeed. She was a farmer's daughter of Irish descent, born near St George, west of Toronto, in 1857.[3] After a basic local education, she married a prominent Conservative businessman (being and remaining a staunch Liberal herself) and moved to the fruit-growing area of Hamilton in 1881. There, some fifty kilometres west of Niagara Falls, four children were born and the youngest, John Harold Hoodless, died. He contracted a common infection known locally as 'summer complaint' through drinking contaminated milk, and perished at the age of fourteen months. In those days, 20 per cent of all Canadian children died before their fifth birthdays;[4] Addie was convinced this was due to the ignorance of their mothers who, like her, knew nothing of the science of hygiene. The Hoodless family's milk was delivered in an open churn, having collected God knew what sort of impurities on its way from the milking shed to their door. If only Addie – and the dairy farmer's wife – had known how to handle milk safely, John's and hundreds of other infants' lives might have been saved. Education was the key.

This was the first of Addie's crusades: a thorough, practical training for girls in the things that really mattered. Intellectual attainment was of no interest to her. Academic ambitions were vain, and the fight for emancipation spurious. Women should embrace the family, and use what domestic influence they had to forge a better world. 'No higher vocation has been, or ever will be, given to woman,' she claimed, 'than that of Home-maker and Citizen Builder.' The hand that rocks the cradle rules the world.

It was thanks to Addie's dogged determination that domestic science became a respected part of the state school curriculum in Ontario, and that dedicated teacher-training facil-ities were established. She was a persuasive and prolific public speaker (dropping the childhood diminutive of her name as her profile rose); the success of her campaign depended on an abil-ity to convince her audiences of her own common sense, and enthuse them to join her in fitting girls for their future role as the mothers of a sturdier nation.

In December 1896 Adelaide was invited to address a meeting at the Ontario Agricultural College in Guelph. The Secretary of a farmers' institute near Hamilton, Mr Erland Lee, was so impressed by her performance that he booked her for the next Ladies' Night at his institute, to be held in the settlement of Stoney Creek the following February. Not everyone at the institute was happy to have a lady speaker, but Lee prevailed. Thirty-five wives were present when Adelaide arrived at Stoney Creek on 12 February, to speak to the mixed audience on the importance of domestic science education for girls. And not just girls: given her audience, Adelaide pointed out that homecraft was something women of all ages could benefit from studying. She sympathised with the boredom and drudgery of life at home on a farm – where she spent her own childhood – and then made a suggestion. Why not form a sister organisation to the Farmers' Institute? A sort of local club where women could meet and learn from speakers, and each other, not about the husbandry of stock and crops like the men, but about how to be most useful at home? Erland Lee asked for a show of hands as an indication of interest in this imaginative idea. Thirty-five arms went up, and a meeting was immediately called for the next week. Naturally, Adelaide was invited.

On the evening of Friday 19 February, 101 women and Mr Lee turned up in a storm at Squire's Hall in Stoney Creek to found the Women's Institute. Lee and his wife Janet, a kindergarten teacher, had been busy canvassing during the past week for potential members, all of whom climbed the rickety outside stairs to the upper floor of the hall, clutching at their hats in a strengthening wind. When Adelaide arrived, driven the short distance from Hamilton by her thirteen-year-old son Joseph (the carriage drawn by Scotty, her favourite horse), the business began. A name was chosen for the organisation: the Women's Department of the Farmers' Institute of South Wentworth; and a committee was appointed with Adelaide at its head as Honorary Chairman. Her address this time was a little more trenchant, railing against the incompetency of a local professor of bacteriology who insisted on ignoring women's need for scientific education, and explaining how much more significant women's work (raising a family) was than men's (growing nice apples).

At the next meeting a week later, a nimbler name was suggested for the WDFISW – the Women's Institute of Saltfleet Township – and a constitution discussed (including time for tea). Janet Lee transcribed the constitution at her dining-room table.

If the homely, very feminine Mrs Hoodless was the figurehead of this new enterprise, then Janet Lee, thoughtful and wise, was its engine. The aims of the Institute were

> to promote that knowledge of Household Science which shall lead to improvement in household architecture with special attention to home sanitation; to a better understanding of the economic and hygienic value of foods and fuels, and to a more scientific care of children with a view to raising the general standard of the health of our people.[5]

The Institute's interests would be divided into six branches: 'Domestic Economy; Architecture with special references to Sanitation, Light, Heat, etc.; Physiology, Hygiene, Medicine, Calisthenics, etc.; Floriculture and Horticulture; Music and Art; Literature and Sociology, Education and Legislation'. Membership was open to 'all women who will take an active interest'; subscription was set at 25 cents, and meetings were to be held fortnightly, on Thursday afternoons at two o'clock.

This first Women's Institute later changed its name again, from Saltfleet Township to Stoney Creek, and it flourished despite the cynicism of the Farmers' Institute, who shook their heads, tutted, and prophesied doom. A second WI was established in Ontario, at Whitby in June 1899, then another in Kemble in 1900, after a talk to the Farmers' Institute there by a female speaker provocatively entitled 'Man Works from Sun to Sun, but a Woman's Work is Never Done'.[6] That year, the government of Ontario promised an annual grant of $10 to each Women's Institute formed, and to distribute any useful literature on request. It was a canny decision, and the first sign of a mutually expedient relationship between the Women's Institute

Movement and the political Establishment that has continued (although Mr Blair might disagree) to this day.

The financial support meant that Institute members were being officially subsidised to improve their own lives, and those of their families. It was in a nation's interest that its citizens, even the female ones, should feel happy and fulfilled. But no matter how earnestly the educational aims of the organisation were publicised, the greatest attraction for much of its ordinary membership was what was later described, with rather saccharine jolliness, as 'fun and friendship'. Belonging to the WI meant having someone to talk to for hundreds of isolated women, one of whom, a dairy-maid, complained that no one knew loneliness like a woman working on a farm. Women's work was usually solitary, while the men laboured together in the fields or conducted their business in town; 'for the likes of me,' she said, 'there's never a body to speak to. Men don't understand.'[7]

Adelaide Hoodless supported the WI for the rest of her life, dying on the speaker's platform at a meeting of a Toronto women's club in 1910. She was a natural crusader. As well as evangelising for home economics education for girls and establishing the Macdonald Institute for Domestic Science at the University of Guelph, Adelaide played an important part in other women's organisations in Canada (the YWCA and the National Council of Women), belying occasional claims as she grew older that her outlook was naive or reactionary. She also collaborated with Lady Aberdeen, the British Governor-General's wife, in setting up the Victorian Order of Nurses, who pioneered health services for upcountry women and children living far from any surgery or hospital. None of these things was done out of idealism, because they were somehow beautiful concepts, for Adelaide was the essential pragmatist. Her intention was simply to leave the world cleaner and tidier than she found it, and educate others to do the same.

Lady Aberdeen left Government House in Toronto for home in 1898, after five years' residence. In June the following year she met Mrs Hoodless again, when Adelaide travelled to London as Canadian delegate to the International Congress of the Council of Women at Westminster Town Hall. There she spoke on 'technical education' for girls – an even more euphemistic name for housework than 'domestic science' – and mentioned, in passing, the Women's Institutes.

> I was able to tell the Englishwomen that the organisation had been recognised by the Government as of value to the State. It was astonishing how this organisation appealed to the old country people [her British audience]. I was deluged with enquiries, even from such important leaders of the agricultural movement as Lady Warwick. At that conference I heard reports from many nations and not one reported such an organisation for women in the rural districts as the Women's Institutes of Ontario. So you see [we] are truly pioneers in this great movement.[8]

It is puzzling that no one, including Lady Aberdeen, appears to have noticed this deluge of enquiries (if it existed) or done anything about forming a similar organisation in Britain. Perhaps Adelaide Hoodless's personality had something to do with it. She was a single-minded woman and something of a visionary, but she limited her scope to better home-making and refused to recognise the need for women to achieve in the world beyond the kitchen sink. Also, Stoney Creek may have been thriving when Lady Aberdeen left Canada in 1898, but at that stage the Women's Institute was still experimental, and its ambitions somewhat eccentric.

Anyway, there already was a Women's Institute in England. Lady Aberdeen was one of its members.

Coincidentally, this one had also been founded in 1897, but with a very different membership and mission from the Stoney Creek WI – and its name was *never* abbreviated. Its instigator was Mrs Nora Wynford Philipps, a suffragist and keen campaigner for equal opportunities for professional women in the workplace. Its first meeting was reported in *The Times*, where its object was described as 'to afford a meeting-place and a centre of information for the convenience of women engaged in all departments of public and professional work, in science, literature, art and domestic life'.[9] Most of those involved in its inception were males; indeed, the whole idea sounds a little like a classy female equivalent of a gentlemen's club. Its headquarters in Mayfair were furnished with a library and other 'fitting accessories', with facilities for 'recreation, education, and information' for undistressed gentlewomen who chose to work for a living, for their own satisfaction or for the benefit of others. It was far more of a ladies' institute than a women's one.

It boasted a full programme of edifying talks by various distinguished speakers, advertised in the Court Circular pages of *The Times* as 'drawing-room meetings'. Subjects ranged from arts and crafts (including a musical soirée with the Ranee of Sarawak), through female education and careers, to 'unprotected women' and 'the customs of other countries'. Here the lines of distinction between this Women's Institute and our more familiar one begin to blur. Current affairs were discussed, along with the desirability of eugenics (*very* desirable), 'women and the rural exodus', penal reform, and various government bills affecting women. Despite a lively interest in matters of the day, the institute declared itself formed on 'strictly non-party lines'. Refreshments were available at meetings, with a choice of tea, coffee, mineral water or a fortifying cup of Bovril.

The similarities continue. The institute allied itself with other organisations – not just the National Council of Women, but the Educational Flower Show and Rural Educational Union, for example, founded by Lady Warwick in 1901. Lady Warwick was one of the VIPs Adelaide Hoodless was so pleased to spot among her supporters at the International Council Congress; perhaps Adelaide wasn't aware then of her notoriety. Frances Greville, Countess of Warwick (1861–1938), was known to everyone as Daisy (celebrated in the song 'Daisy, Daisy, Give Me Your Answer, Do'); she was an indefatigable socialite and the mistress, serially or concurrently, of several important gentlemen, inevitably including the Prince of Wales, or 'Edward the Caresser'. She also happened to be passionate about the unwontedly demure arts of needlework, gardening and natural history. Something of a philanthropist, Daisy opened a school for needlework on her estate in Essex, and a hostel for women students of agriculture at Reading College (which later became the university) in 1898. Once her elaborate and scandalous life as a courtesan had run its course, she turned to socialism, and bought Studley Castle in Warwickshire with the intention of turning it into an agricultural college exclusively for women. All this was in the future when Adelaide met her; then, she was merely one of London society's most extravagant players.

In 1915, before the first British WI came into being, an extraordinary event was organised under the auspices of Lady

Aberdeen's Women's Institute, involving a display of 'what women have done and can do in agriculture'. It was held in the gardens of a resplendent private house in Carlton Terrace. There were demonstrations of butter-churning and milking, while hens, goats, carthorses and a cow wandered neatly around, all in view of Buckingham Palace, and the hostess and her daughter explained what was going on. The house belonged to Lady Cowdray; her daughter was Lady Gertrude Denman, later to become the nearest secular equivalent to a patron saint the WI has ever had.

By this time, just to confuse matters (and endorse my point about the uninspired name), there was yet another Women's Institute movement flourishing in London, established in 1913. These urban institutes were essentially centres for adult education, administered by London County Council (the LCC) and run in tandem with working men's institutes (again, educational rather than the social kind) expressly 'for the benefit of poorer inhabitants'. There were thirty of them. None was anywhere near the plumply prosperous streets of Mayfair and Westminster; instead they were based in the riskier neighbourhoods of Hackney, Deptford, Brixton, Borough and Battersea.

Classes were offered to women at 2s a course (subsidised, if necessary), in 'domestic and health subjects' as well as 'Odd Jobs' including repairing door fittings and fastenings, stopping leaks in washers, screwing on castors, soldering metal instruments, cleaning gas fittings and stopping gas escapes, hanging pictures, repairing string bags, and even recharging electric batteries. The Odd Job classes were offered in 1915, to equip women whose handy menfolk were away fighting, but few of the skills they covered would be unfamiliar to members of our present WI. Nor would be an enterprise involving the LCC institutes held (bizarrely) at the Prince's Skating Club in Knightsbridge, London, in the summer of 1916. This was a 'National Economy Exhibition', visited by the Queen and displaying exhibits by students of the institutes – duplicated at hundreds of WI shows over the years ever since – on cookery, crafts, bee-, poultry- and rabbit-keeping, making do and mending, home hygiene and domestic architecture and design. There was even a competition for the best-cooked potato or cabbage, announced by the Mayor of London, who sensationally declared he would turn vegetarian if the prize-winners were tempting enough. Apparently, they weren't.

Both of these alternative Women's Institutes were urban affairs, despite any political or practical interest they may have had in traditionally rural pursuits. Yet each played its part in preparing the ground for Adelaide Hoodless's movement to take root in Britain when the time was right. Other factors helped. One was the radical Women's Co-operative Guild (WCG), founded in 1883 to encourage social reform and political awareness among its members, the majority of whom were working-class housewives, including farmers' wives.

The WCG had a reputation for activism, but that was nothing new among working women, even then. In England in 1795 bread riots had taken place, when a series of poor harvests and costly wars left stocks of wheat low and prices cripplingly high. The same year saw 'the revolt of the housewives', a series of insurgencies organised by local women not only to protest about the lack of affordable food, but to do something about it. In Aylesbury, Buckinghamshire, a 'numerous mob, consisting chiefly of women', seized all the wheat coming into the town one market-day in March after a difficult winter, and held it hostage, forcing farmers to accept only what the women could afford to pay for it instead of the inflated price demanded by the government. It was then evenly distributed to everyone in need. The same sort of thing happened in Bath, except there the housewives impounded a ship about to export English grain (while lustily singing 'God Save the King') and kept its cargo for the community. In Carlisle in the north-west of England, the women protesters went so far as to set up a distribution committee (very WI) after stockpiling their captured wheat in the Public Hall.

On the only occasion during this housewives' revolt when things seem to have got out of hand and turned ugly – in Chudleigh, Devon, where two flour mills were destroyed – it transpired that the rioters weren't women at all, but great burly men in dresses, trying to take advantage of the spirit of the age.[10]

The campaign for university education helped beckon the WI into being. When the first English university allowed women degrees in 1878, it was a triumph not only for the students involved but for those men and women who had worked behind the scenes for years so determinedly, and with such tact and sensitivity, to make it happen. Between them they introduced the concept of female high achievers and of a woman's right to widen her horizons, without which the WI could never have flourished as it did (indeed, some of the WI's most influential champions in Britain were also pioneers of university education themselves).

It wasn't just academic achievement that mattered in this respect: hand in hand with that campaign went a less spectacular attempt to widen access to more practical, vocational careers for women. Lady Warwick opened her agricultural college for women at Studley in 1903; those preferring to study horticulture could do so from 1901 at Kew Gardens, or at Swanley College in Kent, which catered exclusively for women from 1903. Nurses had been trained at St Thomas's in London since 1860, and women doctors at the Royal Free Hospital since 1877. Isabella Beeton had been teaching her readers about the business of household management for decades, and Norland College, opened in 1892, made a profession out of childcare. All of these initiatives relied on ambition.

The political climate of the late Victorian and Edwardian eras was surprisingly kind to the formation of the WI. Ever since the 1850s the government had discussed the problem of the nation's inconvenient 'super-abundance of females'. Articles in the press warned that the balance of the sexes had grown so unequal (thanks to men being away empire-building) that our 'free and glorious constitution' was in peril of being 'eaten up with women' and reduced to nothing by a petticoat government.[11] How were these swarms of England's daughters to be controlled?

One solution was to encourage them to emigrate, and off went some to Ontario; another was to find ways of distracting them from misrule and occupying them usefully. University was fine as long as it didn't lead to an infiltration of the professions – which of course it didn't, on the whole, until after the First World War. What the leisured classes really needed (thought the Establishment) was worthwhile work for worthy ladies, not a glut of redundant bluestockings. Institutional do-gooding was preferable to academic dabbling – or, worse still, agitating for the Vote – which explains the plethora of charitable societies set up in Britain during the latter half of the nineteenth century.

These embraced a bewilderingly specific array of victims, ranging from Respectable Female Lunatics to Deserted and Destitute Children, the Aged Poor, Fallen Women, imperilled Watercress and Flower Girls, and Poor People who need Trusses. All of them offered the chance for middle-class wives and spinsters to pass their time profitably.

What the working classes needed, conversely, was worthwhile leisure time. Drudgery induced discontent as much as did idleness, hence the formation of the London County Council institutes, and a drive outside the cities to encourage women to look for constructive opportunities to use skill and enterprise, and foster some comfortable kind of fellowship or sisterhood. Edwin Pratt, the author of a widely read study of agriculture published in 1904, quoted research proving that 'more women in the country[side] go insane than in any other class in the community. This is not so much from overwork, but because of the monotony of women's work on the farm.'[12] He went on to recommend an organisation he'd recently come across near Hamilton, Ontario: the Women's Institute. He added how crucial it was to remember that women's lives are made of 'little things', and if you can make them proud of these little things (cooking a meal, cleaning a room, washing clothes, keeping chickens), if you can develop a culture of vocation and shared achievement, not only will the home prosper but so will the nation.

That same year, 1904, a Government Committee on Physical Degeneration was set up in the wake of the Second Boer War (1899–1902). Those who volunteered to fight, especially from the cities, had been found to be shockingly puny and ill-nourished; they were obviously the wrong 'type' (eugenics being an increasingly popular study, as the talks at Lady Aberdeen's

Institute suggest). Unless things changed, there was a danger that the next generation of British soldiers would be unfit for duty. Their mothers needed educating about wholesome nutrition and about the benefits of healthy minds in healthy bodies. Agriculturalists like Pratt recognised this, just as Adelaide Hoodless and the government of Ontario had done.

An editorial in *The Times* in April 1904 mentioned the Canadian Women's Institutes as a stimulating and fruitful means of promoting agricultural efficiency in the countryside, but it does make them sound rather clinical and dull. A better (though slightly sickly) account appeared a few years later, in an article describing a visit by the paper's correspondent to a Canadian farm. There he's entertained by a charming, cheerful housewife who prepares him (and thirteen other diners) a feast of turkey, steak-and-kidney pie, potatoes, stewed tomatoes and corn. They all demolish a mince pie, an apple pie and a 'monstrous deep' plum pie, with peaches and cream, for pudding. Everything, of course, is home-produced.

After dinner he's invited to visit the cellar, where the farmer's wife stores her treasures. There he finds shelf upon shelf of glass jars, glowing like jewels and each containing some triumph of home preserving.

The ordinary jams and preserved fruits are there, as a matter of course; but there are also such marvels as tomato butter and celery relish, 'rummage pickle' and chutney, and pear marmalade flavoured with ginger. These things cannot be described – they must be eaten before they can be imagined . . .

To be a good housewife is a high ambition; no other kind of philanthropy has such powerful and elevating effects, or so well repays the genial tact and quiet energy that a wise house-wife puts into the home management. I am not thinking only, or even chiefly, of cookery. Someone has said that 'the way to a man's heart is through his stomach'; but it is only one of many ways, and by no means the surest.[13]

Once a fortnight or so, off trots this paragon of a farmer's wife to her Institute. Women's Institutes are, says the *Times* man, a delightful movement for 'the all-round improvement of home life'. There are 'hundreds' of them in Ontario (in fact about two hundred by now), where isolated housewives meet and exchange ideas with each other or 'rub shoulders and rub wits', as he inelegantly puts it.

'It used to be very different,' one of these ladies said to me. 'For instance, if we knew how to make an extra nice cake we used to keep the recipe a secret to ourselves; we didn't want anyone else to know how to do it. Now, if we know a good thing, we pass it on ... We women can talk, nobody denies that,' said the lady with a smile, 'but too often, even if we've got something worth talking about, we haven't got enough knowledge to make what we say worth saying. And we are apt to take rather narrow views of things. The Institute is really broadening our minds.'[14]

To reinforce what this obliging WI member is telling him, the reporter mentions some of the talks she's recently enjoyed: 'The Duties of the Daughter in the Home'; 'Economy in Small Things'; 'Patriotism'; 'Ten Books Every One Should Read'; 'Labour-Saving Appliances for the Housekeeper'; 'Simple Meals, Well Cooked and Nicely Served'; 'The Prevention of

Tuberculosis'; and, remembering little John Harold Hoodless, 'The Care and Handling of Milk'.

The time was surely right, when this article was published in 1911, for the WI to flourish in Britain. Adelaide Hoodless had been a passionate evangelist on her visit to London in 1899; Lady Aberdeen's vision and influence were undeniable; other societies and enterprises had created useful precedents; and the political climate was beginning to recognise at last that the needs of women of all classes merited closer attention.

Soon, missionaries would arrive from Canada to spread the word, the chief among whom was a formidable WI member called Madge Watt. Madge reached London in 1913, committed to establishing the Movement in the Old Country. She thought the task would be easy. It wasn't.

2

Taking Root: 1913–1918

Please bring a husband –
or a friend.[1]

The trouble with Madge Watt, according to those she tried to enlist as WI pioneers in Britain, was her bloody-mindedness. The trouble with *them*, according to Madge, was their frustrating Britishness (in other words, their bloody-mindedness). They weren't used to being told what to do by a colonial; no Institute since has ever sat back at a meeting and been dictated to, unquestioning, by anyone. It's the very nature of the WI that social and intellectual hierarchies cannot exist (ostensibly, at least) within its constitution; Madge Watt preached this gospel herself, but with an implicit assumption that she was somehow exempt.

Madge was described as autocratic, impatient and overbearing. But she had unique qualities too, and shouldn't be judged too harshly in the light of the challenges she faced in trying to establish her beloved WI in Britain. She couldn't begin to understand how women here seemed at once so independent (or intractable) in refusing to be told what to do, yet so slavishly bound by the class system. The story of an early WI organiser illustrates the conundrum well. This organiser is trying to set up a new Institute in a village she wisely fictionalises:

[The Chairwoman is full of agitation, which she does her best to communicate to the organiser.]

'We can't have Mrs Henn and Mrs Pullett on the committee together. It is well known that as fast as one walks into the room the other walks out.

'We must elect Mrs Wyandotte. She'll be so hurt if we don't. Shall I just go round and tell them all that they must vote for Mrs Wyandotte?

'Lady Rock will have to be President of course. It's rather a pity that she spends half the year abroad and [is] in London the rest of the time, but of course she's the one to be President . . .

'We can't have Mrs Barnshaw of the butcher's shop on the committee. Quite impossible. You must take her off again.'

'Why?'

'She's a Bolshevik,' says the Chairwoman, whose political sympathies obviously lie in the opposite direction . . . 'She doesn't hold with the King . . .'

I am sorry to hear this, but explain that I can do nothing about it and that Mrs Barnshaw having been duly elected must be welcomed by the rest of the committee as cordially as if her views were more orthodox.[2]

Madge would not have found this in the least amusing.

Madge – or Margaret Rose Robertson Watt (1868–1948) – was an intriguing woman. It is not quite accurate to say that she was entirely responsible for establishing the WI in Britain: sparks of interest were already sputtering in parts of England and Wales when she arrived in 1913. But it was she who helped coax them into flame, and then a blaze that went on to consume the whole country. She looms disproportionately large (given her squat and unromantic figure, like a cartoon Queen Victoria) over the first few years of the Movement's development, and is undoubtedly one of its most significant figures.

Like Addie Hoodless, Madge was born in Ontario, but the two had dissimilar upbringings. Madge's parents were enlightened educationalists and allowed their academic daughter to enrol at the University of Toronto, where she took a Humanities degree in 1890. She dabbled in journalism while still a student, and on leaving Toronto wrote professionally for various periodicals in Canada and New York. Her authorial voice was easy to recognise, being an intriguing conflation of New Woman and old-fashioned Angel in the House. Her career demonstrated how progressive she was, and what a feisty role model for the fresh-faced daughters of a new nation like Canada. But she never missed a chance to extol the qualities of femininity that Adelaide Hoodless valued so highly in her countrywomen, sharing her friend's conviction that 'a nation cannot rise above the level of its homes; therefore we women must work and study together to raise our homes to the highest possible level'.[3]

In 1893 Madge married Dr Alfred Tennyson Watt, whom she'd met at university, and promptly became a home-maker and nation-builder herself. A son was born in 1896, and when Dr Watt was posted to British Columbia (BC) a year later, Madge settled down in a pleasant house just outside Victoria, to raise the family and ornament the local community. She was a founder member of the first Women's Institute in BC and became a WI lecturer and organiser in 1907, a year after the birth of her second son. In 1911 she was appointed (very grandly) Secretary to the Advisory Board of Women to the Department of Agriculture of British Columbia, and her career in journalism came to an end. She was too busy to write. Not too busy, however, to accept a distinguished position as the first female Senate member of her old university in 1912. Life was good: Madge had two bright sons, a professional husband, recognition and respect in social and intellectual circles, a stout heart and a strong constitution.

Then, in the summer of 1913, Alfred Watt died. Worse than that: he committed suicide while being investigated by a Commission of Inquiry for professional misconduct. The stress of the inquiry triggered in him an episode of profound depression – euphemistically labelled 'neurasthenia' at the time – culminating in his stepping from the window of the upper-floor hospital room where he was being treated in Vancouver. The implications for poor Madge were terrible: not only was she now a widow with two children of seven and thirteen, but her husband had died in scandalous and dishonourable circumstances (even though he was posthumously exonerated from all charges). For all her strength and self-confidence, she couldn't stay in Canada.[4]

When Madge arrived in Britain later that same year, she explained to anyone interested that she had come to educate her fatherless boys. The best schools (she was led to believe) were English public schools, and while Robin and Sholto went off as boarders she threw herself into a new life's mission. It was her intention, she said, to transplant the WI from Canada to the Motherland, where she had no doubt it would flourish famously.

Omens were good. The British government's Board of Agriculture had been in existence since 1889, and an Agricultural Organisation Society (AOS) was founded in 1901 expressly to encourage self-help and mutual cooperation in the farming community. The AOS stood for 'the Three Betters': 'better farming, better business, and better living'. The Irish reformer Horace Plunkett, one of its founders, envisaged women playing their part in the 'better living' department and felt (radically) that they deserved the opportunity to find a collective voice to express their wishes and concerns. The best help, insisted Plunkett, is self-help – and so in 1910 the Society of United Irishwomen was born. It was as close to the WI as it was possible to get without sharing the name itself, and was based not only on the precepts of Hoodless's Institutes in Canada but on the American 'Granges', where farmers' wives joined their husbands in social, cooperative and educational clubs. Similar organisations existed in Scandinavia, Belgium and Germany.

Someone had tried to establish something very like the Canadian WIs in England already. He was John Nugent Harris, General Secretary of the AOS, an engaging man with an energetic wife well known for her wicked sense of humour and glass eye. Convinced the way to a country's heart was through its women, he took himself to various branch meetings of the AOS to recommend they be involved in the organisation's future plans. Bearing in mind Plunkett's maxim on self-help, he advised it might be best if women could organise that involvement themselves, just as they had in Canada.

Nugent Harris's idea – shared later, and independently, by Madge Watt – was first to invite wives and daughters to farmers' AOS meetings (as Erland Lee had done in Ontario), and then encourage them to articulate what they would like from a similar organisation for themselves. Getting countrywomen to come to any meeting, however, was almost impossible, and here's where that bloody-mindedness kicked in. Perhaps 'obstinate passivity' would be a more polite term. It was no longer the era of females being better seen and not heard, but it was definitely undesirable to converse with someone without being formally introduced, and you didn't speak to your 'betters' without being spoken to first.

Women knew their place in terms of class and gender, and, judging by the reaction to some of Nugent Harris's early attempts to tempt them out of it, they were damned well going to stay there. In an article dated 1919, the writer Elizabeth Robins explained that problems were inevitable when trying to establish such a radical movement as this among the section of society – rural women – 'most difficult to organise, and least conscious of the need for organisation'.[5] Proud countrywomen had worked alone for generations; keeping themselves to themselves had always been considered a virtue. The task before the infant WI was to get such women to admit how lonely and dull keeping yourself to yourself can be, and so give the lie to their pride.

They weren't exactly encouraged by the community to do so. At one of the villages Nugent Harris visited, the vicar operated a curfew for the women of his parish, forbidding them out after dark. Another worthy gentleman considered it too dangerous to enlighten women in any way, drawing an analogy, appropriately enough, from the farmyard:

Suppose that some friend of humanity were to attempt to improve the condition of the beasts of the field – to teach the horse his power, and the cow her value – would he be that tractable and useful animal he is, would she be so profuse of her treasures to a hapless infant? Could anything be more impolitic?[6]

Even if you should somehow manage to muster a handful of local women to an AOS meeting, said an exasperated Nugent Harris, all they will do is sit, mouths clamped like oysters, glancing apprehensively at the men. They won't speak for fear of being laughed at; they *can't* speak without their husband's permission, and that's unlikely to be granted while the prevailing attitude is one of withering incredulity – 'Clubs for educating women? Well I'm damned! What is the world coming to?'[7]

Madge tried the same approach when she arrived in 1913. Too proud to go for help to Nugent Harris at the AOS, to whom she had a letter of introduction, she sent herself out to as many women's meetings, or meetings with an agricultural bent, as she could find. No one appeared the least bit interested in hearing about 'Home-makers in British Columbia', or this risky-sounding 'Women's Institute Movement'; the class system so inveterate, still, in British society was something she had reckoned without. Canada was refreshingly free of it, but the Old Country was astonishingly feudal, it seemed to Madge. An implacable upstairs–downstairs attitude divided the Big House from its dependants, and nothing could be done in the village, apparently, without the explicit permission and patronage of the Squire and his lady. Besides, the Church community thought itself well catered for by the Mothers' Union or various denominational groups, and anyone with political tendencies could join the Tory Primrose League or, if they must, a suffrage society. The concept of women coming together across social, religious and political divides was incomprehensible. After a couple of years trying, Madge admitted she was close to defeat. 'I was so disgusted at the way my appeals to start Women's Institutes in England were received,' she complained, 'that I decided to give up.'[8]

Ironically, it was Madge's nemeses, the Squire and Squiress, who eventually rescued her mission. Once the titled or educated or wealthy or influential members of the community became involved with the Movement, at local as well as national level, it would be felt that tacit permission had been granted for 'ordinary' women to join in too. At the very first British WI, in Llanfairpwllgwyngyllgogerychwyrndrobwllllantysiliogogogoch (or, mercifully, Llanfair PG for short), the Marquis and Marchioness of Anglesey not only lent a temporary building for the Institute's meetings, but later gave them the land to build their own hall. Their blessing of this novel enterprise gave it the endorsement it needed to thrive. The success of the Llanfair PG pioneers also owed a great deal to John Nugent Harris's energy. He heard one of Madge's last-ditch attempts to enthuse her sex into cooperation at an Agricultural and Horticultural Union conference held in London in February 1915. Even when her own enthusiasm must have been nearing its limit, she spoke well. She was not an impressive figure: short, rather plain, and gimlet-eyed. 'But the energy of her speech, which betokened the keen mind behind it, held one enthralled, and one was conscious that here was a master spirit of a very unusual calibre, capable of carrying through almost any scheme on which she had set her heart.'[9]

What she said about Canadian women's achievements within the WI thrilled Nugent Harris: here was someone who shared his ambition to wake up ordinary women and empower them to help themselves and their country – this being, of course, a time of war – and what's more, she was articulate, and female. The perfect evangelist. He can't have known at this stage how hard Madge had tried already to spread the word, or he might not have been so eager to enlist her help. He immediately booked her for an event coming up in March, a Board of Agriculture conference on agricultural education, and invited her to his office at the AOS to discuss a more formalised approach to founding Women's Institutes here. She was also asked to address the annual meeting of the AOS in London on 24 June, at which Nugent Harris proposed to move a resolution that WIs should be established by the AOS in Britain, and Madge Watt should be appointed their official organiser.

One of his staunchest allies in this new project was a governor of the AOS and Chairman of the North Wales branch, Colonel the Hon. Richard Stapleton-Cotton. Another was the academic Sir Harry Reichel, Stapleton-Cotton's friend and colleague, who was the first Principal of the University College at Bangor. When Madge was asked to speak on 'Women's Work in Agriculture' at the college on 15 June 1915 (a week or so before the annual meeting in London), Nugent Harris made a short speech in support of her, Sir Harry proposed a vote of thanks and Colonel Stapleton-Cotton seconded it. Privately, Nugent Harris is said to have commented that if Madge could persuade the Welsh that the WI would be a good idea, she could persuade anyone. The implication was that if the appeal of the WI could cut across the calcified and divisive loyalties of Church and Chapel, it was bound to succeed.

It is unlikely, incidentally, that Madge could ever have got the WI going in Britain on her own; its potential membership – shy and inexperienced – needed the authority of a group of men like Nugent Harris and Stapleton-Cotton to validate the Movement. Once it had been endorsed by them, as generals in the field, the way was clear for strong-minded women like Madge and the other female pioneers, all appointed by men, to march on and rouse their brand-new troops. This time of world war (about which much more later) was the period that first defined the WI and those women in it as productive and worthwhile members of domestic society. It was important that the members of this innovative organisation should be aware that they also served not just by 'standing and waiting' and saying their prayers, but by coming together officially for the first time in history to work cooperatively and proactively for the good of the country.

So well was Madge's talk at Bangor received that Stapleton-Cotton and his wife Jane decided to catch Madge before she left the area, to suggest another engagement. Would she address a meeting the next day at their own village on Anglesey, Llanfair PG? Of course. A report in the *North Wales Chronicle* noted that 'Mrs Watt, a lady from British Columbia', gave an interesting account of the Women's Institutes in Canada; this was followed up by a proposal from the floor that a similar organisation be set up in the village, which was passed unanimously.[10] Therefore by the time Madge attended the annual meeting in London she was proudly able to claim that she'd already begun to establish the Movement in Britain, before any formal resolution had been passed to help her.

The official 'formation' meeting of the Llanfair PG Women's Institute was held after a busy harvest, on 11 September 1915. Madge was there to supervise the proceedings. The records of this and subsequent meetings still exist, copied into an important-looking 'AOS Women's Institutes Minute Book' in a neat hand and rather blotty ink.[11] First, Jane Stapleton-Cotton was elected the founding President, and a committee was put in place; then Madge took the stage, to explain the workings of a good Women's Institute – which might conveniently be shortened, she waggishly suggests, to 'WI', just as Llanfairpwllgwyngyllgogerychwyrndrobwllllantysiliogogogoch is shortened to Llanfair PG. It's not like anything the women of Anglesey – nor anywhere else in the kingdom – have come across before. An Institute is not ruled, she says, but rules itself. It was important that this should be made clear, since self-determination and democracy in practice were unfamiliar concepts to women in 1915. Four 'freedoms' should always be kept in mind, according to Madge, in anything to do with the WI: Truth, Tolerance, Justice, and Fellowship. Fellowship is the most important. A WI should cater for all tastes, 'be grave *and* gay'. Explore the world together, and learn as much about growing roses in your garden, or trimming hats, as about 'Darkest Africa' or 'Bolshevism'. With canny prescience, she advises members to be adventurous in their approach to meetings. 'If you become dull the young will not join, and your numbers will decrease.' Make sure you always include a 'social half-hour' in the programme: the chance for a chat reduces the amount of whispering during lectures. Have fun, but be fruitful, not frivolous.

Men may laugh at the 'little woman' but the time will come, when that Little Woman without tying herself to railings, or knocking off policemen's hats, will, simply by making her views known throughout the Institute, be able to demand and get healthful improvements in village life, up and down the land . . . Use that Power to its full.[12]

It must have been rather an anticlimax to return, after this rousing call-to-arms, to the prosaic business in hand. It was decided that the Institute would meet on the first Tuesday of the month at 2 p.m. in a garden room 'kindly lent by Mrs W. E. Jones' (in fact a dank-looking outbuilding, cloaked in ivy) until such time as it could find more suitable premises (eventually provided by the Marquis and Marchioness of Anglesey); that 'tea, bread, and one kind of cake' would be served by way of refreshment during the afternoon, and that the subscription rate would stand at 2s.

The first year's Annual Report, published in September 1916, reveals an Institute which obviously hit the ground running. Speakers' subjects ranged from 'Fruit and Vegetable Preserving' (Madge Watt) and 'Child Welfare' (a Miss Dickenson) to 'Salads and Salad Dressings' (from Colonel Stapleton-Cotton – a 'masterly' talk with which he entranced several early WIs). There were practical demonstrations on 'The Fireless Cooker', and (worryingly) 'The Easiest and Most Humane Way of Killing a Fowl'. Occasionally the Institute went out to tea en masse; it listened to harp music and sang 'Land of My Fathers' and 'God Save the King'; it discussed local concerns; it chose a badge 'to be submitted to some woman designer' featuring a dragon or a leek in red and gold; and it carefully articulated the ethos of the Institute: to be non-denominational, non-political, to create a spirit of unselfishness. The motto of the society should be 'Help one another'. It also received gifts, gladly, of cups and saucers, an oil stove, tablecloths, chairs and tea. Three wounded soldiers were invited to the opening meeting, and at Christmas members were asked to bring a husband or man friend: apparently a mutually exclusive choice.

Colonel Stapleton-Cotton's support, both material and

moral, was unstinting. He threw himself into the Movement, forever clattering down the country lanes in his donkey-driven bath-chair (his legs were paralysed) to enlist helpers, and happily comparing notes with members on knitting – at which he was adept – or gardening. When he wrote to Madge Watt in February 1916 to congratulate her on the triumphant progress of the WI, he could not have been more generous. He readily admitted that at first

I was one of the many who doubted the capacity of women to conduct even their ordinary business with success, but I have learned more about women than I have learnt in forty years ... I see and believe that women can and will bring all classes, all denominations, all interests, all schools of the best thought together in that common brotherhood of love and tolerance which every man and woman longs for in his or her innermost heart ... We want to think more, we want to understand one another, we want to think kindly of one another. We are none of us altogether bad sorts ... I can conceive nobody better calculated to make us shake hands all round than woman and her work in these Institutes. Women have the opportunity, the capacity and the will to accomplish that which, judging by results, has been beyond the wit of man.[13]

As a model for other Institutes, Llanfair PG was exemplary. It did, however, break the odd rule. In 1917, it went completely against the letter and spirit of WI law by allowing Lady Anglesey to become a patron, and accepting her inflated subscription of £5. This appears to have been a one-off: not even the Queen was allowed to offer more than the required 2s.

A lady-in-waiting was sent with £1 when Her Majesty Queen Mary joined Sandringham WI – founded by Madge in 1919 – and was promptly given 18s change. Perhaps, given its significance in the history of the WI Movement, the Llanfair PG committee can be forgiven this venal but kind-hearted lapse. There was nothing but kind-heartedness behind their second solecism, which was to allow a man to join. He was, of course, Colonel Stapleton-Cotton, the Institute's closest friend; he and his dog Tinker, who paid his own subscription, were members till they died.

There are other instances of men being directly involved in the WI's affairs. Local solicitors, vicars or doctors sometimes took the Chair at preliminary meetings to decide whether or not a village WI should be formed, most women at that stage having no experience of chairing. The first national organising committee, convened in July 1915, exclusively comprised six men (AOS members) with a female secretary, a Miss Green. Madge was an adviser, but had little to do with executive decisions. Indeed, Nugent Harris remembered Madge and Miss Green being at daggers drawn – not a very edifying example for a women's movement – and eventually Miss Green stalked off, to be replaced by Nugent Harris's popular and emollient wife, Lil. Personally, Madge did not appeal to everyone. 'Mrs Watts's so-called work,' spat another woman involved with the AOS, 'I consider [an] absolute waste of money. If the movement is going to be of any value at all it will not become so ... as a scheme for improving village people.'[14] How wrong that woman was.

Madge might have been granted more of an executive role in these early days had she had better success in founding WIs alone, or been more flexible about how they should be administered, instead of constantly urging the British authorities to follow the Canadian pattern of total governmental control, and refusing to take the idiosyncratic national psyche into consideration. Ironically, she was not a natural democrat. She was 'so sure that her way was the best that she had a tendency to override the wishes of her committee, convinced that at heart they really agreed with her'.[15] Her habit of knitting at meetings was distracting (though fitting), especially as she insisted on using noisy metal needles rather than more discreet wooden ones; her judgement was variously considered 'self-centred' and 'lop-sided', and she never *looked* very nice, bumbling about in a mob cap and what looked suspiciously like an elderly dressing-gown. What couldn't be disputed, however, were her infectious enthusiasm for the Movement, and her experience. So in 1915 she was dispatched as its chief evangelist, metaphorically marching her way east from Anglesey with banners fluttering (or half-knitted socks, from her needles), to conquer a country weakened by war and ready for change.

Singleton in West Sussex and Wallisdown in Dorset each claims to be the first WI in England, started in the autumn of 1915; Madge, naturally, initiated them both. Lady Wimborne and her daughter Lady Chelmsford ran Wallisdown, but the Singleton pioneers seem to have prided themselves on a humbler foundation, holding their meetings in the back room of a local inn, the Fox at Charlton, where one of the founder members was the landlady. This aroused much local suspicion. What kind of an outfit was this, to tempt wives and mothers away from home for secret sessions at the pub?

Despite the obvious benefits introduced by people like the Marquis and Marchioness of Anglesey, the Movement's inevitable reliance in the early days on the cooperation of 'the lady of the manor' was not entirely healthy. When said lady was in sympathy with the WI ethos of egalitarianism and shared enlightenment, as at Llanfair PG or Wallisdown, that was fine. But not every landowner's wife, or even vicar's wife, wished to 'spend sleepless nights and anxious days planning for their own supercession by the labourer's wife or their own servant girl'.[16] This was flirting with Communism. Rural revolution. It was dangerous.

One President brought her meeting to a semblance of order by clashing saucepan lids together; another insisted on driving round the village with her chauffeur to scoop up members both willing and less so for her meetings. When a lady elsewhere fell foul of this newfangled democracy and was not (to her amazement) elected President, she is said to have nailed her front door shut in protest, thus making herself unequivocally unavailable to serve in any lowlier position on the committee.

Then there was the case of the Rector's wife who considered she should have been made President of the newly-formed WI and brought her husband [along] to say so . . . 'Lord B— gave the parish to me and I gave it to Gerald, didn't I, Gerald?' . . . She was so cross that the Church Council meeting was fixed for the same night as the WI, with one item on the agenda: 'The Suppression of the WI'.[17]

How could there be anything but trouble when the early WI membership embraced 'gentlewomen' like this, expected to function shoulder to shoulder with the working women or labourers' wives of the village, and firebrands like Edith Rigby, the founder of Lancashire's first WI? Edith had been a notorious public menace: a violent suffragette whose past offences included sprinkling acid on a golf-course, setting fire to the industrialist Lord Leverhulme's bungalow and to the Blackburn Rovers' football ground, and hurling first black puddings and then bombs (both commendably home-made) at the Liverpool Cotton Exchange when a youngish Winston Churchill was due to speak there in 1913. She'd been imprisoned seven times, had been on hunger strike and force-fed – and yet believed the WI to be utterly wonderful, 'a pillar supporting the temple of national enlightenment'.

Things were not much calmer at national level. Apart from the tensions between Madge Watt and Miss Green, there were constant mutterings among AOS aides – male and female – about WIs being somehow unpatriotic, about the AOS being reduced to a 'mothers' meeting' and, most of all, about the name. There were already Women's Institutes elsewhere. Wouldn't 'Club' be better? The word 'Institute' conjured up the dismal image of a public building, probably a lunatic asylum of some sort; the initials invited flippant and often damaging soubriquets like the Women Independents, the Wild Indians, the Women Inebriates or the Wandering Idiots. It was Madge Watt who insisted the Canadian name be perpetuated in Britain; perhaps surprisingly, her decision has never been overruled.

One of the most urgent problems for the National Organising Committee to tackle, then, was how to keep the wide range of women it hoped to encourage into the Movement from bickering themselves out of existence. The solution was found in the strict protocol instilled at every level, which insisted on immutable regulations regarding the Institute's committees, procedures, membership and remit.

In October 1917, at the first delegates' meeting of WIs (there were 187 at this point, with a total membership of just over five thousand), the National Federation of Women's Institutes was born. A constitution was adopted, along the lines of the Canadian Institute's. Its objectives were to 'stimulate interest in the agriculture industry; to develop co-operative enterprises; to encourage home and local industry; to study home economics, [and] to provide a centre for educational and social intercourse and for all local activities'. All this sounds a little dry, but read the words of the NFWI's Vice-Chairman, Grace Hadow, and suddenly the inclusive spirit of the Movement comes alive:

> The Women's Institute is for all alike: rich and poor, gentle and simple, learned and unlearned – all pay the same subscription, have the same privileges and the same responsibilities. Each member in turn acts as hostess to her fellow members, each puts her own experience and her own practical knowledge at the service of the rest.[18]

A Chairman was elected at this meeting: it was Lady Gertrude Denman, already in charge of a new organising committee for the WI set up the previous year, and whom you may remember co-hosting that rather bizarre agricultural show at her mother's house in Carlton Terrace, London, in July 1915. At the same time, the AOS relinquished its control of the Movement to the women's branch of the Board of Agriculture's Food Production Department (principally because the Treasury refused to grant the AOS the money it needed to administer the WI). The Board agreed to fund the formation of new Institutes and to subsidise the new County Federations emerging around the country, but once WIs were up and running they must finance themselves. This was just as Lady

Denman and her Executive Committee (the forerunner of today's Board of Trustees) wished: autonomy was essential for a movement that claimed, as the WI did, to be independent of any political, religious or cultural allegiance. But it did mean that everyone connected with the establishment of WIs needed to work extra hard at enlisting the support which led to subscriptions and endowments. Luckily, there were some extraordinarily strong characters at the helm: another good reason why the WI survived its first few years.

Lady Denman gave the Movement energy, colour, confidence and impeccable connections. Her deputy, Grace Hadow, was always considered the 'brains' of the Movement. Lady Denman was much admired and slightly terrifying, but Miss Hadow – despite her lofty career as an Oxford academic – was warm, approachable and kind. A little severe at first glimpse, perhaps, being tall and ramrod-straight with an uncompromising hair-do (a scraped-back bun) and rimless pince-nez. But her eyes were gentle and humorous.

After taking a First Class Honours degree in English at Somerville College, Oxford, Grace went on to teach both at Oxford and at Bryn Mawr in Pennsylvania before returning to Oxford in 1929 as Principal of the Society of Home Students (later St Anne's College). She was also Secretary of Barnett House, a centre for public welfare and economic studies and for training students in social work. Her brother, Sir William Henry Hadow, shared her passion for education, being responsible for the Hadow Report (1926) which led to the foundation of secondary modern schools in England. Grace's particular interests were education for women – whether at university level or at home in the countryside – and gardening. She wore an apron made from a railway travelling rug whenever she decently could, in case the chance arose to wield a trowel or pull a weed, and Andrew, the yellow car in which she sped around the country to WI meetings, was legendary.

Like most of the NFWI's first officers, Grace Hadow was also involved in the fight for women's suffrage, but with a little more temperance than Edith Rigby. In 1917, the year before the vote for women of property over the age of thirty was won, and the year she joined the WI, she remembered her militant past with some pride:

It feels quite odd to think that possibly – even probably – before long people will neither shout with laughter nor throw things at one if one mentions women voting. I am glad to belong to a generation which has been stoned – not because I like being stoned (it is tiresome, and often messy), but since some women had to go through that to win the thing, it is a bit of luck not to have been out of it entirely.[19]

It is not recorded who suggested the WI's corporate colours – green and purple – but I'd be prepared to bet it was Grace, in honour of those who fought with her for political recognition. Originally, green, white and violet represented the movement for women's suffrage, signifying hope, purity and dignity, and subtly sharing initials with its uncompromising message: Give women the vote.

Grace Hadow recognised that one of the greatest tasks facing the WI was to fit its membership for responsible citizenship; to teach it to use its vote, so dearly bought, with insight and integrity. The secret ballots by which local WI committees were elected had given British women their first taste of active democracy; after the widening of the franchise to women over thirty in 1918, and in 1928 to everyone over twenty-one, the challenge was to make that vote count for the good of the family and the community. It would be difficult, she argued, to plan a better training for the exercise of the vote – a training 'entirely divorced from all party or sectarian policies' – than WI membership. In the WI women learned not to take, but to give; through their interest in their homes and villages they would come to appreciate the connection between their own affairs and the affairs of the nation, and how they could influence both.

Right up until 1990 it was the custom for the old Executive Committee of the NFWI to include representative members from relevant external organisations; in 1917 those members included John Nugent Harris, on behalf of the AOS, and Miss – later Dame – Meriel Talbot from the Board of Agriculture. Meriel Talbot (also known as 'Slasher' Talbot for her cricketing prowess) was the Director of the women's branch at the Board; her expertise was in food production and international relations, being a founder member of the Victoria League, formed in the wake of the Boer War to foster friendship between the peoples of the world and encourage British emigration to the colonies. She was also partly responsible, significantly, for establishing the Women's Land Army. Though obviously high-powered, she was both sympathetic and encouraging to the WI Movement, believing it to possess 'an almost limitless possibility for the future betterment of our country life'.[20]

The printed report of the 1917 Annual General Meeting of the NFWI is terse, although it notes that Madge got up and spoke, puzzlingly, 'on the privilege of watching the dawn of Imperialism in rural England', which even then must have raised a few eyebrows. In March 1918, *The Times* published a much fuller account of the Movement's progress.[21] 'Societies of women' are being formed up and down the country, the paper tells us, 'to promote the good of their country, of their neighbourhood, and of their own homes'. At their monthly meetings they listen to lectures, watch practical demonstrations, enter competitions, and have almost intelligent debates on chosen subjects. They are taught to give expression to their own ideas. 'The afternoon ends with tea and an entertainment, and the members return to their homes feeling that a new interest has been added to their lives', bless them. The correspondent becomes a little less patronising when talking about the non-corporeal benefits of the WI, the 'drawing together of women of every class and creed working for a common object', then positively enthusiastic when he mentions the war work being done by WIs. But the implication of the article is that here is something safe and fairly anodyne to keep the little woman busy, while the world spins on without her.

John and Lil Nugent Harris used to delight in reminiscing about the early days of the WI. They were well aware that the Movement might initially appear silly and inconsequential to outsiders, but recognised the sturdiness of its central tenets, and perhaps sensed the potential within it to change everyone's lives, not just rural women's. They were never less than affectionate about it – as when John recalled the affair of the hats. This was a faddish period during which WI members refused, or were possibly unable, to remove their fashionable headgear at meetings, with the regrettable result that visiting speakers were rarely seen except by the front row. Wall-mounted hat hooks were John's pragmatic suggestion, where the magnificent things could still be displayed, but more demurely. One of Lil's favourite stories was of a nervous Essex delegate on the stage at an annual meeting at the Queen's Hall in London, whose thoughtful speech was accompanied by the graceful descent of a voluminous and de-elasticated pair of knickers. While the audience watched in rapt fascination and the delegate quaked, Lil – sitting on the stage – waited for the right moment, then helpfully hissed: 'Lift your right foot' – then after a dexterous twitch, 'Now lift your left . . . '[22]

There were two events, both in 1918, that must have gratified the Nugent Harrises enormously, along with everyone else who wished the WI well. These were the opening of the first VCO residential school, and the first National Federation of Women's Institutes exhibition.

Voluntary County Organisers were the lifeblood of the WI. They could claim expenses of up to £3 a month (about £125 today) from the AOS, to travel around the country in an optional uniform available from Harrods, canvassing possible support for local Institutes. If there was enough enthusiasm, they helped to convene a preliminary meeting and form a committee, before moving on to the next target.[23] Madge Watt was the VCO extraordinaire (you'd have to be 'heaven-born', remarked a sweetly smiling Lil Nugent Harris, to come up to *her* standard), and one of her most constructive legacies to the Movement was the training she put in place to pass on her expertise to others. She organised a three-week course, offered in weekly chunks or all in one, at a house in Burgess Hill, Sussex, in May 1918 to do just that. It was a triumph of imagination, organisation and goodwill. The house, Wyberlye, belonged to the local WI President and her husband; students attending the course were accommodated in other members' homes and transported to Wyberlye each day in fleets of borrowed cars. There were lectures each morning on the Movement's (very short) history, on its (infinite) future, and on subjects such as 'How to Help an Unsuccessful WI', or 'Little Helps in WI Work' (ambiguous); the afternoons were spent visiting neighbouring WIs, local food production plants or cooperative enterprises. Each course closed with a lesson on public speaking by a Miss Poppea Peacock, for which Madge Watt nobly offered herself as a 'terrible example'. If Poppea Peacock or anyone else had suggested she really *was* a terrible example, there would have been trouble.

One of the most fascinating sessions at Wyberlye was John Nugent Harris's lecture on the psychology of potential WI members:

A rural audience is composed of people of intense individualism. Ninety-five percent are suspicious, and may appear to be friendly, but in reality are antagonistic, not because they mean to be, but because of their suspicion of promoters of movements that come from towns and cities with the object of improving them. The rural dweller has been, and is being, exploited by those from 'outside'; hence this suspicion, out of which has grown a difficult psychology. This psychology is, however, only superficial in character. The rural mind is at bottom extremely sympathetic, and reflects, when you get its confidence, all the charm and beauty of everything that is pure and primitive and unspoiled by contamination with so-called civilization. It becomes absolutely essential for speakers to such audiences to realize their responsibility in creating an atmosphere, as they have it in their power to mould the audience for good or evil.[24]

The suggestion of savage nobility and social engineering sounds distasteful, and betrays Nugent Harris's roots in a government department trying to maximise the country's resources in a time of war. This is not how the kindly Colonel Stapleton-Cotton expressed himself. It's a canny assessment, though, of the nature of uneducated, isolated, self-reliant women got together and told to be sociable. What he doesn't make clear in this extract is how much he respects these women. Once they relax, once they trust the WI, they are willing to share their experience, open their minds, and learn.

Five months after the launch of the VCO school in Sussex, the twelve thousand WI members of England and Wales held their first joint celebration. It was General Secretary Alice Williams's idea:[25] she decided to hire Caxton Hall in London and invite every WI to submit some sort of entry for a grand exhibition of village crafts – which would also raise much-needed funds for the NFWI. Five hundred Institutes responded out of 773, and when the President of the Board of Trade opened the event on Saturday 26 October 1918, the place was packed with stalls. The Queen and Princess Mary arrived shortly before a hamper of orgiastic rabbits from a successful breeding club got loose and ran amok among the exhibits. Her Majesty chose lots of things to take home to the Palace, although whether she actually paid for any of them isn't clear, and by all accounts she enjoyed herself enormously. Alice Williams organised the entries into classes, which were judged competitively; then all the goods were put up for sale, with a small commission going to the NFWI. The range and quality of work was staggering. Prizes were offered for cheese, butter, eggs, fresh vegetables and fruits, bread, cakes, jam, honey, pickles, bottled and dried fruits and vegetables, dried herbs, starch made from diseased potatoes, baskets, toys, labour-saving devices, articles made from waste, home-dyed garments, home-cured rabbit and mole skins, needlework, knitted goods, and essays on 'Our Institute' and 'How to Plan the Work of a Six-roomed Cottage for a Week'.

Local industries were represented with, among other things, soft and wooden toys, over 3600 of which were ordered during the course of the event, a great favourite being Cuthbert the rabbit. In fact rabbits seem to have been something of a leit-motif for the whole event. There were also tweeds and silks from Tardebigge in Worcestershire, smocks from Ticehurst in East Sussex (which caught the eye of the Liberty buyer), rabbit-skin gloves from Hertfordshire and baskets from all over the place. The five-day show was a roaring success, attracting thousands of visitors who were served 'dainty' teas with cakes and potato scones by WI members in chintz aprons, and entertained with plays, lectures, folk-dancing and music on a central stage.

This exhibition was the WI's first appearance before the British public. Its effect was immediate, and dramatic. Change was coming to Britain's countryside; at its vanguard was a benign assorted army of rural housewives obviously enjoying themselves, achieving things – and, for the first time, speaking in unison.

3

The Women Carry On:
THE FIRST WORLD WAR

Ye shall know them by their fruits.[1]

It was the German submarine blockade of Britain, which began in February 1917, that first put fire in the belly of the WI. Before that, the role of the country housewife in wartime Britain was to be stoical, to endure, and to do her best not to waste resources. This was noble work in itself, as Madge Watt, John Nugent Harris and the other pioneers of the WI were quick to acknowledge. But it was hardly a mission. Everything changed in October 1917, when the National Federation of Women's Institutes was formed. Rumours were circulating that Britain had only three weeks' supply of food in reserve. That summer's harvest had been disastrous; farms were empty of labour, German U-boats prevented the importation of what amounted to half the country's food, and there was a real risk of malnutrition, if not starvation. Old Blighty's heart was growing hollow, but Slasher Talbot seized the moment. 'We have to prevent hunger,' she warned. 'Every ounce of food which can be grown in the country must be grown, and every woman who can give a hand in this vastly important work must give a hand.'[2]

This is the stage at which the AOS (who hadn't the budget to support a mass mobilisation programme of rural women) handed the WI over to the Food Production Department of the Board of Agriculture. From the government's point of view, it was a sensible move. Working hand in hand with the Land Army, the WI could be the greatest asset the Home Front had: Britain's last best hope. The newly formed NFWI Committee, however, had its sights fixed on the future. As mentioned earlier, it had always been a central tenet of the WI Movement, from the old Ontario days, that it should be independent of political influence and accessible to everyone, from the most belligerent patriot to the committed pacifist. Madge Watt and her sister Canadians thought they could manage this impartiality while remaining a government-administered organisation, but Lady Denman was adamant that the WI should not risk being considered a military tool; its role was to keep the heart of rural Britain beating through the dark times, and invigorate it when peace came. This is why she refused the Board of Agriculture's sponsorship, except in the formation of new Institutes and Federations, and insisted on complete democracy and self-determination. It was brave of her to be so assertive (though no surprise, given her character): the WI still needed the support of the government to survive, and had this been withdrawn the Movement might well have perished, virtually stillborn.

Lady Denman's committee issued a pamphlet explaining what a WI was – 'a group of women banded together to help their country and themselves' – and exactly what was expected of its members. They were to 'help their country' in the following ways: by releasing men from the land, increasing the food supply, preventing waste, starting a war savings association, 'considering the question of rural education', encouraging village industries and 'making the Institute the centre of village life'.[3] On careful inspection it would clearly be seen that all these things boosted individuals as much as the nation, and developed the future well-being of the country as well as dealing with the present emergency. This is why the Caxton Hall exhibition had been such a success: it proved how resourceful women were, as well as how talented.

All those rabbits (both dead and alive) meant the country no longer needed to import eleven thousand tons of them for the table, as it had in 1914. By the summer of 1918 there were thousands of rabbit clubs around the country, churning the creatures out for their meat and fur. Also, the scale and quality of toy-making enterprises, especially wooden toys, would gratifyingly threaten Germany's pre-war monopoly. Increased amounts of fruit and vegetables helped feed local communities, and vats and vats of jam not only raised morale but made sure nothing was wasted by way of soft fruit. Both world wars were marked by a glut of plums at home; these, picked and processed by the WI, supplied precious Vitamin C to an ill-nourished population, as well as fruit-stones to provide the charcoal for gas-mask filters. And all that music and dancing celebrated the unbroken spirit of Britain, as well as cheering everyone up.

The exhibition was held just days before the Armistice was signed on 11 November 1918. By then the WI Movement had been established for three years. Between 1915, when Llanfair PG opened, and 1917, when the National Federation was formed, 5198 WI members had been enrolled. This was encouraging, but hard work. Madge Watt remembered frequently being asked whether she knew there was a war on: what use was a club for gossips when the Empire was at stake? In the single year from 1917 to 1918, given a real sense of purpose and direction, the membership more than doubled. At the time of the exhibition it stood at 12,007 – and the year after that it billowed out to an astonishing 55,015. At last the Women's Institute was up and running, and its members – according to a delighted Colonel Stapleton-Cotton – were enjoying 'the chance of their lives'.

To encourage a spirit of identity and loyalty to the WI, a brand-new ladies' magazine was launched in January 1918. It was nothing like its popular contemporaries *Woman's Own* or *The Lady*; this was something altogether more robust. Instead of the usual dewy-eyed beauty on the front cover or a heart-warmingly wholesome mother with her hand-knitted children, *The Landswoman*'s first cover showed two exhausted women, one young and one quite elderly, leading their carthorses home against a wide yellow sunset. It included advertisements – not for costly cosmetics or kid shoes, but for Oatine Face-Cream, Liberty Bodices ('elastic, porous and hygienic') and Woman Power Insurance. Its first editorial was a rousing piece written by Meriel Talbot, praising the work being done by women in the British countryside to combat food shortages and to hold the Home Front during this war to end all wars. It's no surprise to find Miss Talbot at the helm of the new enterprise: *The Landswoman* was the house journal for the Women's Land Army (WLA), which she helped run, together with her colleagues Lil Wilkins[4] of the AOS and the NFWI Committee Chairman Lady Denman.

No surprise either, then, that tucked into a corner of volume one, number one, page 13 is a discreet little article headed 'News from the Women's Institutes', listing new WIs and politely asking if anyone knows where to get the best raw material for making fruit baskets. There's a feature in this first issue about the newly formed National Federation of Women's Institutes too, explaining how it works, who are its officers, and how important its role may be not only in food production but in postwar reconstruction. The WI shared *The Landswoman* until March 1919, when it outgrew its allotted space and published the first issue of its own dedicated journal, *Home and Country* (now replaced by *WI Life*).

The best way to sum up *The Landswoman*'s appeal to both sections of its readership is to quote from a poem by Janet Begbie, 'Carry On!', published in the April 1918 issue:

There's Tom that drove a ploughshare,
    And now he loads a gun;
There's Dick could reap his acre,
    Now soars against the sun;
There's Jack that was a shepherd
    Is watching on the sea,
All dark with death and hatred.
    But England's still, and free!
Yet the harness shan't be rusty
    Because of you and me.
        Carry on! Carry on!
            For the men and boys are gone;
        But the furrow shan't lie fallow
            While the women carry on . . .

We may not die for England,
    We'll work for England then;

She's our land, just as their land –
    Deserve her like her men!
O Tom, we'd give our comfort
    To stand where now you stand;
O Dick, we'd give our safety
    To swoop at your right hand;
O Jack, we may not plough the sea –
    Well, we will plough the land.
      Carry on! Carry on!
        For the men and boys are gone;
        But the furrow shan't lie fallow
        While the women carry on.[5]

The Landswoman had a dual purpose. First, it was designed to inform, entertain, and raise the morale of its Land Army readership. It carried reports on recruitment rallies and Land Lassies' parades (in this war, they tended to be called 'lassies' rather than the less bracing 'girls' of the Second World War). Tips on tractor-driving were included, with inside knowledge on ferrets and on cleanliness in the dairy; competitions appeared on the subjects of 'Cows I Have Known' or 'What to Do on Long Winter Evenings', and recipes for lard-and-carrot chilblain cream and sugar-beet syrup.

The magazine was also a propaganda tool for the Women's Institute Movement. The paths of the WLA and the WI had crossed already, in that a few Land Lassies were WI members (assuming they weren't 'townie' recruits) and one of the tasks of local Institutes was informally to help instruct, feed and even accommodate Lassies whenever possible. The tone of articles aimed at WI members is not quite as sprightly as the Land Army's material; it's rather more sober and grand. Members of the WI are told that as 'Daughters of Britain' they have a duty of service to work together for the Motherland to help win the war.

It is ironic that many Institute archives no longer exist because their members decided to donate them to the war effort (the Second World War, this time). When the call went round for waste paper, they did their duty and threw their minute books and old programmes into the salvage bins. Enough survives, however, to give us a good idea of the variety of work being done by the WI as the 1914–18 war drew to an exhausted close.

One of the most enterprising Institutes of all was at Criccieth in North Wales, founded by Dorothy Drage. Criccieth was one of the few WIs to anticipate Meriel Talbot's 1917 directive to cooperate in food production, by setting up the first WI market in May 1916. This wasn't a stall like the present-day ones, selling goods to individuals; it concentrated on the wholesale market, collecting produce from WI members and others, marking it up – but at slightly lower prices than the local competition – and selling it on. The profits were shared, with the WI keeping a penny in the shilling (or a twelfth) to cover expenses. The market opened at 9.30 a.m. twice a week between May and September; any stock still unsold at 4 p.m. was then offered to private customers. From one point of view the market was a huge success. There was a £250 turnover the first season, equivalent to about £10,000 today. It incorporated an egg production business, and even inspired the first NAAFI (Navy, Army and Air Force Institute) canteens. But it fell victim to that success when already established suppliers complained it was undercutting them and threatening their livelihoods. The

National Federation withdrew its support, and though the market continued to function under an independent committee for a while, much to Mrs Drage's chagrin it ceased to be a part of Criccieth WI.

The records of other WIs around the country show how hard they were working to produce food for the non-commercial market. As well as the ubiquitous rabbit clubs there were several pig clubs, where the animals would be raised cooperatively and their meat shared out among the members. This had the added advantage of using up scraps, as did the rearing of poultry for meat, eggs and feathers. At Madron in Cornwall Girl Guides were mustered to collect fresh kitchen waste in a barrel on wheels built and donated by the local carpenter. The pigs were killed by a WI husband, none of the members having the stomach to do it, and then sold to the public rather than distributed among themselves, just in case 'feeling [ran] so high that it might defeat the object of the Institute to bind women together'.[6]

Scaynes Hill WI in Sussex was a much more confident outfit. The rabbits in its rabbit club were proudly described in *The Landswoman* as not just any old rabbits, but 'patriotic rabbits'. Members ran a soft-fruit cooperative, buying eight dozen bushes between them, as well as growing a hundred 'superlative raspberry canes' donated by Colonel Stapleton-Cotton. The Colonel also made them a gift of fifty blackcurrant cuttings. The fruit would be preserved in bottles (peripatetic demonstrators showed WIs how to do this most efficiently) or in cans, with newfangled canners that could either be bought outright or hired at 2s 6d a day.

A WI member from Lincolnshire explained how fiddly and time-consuming canning could be:

I used to set off at nine o'clock on Thursdays, market day, to drive a load of fruit in my governess cart for four miles . . .

Arrived at my destination I sorted out my baskets, put up my pony and trap, and settled down to work with, perhaps, but not always, the help of a volunteer. The canning was done in a large wash-house. The fire was lit under the copper by the time I arrived, and I would set about preparing and grading the fruit . . . A paraffin stove boiled the kettle and syrup. I also remember an alarm clock being useful as one of the most difficult tasks was to time the boiling so that one lot was ready to go in when another came out. Temperatures were up and down and had to be watched carefully. But oh! That soldering iron! How the solder would slide about and look untidy.

There was no time for lunch, and as the day wore on only a few dozen cans were finished. Anxiously I looked for bubbles coming up during boiling, and hoped for the best. The cooling was done in milking pails and then the cans were left on the tables to their fate for seven days. The most thrilling moments were those when, arriving the following week with more fruit, one opened the wash-house door and saw no cans looking bulgy but all slim and in their places ready to be labelled.[7]

Some WIs ran jam 'factories'. Cirencester, founded by Grace Hadow, had one; so did Hextable and Swanley in Kent. Hextable and Swanley's was set up in the disused laundry of a student hostel (probably for Swanley Horticultural College) with the help of the local Women's War Agricultural Committee, the government body principally set up to organise the Land Army. At the beginning of the fruit season a notice was issued to the villagers, stating that berries, stone-fruit, rhubarb and marrows could be sold to the factory superintendent on certain fixed days, and especially inviting small cottage-garden growers to bring along their produce. The jam was boiled and bottled by relays of volunteers from the village, under the careful eye of 'a lady who is an expert preserver'. Every Friday evening there was a labelling party, and on Saturday the shelves of a room adjoining the laundry were stacked with princely ruby, amber and carnelian jars, ready for the weekly sale.

First in line when the 'jam shop' opened were families who lacked the fruit to make jam of their own; an hour later, anyone could buy a jar or two, with a limit of two pounds per family per week. There was a special allowance of sugar for those making jam for more than their own consumption, and if the supply dwindled too quickly, glucose or sticky corn syrup could be used instead.

Cookery demonstrations were features of every WI's programme, sometimes using 'haybox' cookers – literally, a box of dried grass which would stew already hot dishes very slowly – or risky gas rings made from biscuit tins. They taught members how to cope with shortages (add vinegar to the pastry dough in place of half the fat, or beat margarine together with custard powder to make a (rancid-looking) paste which 'tastes like fresh Devonshire butter'). Advice on how to cook economically for large numbers of people gave confidence to those enterprising WIs who volunteered to open wartime canteens for local schoolchildren or labouring men and women.

These canteens were originally designed to minimise food waste; it was a bonus that many of them also turned in a profit for the WI. School lunches were not yet widely available, particularly in rural elementary schools. Children tended to bring 'doorsteps' of bread from home, which often ended up unfinished, and if no handy Girl Guides were around to sweep them up for the pig club the crusts were thrown away. A scheme for WI members to work together sourcing, cooking and selling food for lunch was much more efficient. At West Malling, 2d for girls and boys and 1½ d for infants bought them a nutritious hot meal, perhaps pasties and milk pudding, prepared on a tiny kitchen range in the Scout hut and served using cutlery and crockery lent by the village grocer on tables spread with white cloths and little pots of fresh flowers. If the weather was fine, the tables were set outside in the playground.

The collection of herbs and bark to be made into medicines and dyes fell easily to the WI. Parties of Institute members marched into the fields, perhaps singing a rather dire anthem called 'Daughters of Britain, Work with a Will', currently being marketed as the national WI song, to gather sphagnum moss for dressing wounds, thistledown to fill quilts, dried ferns to stuff dolls, and wisps of sheep's wool caught on hedges for spinning into yarn. This was the first age of national 'make do and mend'. There were WI classes on tinkering (repairing saucepans, buckets and so on); on upholstery and basket-making, and on cobbling, recommending old motorbike tyres for soling workmen's boots and more elegant bicycle tyres for ladies' and children's shoes. An eighty-five-year-old member of Wroxall WI on the Isle of Wight described how painful it was for arthritic fingers like hers to weave the withies into anything useful, 'but most women realise that the harder we work with head or hands the easier it is to bear the ache in our hearts, and efforts in this small corner of our dear country show how bravely women come forward to help, as far as in them lies, our dear men and Motherland'.[8]

Elsewhere, at Bottisham in Cambridgeshire, four hundred pairs of socks were being knitted for soldiers, and in Bepton (Sussex) a band of dedicated women was busy converting old vests into 'knicker-gaiters' by sewing the long sleeves together – not, thank goodness, for our brave lads abroad (whom one can imagine helplessly hobbled by these bewilderingly sealed garments), but to keep local children warm when the fuel ran out in winter. First aid was always a popular subject, and while teaching audiences what to do in a medical emergency most instructors welcomed the opportunity to disabuse them of generations of dangerous country lore. Don't, for example, apply dusty cobwebs or brandy-soaked bandages to wounds; and the cure for boils and 'gatherings' (infected spots) is not, and never was, to be found in the application of frogs' legs or bacon.

The same sort of advice was available to those hoping to do the spring cleaning for next to nothing. Chimneys can be swept quite efficiently with a gooseberry bush tied to a pole (replacing the extravagant brush-head made of dead hens commonly used in times of plenty before the war). Gilt picture frames come up beautifully when wiped with a little boiled onion water, and the best (if not the speediest) way to clean grubby wallpaper is to rub it all over with bran.

Every WI was encouraged to raise as much money as it could for the war effort. A report in *The Landswoman* of September 1918 shows how committed even the humblest of Institutes could be to this national imperative. It's from the secretary of the Knapwell, near Cambridge, branch:

At one meeting three school desks were covered with vests, pants and shirts for the Red Cross, £27 being raised to buy these articles at a jumble sale. They also collected £51 17s [a little over £1000 today] for War Savings from July, 1917. The village is full of varied activities. Rag mats are made and sell well, and one member gave a large one, which realised two guineas, to the wounded soldiers' fête. Since the war began Knapwell has raised £225 15s [nearly £5000 now] for the Red Cross, Serbian Relief Fund, Prisoners of War Fund, War Savings, YMCA, etc., and sent over a hundred garments to the Belgian refugees . . . Part of the money was given at fortnightly meetings, and part raised by jumble sales. Someone gave sixteen people 3d each to trade with, and the result was that £5 was made in six weeks. One girl had done crochet d'oyleys [sic], and made £1 7s 6d out of her 3d . . .[9]

There are only fifty-three inhabitants over sixteen years of age in Knapwell, we are informed, and no 'wealthy people' at all.

The Women's Institute Movement was fast becoming a national asset. Just as important – in fact more so, Lady Denman might argue – was its personal value. This was one of the long-term aims the early leadership of the WI was so anxious to promote: the nurturing of a new sense of responsibility, confidence and solidarity within what some already considered to be 'the greatest women's movement that has ever been started'.[10] The time was right, with the Great War coming to an end in November 1918, the passing of the Representation of the People Act that spring giving women over thirty the vote, and decades of material and social reconstruction lying ahead. The world was changing, and for the first time women, as a body, would help direct that change. But the constitutional opportunity to do that was one thing; quite another was the belief that it could, indeed, be done. A student at Madge Watt's VCO school in Burgess Hill put it neatly: the WI membership must cherish 'the vision of what should be, the understanding that it can be, the faith that it shall be'.

The first thing to do in empowering rural women was to tackle the boredom and low-level discontent Adelaide Hoodless had recognised in the isolated homes of backwoods Canada. The obvious solution, of course, was to join the local WI. The second issue of *The Landswoman* published a rather crass sketch to hammer home that simplest of messages: 'A Village Without and With a Village Institute'. The narrator is on holiday visiting her friend, a 'town-bred' young wife, who has moved to the country. It's one of the loveliest places in the kingdom, but the friend looks listless and drawn. She says the mountains hide the outside world, and heighten her sense of loneliness. The locals are nice enough, but it's always been the custom not to trust strangers. The village has no social life; there is nothing to do, nowhere to go, 'and this is the dullest place on the face of the globe'.

Then – guess what? Someone starts a WI. On her next visit, the narrator finds an animated, excited friend, bustling around doing her duties as secretary (while never, of course, neglecting her housework). Now there's a sewing class, a cookery class, a dressmaking class, a poultry club, a rabbit club (naturally), a coal club (where wholesale fuel is bought cooperatively at lower prices for everyone), a jam-making circle, a library club, an entertainment committee, an allotment group and a war savings association. 'The President, who formerly was the lady who lived in the Hall and knew very little about their lives, is now the leader of the Institute's activities; she wants the Institute to be a success just as the members do, so a common interest has brought all the women of the village to a common meeting ground.'[11] All this sounds a touch simplistic, but judging by the burgeoning number of Institutes and members and by the soaring profile of the WI across England and Wales, thousands of women were finding just the same sort of fulfilment as this young townie had. The same thing was happening in Scotland, but the Scottish 'Women's Rural Institutes', although inspired by a manically itinerant Madge Watt in 1917, developed separately. They shared the ethos of the NFWI's founders, but had their own organising committees, their own magazine, *Scottish Home and Country*; even their own tartan. The relationship between the two parallel movements was always warm and supportive.

However tempting it might be, we shouldn't get the idea that the whole of rural Britain relaxed into some sort of utopian sisterhood all at once. In the basement of the National Federation's headquarters in London are shelves of Voluntary County Organisers' reports, filed whenever they attempted to set up a new Institute – or close one. Many WIs didn't survive their first couple of years. The reasons given for failure by VCOs are tantalisingly cryptic. Comments include 'too contented to make much effort', 'the officers are quite useless, though the treasurer is very "worthy"', 'only the men spoke' (what were they doing there?), 'an unsuitable place for an Institute', 'detrimental to the reputation of the Movement'. Details, sadly, are unforthcoming.

The early records of Glynde WI in Sussex are pathetically short. It was set up in 1917 with an assiduous President, Mrs Pickard, and twenty-eight reluctant members who were supposed to meet in the Working Men's Clubroom. Mrs Pickard tried her utmost to make it a success, but no one was interested in a slightly obsessive programme of speakers on 'Laundry Agents' (detergents), 'Personal Hygiene' or 'How to Get Rid of Flies'. Nor could she get an upholstery class going, or a course on bee-keeping. Worst of all, she didn't serve buns at the meetings. After a couple of years, Mrs Pickard admitted defeat. Democratic to the last, she put it to the diminished membership of twenty-four that they should vote on whether or not the Institute continued. She wrote to everyone, asking them to return a signed slip with 'YES' for carrying on or 'NO' for closing down. The result was one 'YES', twenty 'NO's and three couldn't-care-lesses. Glynde WI was therefore dissolved.

Mrs Pickard decided one of the problems at Glynde, an estate village, had been the high proportion of working women in the Institute, who – one gets the impression – were rather press-ganged into joining. Meetings were sparsely attended because members claimed to be still out in the fields. She tried to include them by gamely conducting a survey into what 'the village working-class' considered essential requirements in a 'good cottage', but their hearts weren't in it. They didn't see the point. It was possible to try *too* hard to galvanise an infant Institute. Lady Plymouth, a President in Worcestershire, was perhaps a little wiser than the strenuous Mrs Pickard. 'Difficulties and discouragements fade like the mist in the morning,' she advised, 'when we realise that they are common to us all. Sometimes the best way to solve a difficulty is by masterly inactivity, and by remembering that we are pioneers working for the future, and thus we can afford to be patient.'[12]

The best Presidents were those who made a conscious effort to include everybody. It wasn't easy, so close to the sclerotic conditions of pre-war society with all its impenetrable rules of precedence. The WI had its hierarchies, too, but they depended (nominally, at least) on the ballot box. Alice Freeman was a bright young woman from Warwickshire, who had left school at ten to work on the carrier's cart. Joining the WI, she said, was 'the best day's work' she ever did. Her skills as a communicator, her sympathetic nature and irrepressible enthusiasm were quickly noted by the Movement's leadership, and before she knew what had happened she was sitting round a committee table with the great Lady Denman herself – feeling horribly out of her depth.

> Then Lady Denman (the chairman) said, 'Mrs Freeman, don't look so frightened. We are not going to eat you ...' When we adjourned for lunch she asked me what was the matter. I said, 'You are all educated people and I have no proper education or anything. I can't see what use I am going to be' ... She said, 'You'll be as much use as any one of us. Education doesn't mean a thing. It's experience that counts.'[13]

Alice went on to become a legendary VCO, cycling thousands of miles in a thirty-year career with the WI. Margaret Rotherham, a future member of the NFWI's Executive Committee, remembered her as 'very determined, and brave as brave', and wished there were a few more like Alice 'on the same strata as the WI members' to help bed the Movement into village society.[14] Lady Denman's Vice-Chairman, Grace Hadow, thought one of the best examples of the WI's spirit of democracy was an elderly cottager she came across in 1918, proud to admit that she'd 'come to every Institute meeting this last year, and I ain't felt patronised yet'.[15]

Miss Hadow's ideal, that 'rich and poor, gentle and simple, learned and unlearned' should come together as sisters in the Movement, was realised – in general – remarkably quickly. This was largely thanks to tea. Good-natured gossip is a great leveller; it's only when whispered behind cupped hands that it becomes divisive. Tea-time was when the support so necessary to a community of women in wartime was allowed to express itself, in mutual comfort for lost husbands, fathers, brothers and sons. When asked what the WI meant to her, one bereaved member admitted how important that camaraderie was. Both her sons had been killed, and she felt it her duty to them to make the village they had loved a better place. The WI helped her do this. But it also helped keep her alive: without the company and sympathy of her fellow members she might not have found the strength to carry on.

Madge Watt must surely have had a soft spot for those WIs she set up personally on her first Royal Progress in 1915. It took her about eighteen months to work her way from north-west Wales to south-east England (with a break in 1916 when one of her sons, now a soldier, was sent home wounded). On reaching Essex in May 1917, she was exhausted. And there wasn't much of a welcome to lift her spirits: Lady Petre of the Women's War Agricultural Committee had arranged for Madge to give a talk to likely WI officers at Chelmsford, but not a single volunteer came forward to organise a village meeting. A crestfallen Lady Petre suggested there might be too many Tory husbands around. A number had already informed her that their little women would not be joining any enterprise designed to distract them from wifely and motherly duties, and to befuddle them with political nonsense. There was also opposition from branches of the Mothers' Union, the nationwide association of Anglican women founded in 1876, who were convinced WIs were being set up in direct opposition to them. When Madge explained that the Women's Institute Movement was not a militantly infidel organisation, merely a non-denominational one, they were usually mollified. In fact many women belonged to both.

Querulous husbands were not so easy to convince, but eventually Madge persuaded a group of women at Boreham to start a WI in the Scout hut (with a nice, uncontroversial talk on bee-keeping to open the proceedings), and with Lady Petre evangelising at full tilt, word spread astonishingly quickly. By the end of 1917, there were twenty Essex Institutes in business. One of the liveliest of all was in Epping.

Epping WI plays a significant part in the history of the Women's Institute Movement in Britain. It was an Epping member, Mrs Trenow, who put forward the very first NFWI resolution, thus marking the beginning of the organisation's trademark involvement with campaigning and public affairs. Ever since the second one was held in October 1918, it's been a feature of NFWI AGMs to discuss resolutions put forward by 'ordinary' WI members. The process of placing resolutions has changed over the years, but broadly it involves members proposing that a specific idea should be discussed at village or county level; then, if there's enough support for it and it's considered a potential catalyst for change, it's forwarded to a consultative selection committee, debated again, and can finally end up before the AGM. Every WI in the land will be notified about the resolution at this stage, so they can decide how they want their representative delegate at the AGM to vote, or whether she's allowed to use her discretion. If the resolution is designed to trigger a change in the law, it must be carried with a two-thirds majority at the AGM before becoming an official NFWI mandate and the basis of a new campaign that will involve the lobbying of relevant government ministries.

The 1918 resolution proposed by Mrs Trenow was as follows:

> That the provision of a sufficient supply of convenient and sanitary houses being of vital importance to women in the country, County Federations and Women's Institutes are urged to bring pressure to bear upon their local councils and, through the National Federation, upon the Local Government Board to ensure that full advantage is taken in their districts of the Government scheme for State-aided Housing.[16]

This grew out of Liberal Prime Minister David Lloyd George's promise to create 'Homes fit for Heroes' by requiring local authorities to subsidise healthy, well designed housing for returning soldiers and their families, in town and country (Lloyd George's wife and sister-in-law were both WI members). Merrie England was to be born again, and the WI must play its part. It was a measure of the WI's high profile, only three years into its existence in Britain, that the government was able to acknowledge how important a part this would be. 'Housing is essentially a woman's question,' ran a Ministry of Reconstruction report in 1919. 'Bad as may be the effects of present housing conditions for the man, they are worse for the woman, since she has to endure them the whole day long.'[17] That's what poor Mrs Pickard had been trying to do in Glynde when she conducted her survey on working-class dwellings: find out exactly what women wanted from the bright, new, shiny homes of Britain's future. The members of Glynde weren't that bothered, it seemed.

They had obviously not read *The Landswoman*'s editorial for January 1919, which was positively rhapsodic in its exhortations to strive together 'For Home and Country'. The New Jerusalem is being built, it declaimed, in England's Green and Pleasant Land (this was before – but one of the reasons why – Blake's 'Jerusalem' became the WI anthem), and Institute members, 'who represent a great band of united women', have a leading role in this glorious task. They must increase food production, improve farming methods, and breed and bring up healthier children.

This last mission was discussed at length, both within and beyond the WI: too many names on the lists of the fallen were those of 'only children'; too many fighting soldiers were handicapped by indifferent health and poor stamina. Britain needed restocking with large families of vigorous young people 'to live, not to die, for their country'. It was the responsibility of mothers and mothers-to-be to keep themselves sound of mind and body, and produce not the 'C3' specimens of the pre-war generations but a sturdy, intelligent, wholesome population classified, rather chillingly, as 'A1'.

It was also their responsibility to demand education for all members of the community, in village schools, colleges of agriculture, and in classes administered by such organisations as the WI, the Workers' Educational Association and local authorities. Thriftiness must become not only a habit but a virtue, together with cheerfulness. 'The stability of the nation rests on a happy, contented people, and on the women the creation of happiness mostly depends.' There were some (naive souls) who thought the WI Movement would fold as soon as the war ended, for lack of anything to do. No chance: there was more work now, in reconstruction and regeneration, than ever.

Mrs Trenow's resolution at the 1918 AGM was debated with considerable passion. With no running water, no drainage and dark, poky rooms, the traditional cottages of England were described as little better than 'men-sties'. Ideally, each should have three bedrooms, a parlour, a kitchen, a scullery with washing copper, and a plumbed-in bath. It was a scandal, complained a delegate called Mrs Bland, that so many women were forced in this day and age to walk a quarter of a mile to fetch the family's water. Mrs Boyce agreed, declaring it a disgrace that any English child's life should be entrusted to such insanitary conditions.

The resolution was passed. A couple of years later there was another: to place as many women as possible (now trained in committee procedure by their WIs) onto the parish and district councils responsible for enacting these ideals. Essex triumphed again: the entire membership of Birch and Layer Breton WI turned up at the annual parish assembly when its President, Mrs Charles Round, stood for election as the first female councillor. Much to the consternation of the incumbent men, she got in.

This involvement with local non-party politics soon spread across the country, and the NFWI was delighted. Here was a movement, in action, generous enough to include the most isolated rural villager with hardly any schooling along with academics like Grace Hadow; callow but enthusiastic young VCOs such as Alice Freeman, and the likes of Lady Denman, who was one of the best-connected aristocrats in the country; the most pompous of provincial Presidents, and militant suffragettes. Membership empowered them all, both politically and personally. At last they were recognised for the contribution they could make to society. 'The knowledge that *their* work and *their* brains are being used for the betterment of future homes,' wrote NFWI General Secretary Alice Williams in 1918, '... must be an incentive and an encouragement to many women who never before had any idea that in them lay the ability to do anything but drudge.'[18]

That advertisement for Woman Power Insurance in *The Landswoman* has a startling strapline: 'Woman Power throughout the Empire stands out dominantly as the most wonderful feature of the war.'[19] Even more arresting is the notion, heavily endorsed by the WI, that women should be *worth* insuring. What had first been perceived by the public as a comfortable little club, or 'Mother's Afternoon Out', was fast becoming part of Britain's fabric. And it was increasingly obvious that – as one press commentator put it – there was a lot more to the Women's Institute than even its inventors could have guessed.[20]

The list of resolutions put forward at Annual General Meetings during the first ten years of the NFWI's existence reveals an almost shocking liberality. After the first, Mrs Trenow's on state-aided housing, and the next one on the public representation of women on decision-making committees, various campaigns were mounted: in support of the Bastardy Bill, whereby fathers were required to maintain their illegitimate children (this was in 1920, reflecting a wartime legacy of fatherless babies); for better awareness and treatment of sexually transmitted diseases (1922, following numbers of returning soldiers infecting their wives); for more humane slaughterhouses (1923); for an increase in the number of women police officers (1924); and for an investigation into maternal mortality (1925).

Traditionally, these are not subjects rural housewives were expected to bother their busy little heads about, never mind discuss; it was staggering that thousands of them were now expressing their opinions on such fundamental matters, and daring to lobby the highest authorities in the land.

It was increasingly obvious after the First World War that the WI's appeal reached wider than might be supposed from its original remit to improve the lives and conditions of village women. The Queen was a prominent supporter of the Movement, as President of Sandringham WI in Norfolk, as a visitor to various county and national exhibitions and as a guest of honour at AGMs. So were other high-profile individuals, who were either members or friends and relations of members – such as musicians Ralph Vaughan Williams, Malcolm Sargent and Adrian Boult; authors Virginia Woolf, John Buchan and E. M. Delafield; the activist and academic Gilbert Murray; almost the entire Lloyd George family; Neville Chamberlain; Winston Churchill and Lord Leverhulme (these two despite the best efforts of suffragette and WI member Edith Rigby, who, as noted earlier, attacked them both in her salad days); a goodly proportion of the House of Lords, and successive Home Secretaries, including Sir William Joynson-Hicks, who in 1925 described the WI as 'one of the most remarkable movements of modern times'. By then it had attracted over two hundred thousand members: all representatives, according to Chairman Lady Denman, of 'the normal womanhood of the country'.

One reason the WI was taken – and took itself – so seriously was Lady Denman. The Movement could thank Adelaide Hoodless for its inspiration, Madge Watt for her indefatigability, Lil Wilkins of the AOS for her commitment, pioneers like the Nugent Harrises and Colonel Stapleton-Cotton for their vision and Grace Hadow for her wisdom. It also owed a great deal to the circumstances of the war, which gave it impetus and a role to play in national life. But without the woman who led it until 1946 it would never have flourished as it did. She invested it with her own strength of character, and inspired its members towards confidence and influence. Lady Denman drove the WI forward – relentlessly.

4

Golden Eagle: LADY DENMAN

Lady Denman was that rare sight:
a rich woman going through
the eye of a needle.[1]

I used to spend an unusual amount of time between the ages
of about eight and twelve compulsorily motoring around the
moors of North Yorkshire with my parents, visiting weekend
farm sales. They collected furniture, so I went for pocket-money
job-lots of books and the inevitable boxes of photographs to be
found in a corner of the chicken shed or in the loft. I was fasci-
nated by these little archives of stiff-backed men and women, all
with the same pained, stoical expressions, as though trapped
behind the cracked glass and dirty clots of cobweb. Why did
they all look so sullen? I decided that history must be full of
ordinary, miserable people who can never have laughed or
relaxed. How glad I was that my generation was obviously the
first one ever to smile.

Most photographs of Gertrude Denman are like this. She
looks deadpan, neat and tidy; aloof, even, with her long nose

and down-turned lips. She's surely some sort of aristocrat, doesn't suffer fools gladly, and probably takes herself far too seriously to be much fun. Her face, in its conventional cast of formality, gives nothing away. There is one image, however, which suddenly lets the sunshine in. It's not very clear, taken by a friend on a trip into the Australian bush, but it's radiant with personality. The date is 1912, when Gertrude is twenty-eight, but she looks about fourteen. Everything about her is unconventional. Unruly long hair frames her face from a central parting and streams down to her hips. She's wearing a workaday shirt tucked into baggy jodhpurs, with black riding boots up to her knees. She's in the middle of mending or constructing something (this was a camping trip, and there's a pile of equipment on the scrubby ground), and she's grinning. Not just smiling, but grinning. This image says more about Gertrude Denman than any of the stuffy official photographs that were taken over the years. Yet it begs all sorts of questions, too.

Gertrude Mary, known to her family as Trudie, was born in London in 1884, the second child (of four) and only daughter of Weetman Pearson and his wife Annie Cass. They were invigorating parents. Weetman, aged twenty-eight when his 'Trudles' was born, was to become the 1st Viscount Cowdray. Pearson business interests encompassed massive engineering works, including the Hudson and East River Bridges in New York, the Blackwall Tunnel in London and the Sennar Dam on the Nile. There were family oilfields too, and a munitions manufactory, as well as a publishing house which owned the *Westminster Gazette* and various provincial newspapers, and which today is at the core of an international media corporation.

Annie was a keen suffragist and a forceful supporter of Good

Causes. She was the daughter of a staunch Yorkshire Tory, and one of that class of women described so well as Ladies Bountiful. Moneyed wives and daughters like her were with very few exceptions denied a serious education or vocation; instead, they turned to what was sometimes a rather aggressive brand of philanthropy. Some of her bountiful contemporaries were overwhelming. The 3rd Marchioness of Salisbury (whose daughter-in-law, incidentally, was later Gertrude's rival for office) was described as 'dominating, wilful and stormy' with a 'reckless energy and impatience', while other worthy ladies tended to veil 'an iron will and considerable business acumen' beneath a harmless-looking expression 'of sweetness, sympathy and resignation'.[2] Annie Pearson, although famously dynamic, was more sympathetic. She concentrated on Florence Nightingale's noble profession, helping found the College of Nursing and opening the Cowdray Club in Cavendish Square for its members. It was important for her to be *seen* to be doing good, and to be recognised as socially superior. She was an unsettling mixture of radical and snob. Riding a bicycle (as she did) and agitating for the Vote were unusually daring activities for a woman of her background. But the bicycle was a solid silver one from Tiffany's in New York, and her attitude to emancipated women did not extend to her own daughter, who she insisted should marry not for love but for power.

Trudie was closer to her father than to Annie. Weetman was similarly energetic, maintaining a political career alongside his industrial and business interests – he was the Liberal Member of Parliament for Colchester from 1895 until raised to the peerage in 1910 – but his dynamism was tempered by Trudie's favourite quality: common sense. He wrote a letter to her in 1903, when she was nineteen, which she kept all her life:

'Tis always well to remember that a reputation is a most dangerous possession. Those who own it have, willingly or unwillingly, the almost irresistible temptation to live up to it. The beautiful woman takes to dyeing and generally touching up (by adding to or taking from – the latter case in so far, of course, as possible) in her thirties or forties; the brilliant woman must shine at whatever strain or effort to herself and perhaps misery to others at being made to appear ignorant or foolish; the rich must continue to spend when possibly they would be much happier (and truer to their own interests) by being careful . . . No! The only true course to follow is to remain as near commonplace and average as your surroundings will allow you. This conduct will save many heartburnings, many disappointments and many false positions. But, at the same time, it is necessary to have large reserves, so that at any time you can push your way to the front should it be necessary or advisable to do so . . . Hence be careful to avoid having nothing behind. If you can make a splendid show in the window, do so, so long as there will be no disappointment when the interior of the shop is examined.[3]

'Splendid shows' never interested Trudie much. She was educated by a glum succession of governesses and at a small private school in London before being sent away to be 'finished' in Dresden. At eighteen she was duly launched at Court as a débutante, with all the other young ornaments of Empire. She must have been the most reluctant of the lot. Embarrassingly shy, she would far rather have spent the whole of her childhood at the Pearsons' enormous country estate at Paddockhurst in Sussex, making alarming bonfires from trees she axed herself, riding recklessly out to the hunt, shooting rabbits, playing hockey or tennis, and smoking. None of these, save perhaps the tennis, was a particularly feminine pursuit. Besides, she admitted delighting in 'behaving badly' – which probably meant no more than being unconventional. She read books on philosophy and economics rather than the frothy novels she was supposed to, and preferred the servants' company to friends of her own age and class. She was not a beauty, thanks to a broken nose proudly sustained in a sibling argument (earning her the nickname 'Golden Eagle'), nor particularly fond of dancing, dressing up, sitting through elaborate meals making inane conversation, or playing any part at all in the horribly defensive charade of London society.

When Annie Pearson advised Trudie to take seriously the unexpected marriage proposal of an army officer, Thomas Denman, made during her débutante season, Trudie was appalled. She didn't love the man. She barely even knew him. But Denman was considered by Annie to be a good match: though he wasn't wealthy, his breeding was good, his record in the Boer War honourable and his political ambitions lofty. At twenty-eight he was already a Liberal peer – the 3rd Baron Denman – and had made a promising impact on the House of Lords. To be fair to Annie, it has to be said that Denman appeared a likeable and witty young man and shared several of Trudie's interests, particularly hunting, and sports and games for which he had a flair. More unusually, he also shared her repugnance for pomposity and empty protocol. And he was loyal.

Trudie felt nothing for Thomas, however, but ordinary friendship. Bravely, she defied her mother and refused him, whereupon Annie dramatically succumbed to a nervous illness. The implication was that her perverse daughter was wilfully responsible; Annie was unlikely to recover unless Trudie made her happy again. Weetman supported his wife, and sternly instructed Trudie to make it her 'special care' to restore Annie's health and good spirits. Thus blackmailed, Trudie gave in, and accepted what was no more than an arranged marriage. On the morning of the wedding, 26 November 1903, she made one last attempt to salvage her integrity by refusing to go through with the ceremony. But the indomitable Annie prevailed. The Bishop of Chichester was waiting and St Margaret's, Westminster (the most fashionable church in England), was full. It would be the worst sort of form to back out now.

For her going-away outfit the new Lady Denman wore a hat on which sat an entire brown owl, stuffed and staring blankly into space.

A son, Thomas, was born to the Denmans in 1905. That same year Weetman presented them with a Victorian mansion, Balcombe Place, and its three-thousand-acre estate. It was next door to Paddockhurst, and Trudie loved it. Her daughter Judith (who went on to read Engineering at Cambridge) was born there two years later. There was a village on the estate, and when she wasn't out lumber-jacking in the woods or shooting things with the pistol she habitually carried, or driving a pony-cart with a frying-pan for a whip, or – most likely of all – fox-hunting, Trudie occupied herself with modernising her two hundred-odd cottages, installing sanitation and running water.

Occasionally forced to stay in London, she joined, at her mother's behest, the Executive Committee of the non-militant Women's Liberal Federation, working towards electoral reform. Future WI stalwarts Megan Lloyd George and Professor Gilbert Murray were also involved. In two years

The committee of Canada's National Council of Women at the time the world's first WI was founded, with Adelaide Hoodless seated front left, and Lady Aberdeen holding the book in the centre.

The redoubtable Mrs Watt, known to everyone as Madge, who exported the WI from Canada to the UK. The portrait is by her son Robin.

Adelaide Hoodless, founder of the Women's Institute movement.

Gertrude Denman in the wild: an improbable glimpse of the Governor-General's wife on walkabout in the Australian Bush in 1912. Gertrude was National Chairman of the WI from 1917–46. Inset: Lady Denman's official image.

Margaret Wintringham, known fondly by early WI members as 'our Institute MP'.

Idealist and academic Grace Hadow, to whom the WI movement owes so much.

At Scaynes Hill in Sussex, WI members were taught tinkering and cobbling to help 'make do and mend' during the First World War.

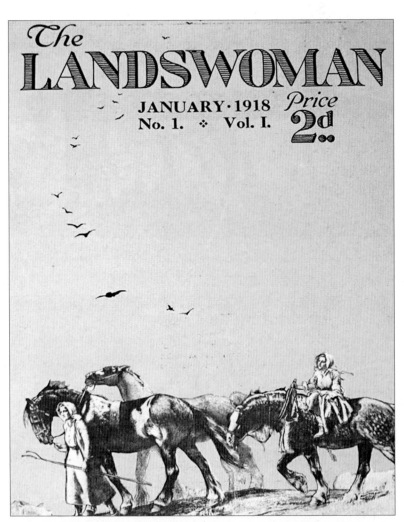

The Landswoman was published between 1918 and 1920 for members of the
Women's Land Army. It also included snippets of WI news before *Home and Country*
first appeared in March 1919.

These cartoons of 'WI Hats' were published in *Home and Country* in 1923. The women wearing them are timeless.

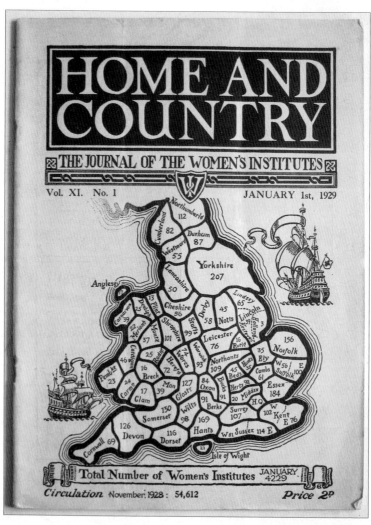

During the 1920s *Home and Country*'s cover featured a map of England and Wales
showing the number of Institutes in each county multiplying month by month.

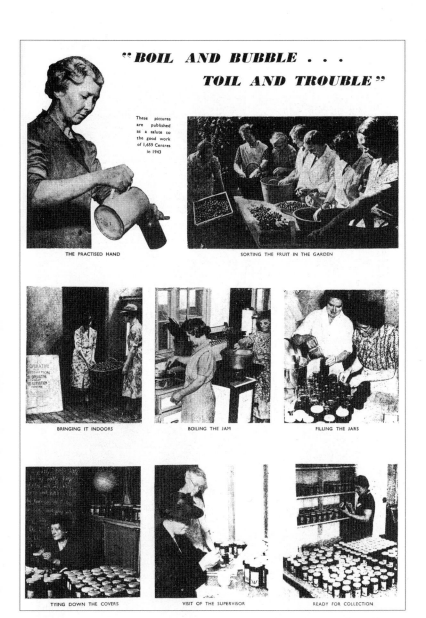

"BOIL AND BUBBLE . . .
TOIL AND TROUBLE"

These pictures are published as a salute to the good work of 1,659 Centres in 1943

THE PRACTISED HAND

SORTING THE FRUIT IN THE GARDEN

BRINGING IT INDOORS

BOILING THE JAM

FILLING THE JARS

TYING DOWN THE COVERS

VISIT OF THE SUPERVISOR

READY FOR COLLECTION

The 'jam-busters' at work: the WI's defining occupation during the Second World War.

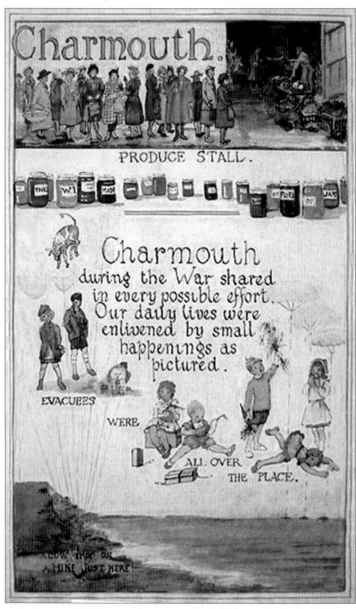

A page from the Dorset Federation of Women's Institutes War Record Book, picturing Charmouth WI's produce market; local evacuees; and the memorable day a cow was blown up by a land mine.

there, and largely thanks to the surprising Annie, she learned more that would be of use to her in the future than in all the years of her so-called education. It's where she developed her knowledge of and trust in procedure and in the mechanics of public service, and where she first witnessed the power of political persuasion and delegacy. It's also where she conceived, or formalised, many of the ideas that would underpin the infant WI: not least of all that women had far more to give to society than had ever been asked of them, and that class distinctions and a spurious notion of decorum corroded their lives. Trudie couldn't understand why women had to wait to be introduced to one another before speaking; why those of a lower social stratum were generally considered incapable of coherent thought and forbidden to address their 'betters' without invitation; why good manners were more desirable than good ideas; and why, given high ideals and strict integrity, a woman mightn't do exactly as she pleased.

Trudie resigned from the Liberal Federation in 1910, on the startling news of Lord Denman's appointment as Governor-General of Australia. He was only thirty-six: this was a singular honour for one so young and inexperienced. Either that, or (it was rumoured) a desperate attempt by his rivals in Parliament to get him out of the way, at Australia's expense. Whatever the reason, Trudie's parents were delighted and swiftly offered a gift of £50,000 to underwrite a suitably lavish lifestyle once they got to Melbourne. Thomas's unstuffy personality fitted the character of the young Commonwealth country well. The Denmans' predecessors at Government House in Melbourne had been the Earl of Dudley and his lady; he was an extravagant gentleman of the old Imperialist school, described as oppressively pompous. His wife appeared rather too decorative for

Trudie's taste. Australia was ready for a change – and so were the Denmans.

The two were warmly welcomed on their arrival in July 1911 as 'the perfect odd couple'. Here was a British bigwig who looked almost comically dismayed when ladies curtseyed to him, and a First Lady in her mid-twenties who squirmed with embarrassment at the absurd loftiness of her temporary station in life. They did have dignity, but were refreshingly unspoiled too. 'They are in everything not merely placid, critical spectators, but cheerful, enthusiastic gaiety-makers. They enjoy themselves thoroughly, and help everybody else too. It is the proper spirit to have in Vice-regal personages. It helps them, and it helps us.'[4] The press went into raptures over Trudie. She readily 'climbed down from the high horse of Vice-royalty' and was clearly far more comfortable hurling herself around a tennis court, 'hot and perspiring', with 'ordinary people', than playing la-di-da in Government House. But a certain amount of la-di-da could not, unfortunately, be avoided. 'I am so grand,' complained Trudie in a letter to her younger brother Geoffrey,

that I am not allowed to go to any but epoch making functions of a national character. I have to avoid doing anything merely civic or parochial, as that is the department of the State Governors' wives. I am also too grand to go into a shop. Can you wonder that most of the Governors' wives are bored to tears? . . . It is such a strain wherever one goes finding people to whom one must be polite. But we generally get a day's racing or hunting each week and odd games of tennis and, when wet, we play hockey in the ballroom. This last amusement must on no account be mentioned.[5]

She also played golf (a recent passion) down the corridors, dotting cushions around to act as inverse bunkers.

Sadly, marriage had not brought the Denmans any closer. There were practical as well as temperamental reasons for their incompatibility. Trudie's prodigious smoking habit, for example. For all his love of physical exercise and his bravery on the battlefield, Thomas had never been particularly healthy. He suffered all his life from chronic hay fever, bronchitis and asthma, which Trudie's smoggy company can only have exacerbated. When you're as robust and unforbearing as Trudie tended to be, there's nothing more irritating than someone who constantly drips and sniffs. So her favourite times in Australia were those she spent away from Thomas and Government House, in the outback. She would travel incognito, either riding astride (a skill she learned in Australia) or driving one of the two maroon-liveried cars they had brought with them from England. She adored caravanning and camping, both of which she was able to enjoy in the bush, and was rarely happier than when roaming around doing all the things she used to do at Paddockhurst and Balcombe Place: indiscriminately lopping down trees and burning them, hunting (except that now her quarry was more likely to be a kangaroo than a fox), and smoking.

Trudie fulfilled whatever official duties were required of her, inspiring Australian journalists into rapturous descriptions of her gowns, jewels and opulent hospitality. But she never saw the point of ceremony for its own sake. All work should be charged with purpose and proactivity. The Bush Nursing Scheme is a case in point. Lady Dudley had initiated a programme in 1909 to train women for medical work in the outback (like Canada's Victoria Nurses); when Trudie inherited her position as unofficial patron, she was disgusted to find only one Bush Nurse had actually been appointed. Recognising the desperate need of women and children in rural Australia, the golden eagle took the organisation under her wing, convening meetings, fund-raising, encouraging fellow workers and networking wherever she could, until by the time she left there were almost twenty nursing centres in Victoria alone and the scheme had been given the momentum it needed to grow nationwide. Perhaps Trudie connected the ethos of Bush Nursing with her mother's charitable interests; she was certainly convinced that she was able to help, and there was never any distinction in her mind between conviction and action.

Like Addie Hoodless in Ontario, who was also involved with Bush Nursing, Trudie became closely concerned in Australia with the National Council of Women. She had much to learn from them: political enfranchisement had already been introduced to the country between 1894 and 1908, and each state was anxious to train its membership in good citizenship and effective petition. What they learned from Trudie was to work cooperatively. She suggested the six state branches of the NCW should meet nationally, and addressed their first annual joint conference in Sydney in 1912. From then on the NCW became an integrated and powerful element of Australian public life.

At home in Melbourne, Trudie spent whatever spare time she had raising money – with the help of her friend Dame Nellie Melba – for two of her favourite causes: the local Repertory Theatre Club and the Arts and Crafts Club. The divine Dame Nellie was well known for sailing pretty close to the wind, once remarking when presented with a disappointingly slack jelly for dessert that there were two things in life she liked stiff, and jelly was one of them. No doubt the Dudleys would have blenched at such vulgarity, but it's easy to imagine Trudie roaring with delight. One joint Trudie–Nellie triumph was an enormous charity exhibition of antiques and silver held at Government House, to which twenty thousand paying visitors came over several days. It brought in over £1000 – equivalent to about £50,000 today.

It's difficult to avoid marking everything Trudie achieved in Australia as a portent of her future career in the WI, but it has to be said that rural nursing services, political awareness and good citizenship, involvement in drama and crafts, a fund-raising exhibition – plus an undeniable capacity for fun – could have offered no better training for the pioneer Chairman of the NFWI.

The most splendid engagement of the Denmans' residence in Australia happened on 12 March 1913, by the Molonglo River some 160 miles south-west of Sydney, when the laying of the new capital city's foundation stone took place in a naming ceremony. Despite all the parades, gun salutes, bands and fanfares, it appears to have been a rather haphazard and jolly day out for everyone concerned. Surviving film footage shows nearly everyone smoking (except poor Trudie, who wasn't supposed to do so in public), several dogs capering around the horses' and dignitaries' legs, and Trudie herself, thin and elegant in a gown of white net over green and an enormous hat, shuffling about as if not entirely sure what she was doing there.[6] The choice of name for the nascent city had not been easy. Everyone had their pet favourite, be it Denman, Southern Cross, Radiance or – horrifically – Sydmeladlperbrisho, combining elements of all six existing state capitals' names.

Once the final decision was made, the result was kept secret until The Day. It was written on a card which was slipped inside a gold cigarette case, ready for Trudie to perform the official ceremony. Unfortunately, no one was quite sure what it meant. Some insisted it was an Aboriginal word for a meeting-place; others whispered it was really a rather unseemly reference to a lady's bosom, after two nicely rounded hills nearby. Nor could anyone pronounce it with any authority. Prime Minister Andrew Fisher left it to chance, deciding that however Trudie happened to say it, so it would remain. When the time came for the christening at noon, the crowd fell (comparatively) silent. Trudie was handed the cigarette case, withdrew the card, and in her resonant, low-pitched voice declared: 'I name the capital of Australia, Canberra,' stressing the first syllable. She was greeted with three cheers, barking, various explosions and a very large lunch.

Soon after this, she returned to England. The official line was that her diplomatic duties had exhausted her, and brought on some unnamed but debilitating illness. Her friend and biographer Gervas Huxley, however, suggests that there were darker reasons for her departure. Mirroring her disintegrating relationship with Thomas was a growing and dangerous mutual attraction between Trudie and a member of the diplomatic staff at Government House. A serious affair would have been unthinkable: Trudie's character was as loyal as Thomas's and her personal standards aimed uncompromisingly high. She and her admirer (lover?) needed time to accept her unavailability. That's why she disappeared.

By the autumn of 1913 she was back, but not for long. Thomas was suffering from increasingly frequent episodes of asthma, and together the Denmans decided enough was enough. A replacement was arranged, although Prime Minister Fisher reckoned Thomas the best Governor-General Australia had ever had. A farewell party was held for Trudie by the National Council of Women. Everyone, they said, would miss her 'vivid personality, sound business head and untiring energy'. She was 'the last woman Australia would willingly part with'.[7] A gem.

In May 1914 the family set sail for home.

The Denmans arrived in England days before war was declared. Thomas went straight off to join the Middlesex Yeomanry, while Trudie submerged her energies (presumably renewed by the voyage from Australia) in a newly established charity close to her heart. The Smokes for Wounded Soldiers and Sailors Society, or SSS (there should really, surely, be four Ss), supplied millions of cigarettes and mountains of tobacco, pipes and cigars to military hospitals and for distribution at ports and stations around the country, to greet and comfort those servicemen who had 'caught a Blighty one' and been sent home. Trudie volunteered the ball-room of the Denmans' London home, at 4 Buckingham Gate, as a packing room; it buzzed with volunteers, and must have reeked gloriously of gaspers.

Outside, in a garden a stone's throw from Buckingham Palace, Trudie kept chickens. Poultry was a new enthusiasm: she and her close friend Nellie Grant spent hours together trying to devise the perfect backyard hen-house unit, which could be ordered through them for installation almost anywhere with a few square feet of space. With characteristic commitment, Trudie's interest in poultry quickly matured into a passion; she became Chairman of the women's department at the Poultry Association, and avidly attended conferences and lectures on the subject. It's not hard to appreciate why: here was something women could do on the Home Front, especially countrywomen, that was practical, satisfying, productive and skilled. No wonder she was so keen to help with her mother's bizarre agricultural show (for the other, posher Women's Institute) in the grounds of the Cowdrays' home around the corner in Carlton House Terrace on 11 July 1915: poultry was something of a speciality.

Neither the Smokes nor the chickens, however, were able to dispel a growing sense of unease over Trudie's relationship with the absent Thomas. Her younger brother was one of the first casualties of the war, killed on the first day of the First Battle of the Marne on 5 September 1914; the following spring the Australian friend from Government House died at Gallipoli. Both these shattering events must have brought home how desperately short life was; too short to waste on regret. She was never comfortable with dissimulation of any sort, and quick to deride it in others. Yet here she was, pretending to be happily married – or tolerably so. Despite the anxious advice of her parents, in whom (perhaps surprisingly) she must have confided, Trudie wrote to Thomas and suggested that, for both their sakes, they part.

Thomas was aghast, and begged her not to leave him. Apparently, when Trudie was a child and having to cope with shyness, those miserable governesses and a boring school, her closest ally in life was her dog. It followed her everywhere; she told it everything; she loved it completely. The grief she felt when the dog died was such a shock, and so terrible, that the young Trudie vowed never to have a dog again (and she didn't). Perhaps there was something of this defensive steeliness in her eventual decision, in the autumn of 1915, to remain as Thomas's wife. Perhaps she persuaded herself that it was acceptable finally to commit to being Lady Denman, so long as she didn't feel guilty for not loving him as she should – and she wouldn't feel guilty, so long as she loved no one in his place. The Australian was dead, and there is no suggestion that anyone else was ever romantically involved with Trudie; she and Thomas lived more or less together until her death in 1954. He died less than three weeks later.

In October 1916, Trudie's explicit association with the WI began. So much she had done in her life had been leading up to this, but it was only when Lil Wilkins asked her to join the relevant subcommittee of the AOS – alongside Mrs W. E. Jones, the owner of the garden hut in which the first ever WI meeting was held in Llanfair PG, and the dynamic Dorothy Drage of Criccieth – that an official link was formed. Trudie and Lil Wilkins must have met through their mutual interest in small-scale farming. Lil was the author of the definitive work on the subject, *The Smallholdings of England*, published in 1907, and Trudie had tried to institute a scheme (together, predictably, with a poultry-farming enterprise) at Balcombe Place. Lil appreciated Trudie's independent spirit and her pragmatism: right from the earliest beginnings of the WI as a national movement, Lil had been anxious that it shouldn't become too closely identified with the political Establishment. Trudie, as a suffragist and someone who obviously felt all countrywomen should have a voice, could well be very useful. Her lack of 'side', or snobbery, together with her experience on the committee of the Women's Liberal Federation and in running the SSS (of which she was now Chairman), made her an ideal candidate.

Trudie was not the only candidate, however. Samuel Bostock, a fellow governor of the AOS with Lil Wilkins, preferred Lady Salisbury. Cecily Alice Gascoyne-Cecil, Marchioness of Salisbury, had been Lady of the Bedchamber to Queen Alexandra; she was married to a prominent Tory politician whose father and cousin had both been Prime Ministers; her mother-in-law was a renowned and formidable philanthropist, and her society connections were impeccable. Bostock outranked Lil, and Lady Salisbury was duly invited to head the Women's Institutes subcommittee. But she refused. Trudie was second choice (though whether she knew this is unclear) – and accepted with pleasure.

Within the year, as mentioned earlier, the AOS was instructed to hand over responsibility for the quickly growing WI Movement to the women's branch of the Board of Agriculture's Food Department, headed by Meriel 'Slasher' Talbot and originally formed to set up the Women's Land Army. Trudie was astute enough to recognise that at this point the future of the WI could be fixed for ever. If it became an organ of the government, which Madge Watt advocated, its value as a tool for self-government for women would be lost (remember, this is still before the Vote). Its character as a non-sectarian, non-party-political organisation – so crucial for inclusiveness – would be nullified. Above all, its credibility as an organisation for identifying social problems and pressurising the relevant authorities would be eroded. 'I was convinced,' remembered Trudie later,

> that country-women were overlooked by the authorities and that unless they got together to put their case this unhappy state of things would continue. The 140 Institutes scattered through England and Wales were not then a Federation – a few of us had been discussing the need for a proper constitution, but how was I to convince a Government department that if these village societies were to be controlled by a Ministry or by Local Authorities their value would be nil?[8]

As chairman of the WI subcommittee, Trudie was called to a meeting with Meriel Talbot to argue her case for independence within the Board of Agriculture. 'I arrived at my interview prepared for battle and ready to spin a yarn that there'd be a riot in the countryside if the Women's Institutes became official organisations. Luckily my truthfulness was not put to the test, for Dame Meriel took it for granted that the Institutes must unite to manage their own affairs.'[9] One wonders whether the government would have been so indulgent of the WI had its membership been male. But as an organisation of largely unsophisticated women rather than politically subversive men, it was deemed unthreatening and quite possibly useful, especially as most of its members were suitably modest – in public, at least. 'We cannot be experts on big social questions,' admitted one of them, in coy response to a press report accusing WI members of generic stupidity, 'but we are not out to be experts, merely to apply our common-sense to the big questions of the day ... Experts ought to be on tap and not on top.'[10]

Thus the National Federation of Women's Institutes came into being. Elected Chairman at the first meeting in October 1917, Trudie was re-elected without fail for the following twenty-nine years.

Trudie and her first Vice-Chairman, Grace Hadow, complemented each other on the Executive Committee until Grace's untimely death in 1940. Both powerful characters but with different strengths, they had a healthy awareness of their own limitations and a great deal of mutual admiration. Grace was gentler and more cerebral than Trudie, whose nickname began to suggest a certain noble ferocity. Feisty and direct, as we have seen, Trudie grew increasingly impatient with those around her who dithered, lacked confidence or simpered. She could be quite daunting: very efficient, extraordinarily talented at bringing out the best in people individually and collectively, but not – beyond close family and friends – particularly warm or affectionate. Madge Watt, whom a later Vice-Chairman of the NFWI called 'a darling old bumbler',[11] was one of the few people to criticise Trudie for a perceived lack of sensitivity. But her criticism was not unalloyed by jealousy. Madge was visiting Norfolk on WI business when the news came through that Lady Denman had been elected Chairman, and is said to have given vent to her anger in the train on the way back to London, indiscreetly declaring the appointment 'a scandal'. *Madge* was the right person for the job, according to Madge, and the Movement would only suffer under Trudie.[12]

The committee of Llanfair PG WI had its reservations, too: in December 1919 they voted to write to Lady Denman in protest at what they considered to be an 'exorbitant' increase in the proportion of the membership subscription to be directed to county and NFWI headquarters – from 2d to 6d, a quarter of the year's fee. When Trudie was invited to Llanfair PG's summer garden party a few years later, despite being asked to choose the date herself, she doesn't appear to have attended.

Presumably those who derided the WI, and there were plenty, had little respect for Trudie, by association. Various letters appeared in the broad-minded house magazine *Home and Country*, pointing out the wicked folly of tempting a woman from her domestic duties in the afternoon or – worse – the evening. One, from a WI husband, condemned 'this D——Institute' as 'the curse of a married man's life' – 'Surely a married woman's place is at home when her man comes home from work? If I came home at 6 (which I don't) and had to get my own tea, things would happen . . . '[13]

An article describing the 1923 AGM, again published in *Home and Country*, ridiculed the whole exercise. The speakers were all middle-class women in laughably elaborate hats, it said, either mumbling, blaring or droning their scripts, and rarely offering any justification for their arguments other than that they believed in them deeply, and/or that they were women. 'The inevitable result of that position is that you begin to criticise almost automatically the things men do "because they're men"!'[14] The author (a man) went on to praise Lady Denman for her stern chairmanship – and then to sympathise with a speaker who was brutally cut off by her in the midst of a flowing speech. 'She had a wrong idea of the sort of stuff wanted for the conference. It is only fair to say that she took her discomfiture "like a brick".'

On the whole, however, Trudie was much admired. Gertrude Anson, an early VCO, characterised her as lucid and fairminded, with a strong, rich voice; she was always well dressed with 'a perfect hairdo and marvellous pearls'.[15] She used to sleep, it was said, with the standard work on parliamentary procedure under her pillow, but surprised many with her sense of humour. She strode, never sauntered; she was 'a capable business woman, a good housekeeper, shy, devoid of sentimentality, and full of sympathy for those in trouble'.[16] Her addiction to nicotine alarmed some, especially the fluffier sort of gentlewoman who thought it unfeminine or impolite to smoke, but that never worried Trudie.

In many ways, the WI was Trudie's life's work. But she seemed to possess an almost superhuman knack of running several lives' work concurrently. She was a prolific Chairman, combining her position at the NFWI with twenty-four years at the head of the Family Planning Association, twenty-one at the Cowdray Club (her mother's brainchild), ten as a trustee of the Carnegie United Kingdom Trust, six as President of the Ladies' Golf Union, and five as a member of the executive committee of the Land Settlement Association (encouraging the smallholding scheme). Add to that four years as a fellow and council member of the British Eugenics Society (not resigning – perhaps naively – until 1943, when the 'science' of eugenics was already chillingly embedded in Nazi Germany). She served on the board of the Westminster Press and of S. Pearson & Son, the major family businesses. In 1925 she was commissioned by the Ministry of Agriculture and the Board of Education to produce the Denman Report (published in 1928) on 'the practical education of women for rural life'; she was a JP, one of England's first women parish councillors, a Covered Courts Lawn Tennis doubles champion for 1920, and a member of Balcombe WI. She was made a CBE in 1920 for services rendered during the war, a DBE in 1933 for her NFWI work, and was awarded the GBE – Grand Cross of the British Empire – for organising the Women's Land Army, in 1951.

Towards the end of her life, when Trudie had given up most of her public positions, there was one she refused to relinquish. That was her leadership of the Family Planning Association. She never forgot the despair of many of the women she had met in the Australian outback, rendered helpless as any chance of some hard-won prosperity for their families dwindled with the arrival of more and more children. Mothers with families of perhaps ten or more were worn out and finished by the time they reached the end of their thirties, leaving their widowed husbands to make the impossible choice between working and so neglecting the children, and staying at home and sinking into poverty. Besides, Trudie had always believed in well informed choice. Women had as much responsibility in managing the population as men. The FPA empowered them – especially the socially disadvantaged – to use that responsibility wisely and do something practical about it.

Trudie's work with the FPA was not widely publicised. She is best remembered now for her role in the WI and for her well documented directorship of the Women's Land Army during the Second World War. The Land Girls were as close to her heart as those she called 'the salt of the earth', the members of the Women's Institutes, and she only resigned as Director of the WLA when the government refused to allow those who had served in it the official acknowledgement and privileges enjoyed by veterans of other women's services. She was said to love racing around England in her car, dressed in breeches, with a half-smoked cigarette hanging from her mouth and wielding a huge wooden football rattle to attract attention, recruiting new members to the WLA. She never lost an opportunity to bring them and the WI together, and was much prouder of the Land Girls themselves than of her part in their success. It was the same with the WI. Meriel Talbot, who helped found both movements, knew how vitally important Trudie really was: 'Perhaps I did little active service for the Institutes,' she once said with a twinkle in her eye, 'but I did give them Lady Denman.'[17]

5

Marthas, Marys, Pigeons and Crows: THE 1920S

We are yet bound together in one great,
unbreakable sisterhood.[1]

It is the autumn of 1925, and a typical day unfolds at the headquarters of the National Federation of Women's Institutes at 26 Eccleston Street, near Victoria Station in London. The building is leased by the NFWI from Lady Denman, who bought it in 1921 for the purpose; it is a comfortable four-storey terraced house, but already too small for those who work there and visit.

Almost everyone inside, bizarrely, is wearing a pale-blue cotton coat, from General Secretary Inez Ferguson downwards. This gives the place the surreal air of a private sanatorium with no patients, or a laboratory where the equipment is kept sinisterly out of sight. Members of the Executive Committee tend not to wear the overalls; they come to meetings in smart costumes and obstructive, flowery hats (except for the tall, bare-headed Miss Hadow and little Madge Watt, with her mob cap or crown of silver hair). There is a WI uniform available for Voluntary County Organisers at 68s, but it's neither attractive nor popular, consisting of a brown corduroy coat and skirt, a white or brown silk shirt with a brown tie, and a boring brown hat. There's also a slack-belted corduroy overcoat available (in brown), and a vaguely alternative hat (same colour). The skirt hangs lifelessly just above the ankles, and the overcoat looks dreadful.

All the windows are open to dispel the cigarette smoke, and the chatter of busy women drifts out onto the street. Miss Ferguson is slight and neat; she's a graduate of St Hilda's College, Oxford, where she read Classics. After that she took a diploma in Economics, then worked in the offices of the National Union of Women's Suffrage Societies and as the Press Secretary of the National Union for the Society of Equal Citizenship, before being appointed General Secretary of the NFWI by an admiring Lady Denman four years ago, at the tender age of twenty-six. She succeeded Margaret Hitchcock, who was also a committed suffragist and is still remembered at NFWI HQ for her stern exhortation to the newly enfranchised women of England to 'use their votes to insist that the morality of men conform to that of women'.[2] It's Miss Ferguson's job to coordinate the administration of the entire Movement, and to run 26 Eccleston Street. Her assistant, also an Oxford graduate, is Mavis Hay.

The Honorary Treasurer is in for a meeting with Lady Denman: she's Helena (Nellie) Auerbach, a colleague of Inez from the NUWSS (where she also acted as Treasurer) and Vice-President of the Jewish League for Woman Suffrage. Mrs Auerbach is in her mid-fifties; she's been in post since 1919, a confident, imaginative and efficient servant of the WI, with – according to Trudie – a 'clear brain and fighting spirit'. She is, incidentally, an evangelistic vegetarian.

Margaret Wintringham is also in the building. She's been a member of the Executive Committee (then called the Central Committee) since 1922, and is one of the NFWI's rarest assets: a Member of Parliament – or, strictly speaking, an ex-MP at this point: she served from 1921 to 1924. Margaret was the first woman to be elected to a rural seat and only the third to be elected at all, after Constance Markievicz (who didn't take her seat) and Viscountess Nancy Astor. She was born Maggie Longbottom in West Yorkshire in 1879, and trained as a primary school teacher before becoming headmistress of a school in Grimsby, Lincolnshire. She married a local timber merchant, Tom Wintringham, in 1903. The couple were unable to have children, and Margaret busied herself during her married life with work for the National Union of Women Workers, the British Temperance Society, various suffrage societies and – as soon as it reached Lincolnshire – the WI. She helped found and organise local Institutes, often driving potential members to meetings herself, and always with her own enormous teapot in the back of the car, having a perfectly understandable aversion to urns and geysers.

In 1920, her husband was elected Liberal member for Louth; when he died suddenly the following year, Margaret was invited to stand in his place. She had never been shy to declare her political allegiance; she was an indefatigable worker, a pioneering female JP, a committed Liberal campaigner. This likeable, unsophisticated countrywoman looked the very picture of homespun solidity – quite the opposite of the elegant and soignée Lady Astor – and Lincolnshire's farming stock warmed to her. The only problem with the election campaign was that Margaret refused to compromise her mourning for Tom by making any speeches, and the Tories had lined up a heavy-weight and eloquent candidate to oppose her. But thanks to her political contacts, Margaret could enlist a flying picket of the strongest and most persuasive of women to speak on her behalf, including feminists Eleanor Rathbone and Ray Strachey, and in September 1921 she won the by-election.

There was plenty of talking to be done once Margaret arrived at Westminster, and she soon established herself as an effective constituency MP and campaigner for women's issues. Trudie Denman proudly called her 'our Women's Institute MP' and relied on her to raise WI concerns at the highest level. This Margaret was happy to do, working particularly hard to retain women police officers (introduced during the war but in danger of being phased out), to widen the vote to all women of twenty-one and over, and to support free state education from nursery level to university. Neither Trudie nor Margaret saw any conflict of interests in Margaret's dual position of MP and Executive Committee member, given the non-party-polit-ical ethos of the WI. As another intensely political WI member put it (Eleanor Acland, the wife of a Liberal MP and a formid-able activist herself): 'I think that most strong party women will agree that it is a great pleasure and satisfaction to escape from the atmosphere of party politics and to join with our fellow-women of different parties to promote non-party ends, which still, thank goodness, form a large share of our common life.'[3] Perhaps surprisingly, given their opposing political views, wildly different backgrounds and almost comically dissimilar appearance, Liberal Margaret Wintringham and Tory Nancy Astor became close friends and – in many ways – allies. Both campaigned to encourage and empower women and achieved much when they worked together, even though Nancy was (according to Margaret) the dashing 'prancing pony' of the relationship while Margaret plodded along like 'a slow old carthorse' at her side. They remained close when Margaret lost her seat in 1924 and receded into the background of public life. She tried to re-enter Parliament, but failed; instead she continued with her WI work, and became a serial committee member in both Lincolnshire and London. A colleague on the Rural District Council remembered Margaret waddling into meetings invariably late, with a disarming smile and an apology (*so* busy today) before leaving early to attend the next one. She eventually spread herself too thinly to do much good – but here in 26 Eccleston Street, in 1925, she is still possessed of considerable power. The NFWI is lucky to have her.

Grace Hadow is not in today. She's engaged on library business, driving a van of books donated by the philanthropic Carnegie United Kingdom Trust to some distant WI.

There are seventeen members of the National Federation altogether, chosen (after 1923) by secret ballot. Most of them have retreated to their counties. Madge Watt is around, back from Canada and checking at the *Home and Country* office that her name is still emblazoned on the magazine's masthead, as she has requested, as the founder of the WI. It is.

When everyone is present for NFWI Consultative Council meetings, for example (to which County Federation representatives feed through ideas for future resolutions), or for full Executive Committee meetings, there's hardly a free moment nor any room to breathe. Subcommittees function between full meetings, covering education, public affairs, literature, music, agriculture and horticulture, health and handicrafts, and there's always some edict or other, a procedural handbook or perhaps a new set of rules for competition-judging to be printed, stuffed in envelopes, addressed and posted.

Members of the Executive Committee did an informal audit of their joint and several activities a couple of years ago, in the summer of 1923. Between them in a matter of months they organised three VCO schools, made scores of visits to individual Institutes, held three schools for the WI's Guild of Learners of Homecraft (which administered national craft exams and judges' courses), overhauled the NFWI's finances, gave evidence to a government departmental committee investigating food prices, set up a correspondence school for students of agricultural economics and published a series of short talks for WI members, as well as all their usual administrative tasks. The house buzzes audibly with industry and energy the whole time: a beehive with a hierarchy of queens and a little pale-blue swarm of willing workers.

Twenty-six Eccleston Street is also the headquarters of the Movement's six national (as opposed to county) organisers, with the beloved Mrs Lil Nugent Harris at their head – although she's considering resigning by the end of the year. Since 1923 Pollie Hirst Simpson has been one of Lil's fellow organisers, and the two friends make a pair as unlikely as Mrs Wintringham and Lady Astor. Lil, who also edits *Home and Country*, appears a fluffy, bird-like character, with a benign Irish lilt and a sparkle in her remaining eye. Miss Simpson, on the other hand, looks like the future Harold Wilson only slightly in drag, with a man's haircut, a collar and tie and a loud, gruff voice. Where Lil encourages with kindness, Miss Simpson terrifies. 'I have no time for the woman who comes [to meetings] and sits herself down and waits to see what everyone else is doing,' she barks, 'and then on the way home says she does not think much of it.'[4] She hurtles around to unsuspecting Institutes in her NFWI car and keeps a clockwork mouse in her pocket to wind up and let loose if her audiences ever dare relax too much. Despite her apparent ferocity, however, Pollie is also much loved. She is full of anecdotes, which she tells with hoots of klaxon laughter, and never denies the popular WI myth that beneath her stout and masculine clothes she wears the most outrageously sexy lingerie.

There is a fairly constant stream of visitors to the house all day. Some of them are Institute Presidents or VCOs, come to talk over personnel or procedural problems. A Norfolk WI has been refusing to pay its dues to the County Federation; a Middlesex one declines to respond to any missives (of which there have been many) from HQ. How should we deal with Lady X, a President who is described, despairingly, as 'an auto-crat of autocrats' and who doesn't allow 'her' members to meet when she's away – which is ridiculously often? Is there really no alternative to a Cumbrian WI having to meet in the local police cell for want of anywhere else?

Ex-suffragette Edith Rigby might breeze in on a visit from her Lancashire Institute, to reminisce about those heady stone-throwing days on rallies with Mrs Pankhurst and her militant friends. Meriel Talbot's colleague at the Agricultural Organisa-tion Society, Samuel Bostock, is a familiar face, as are Messrs Dobson and Dallinger from the Ministry of Agriculture: they are all representative members of the Executive Committee. An increasingly exasperating visitor is the journalist and first his-torian of the Movement John Robertson Scott, whose repeated requests for information and 'copies of almost everything, including circulars', to complete his *Story of the Women's*

Institutes (published just before Christmas 1925), are turning Lady Denman 'a little tart'.[5]

Between interruptions, members of staff concentrate on collating and sending out information for County Federation officials, VCOs and Institute secretaries. *Home and Country* regularly publishes letters from disgruntled WI members complaining about the amount of bumph sent from on high, but Trudie Denman believes it's good for them to learn to prioritise and deal quickly and efficiently with correspondence. When it's time for the monthly newsletter to go out to organisers, the helpers (including the doughty General Secretary Miss Ferguson) crowd round a dining-room table to lick envelopes and stamps. This, according to another *Home and Country* correspondent, is an occupation fraught with hidden danger: sadistic Post Office clerks like sliding stamps to their customers across grubby counters gummy-side down; furthermore, envelope flaps collect all manner of germs, which are then transferred to innocent tongues with potentially dire results. Happily, despite encountering hundreds of these death-traps, Miss Ferguson survives.

The year 1925 is a significant one for the NFWI's finances. When Treasurer Helena Auerbach took over from Alice Williams in 1919, everything was changing. The war was over, and having elected for independence from the government (which is estimated to have spent a massive £50,000 on it in total),[6] the Movement was now responsible for governing and financing itself. Grants of diminishing amounts were promised from HM Treasury to help ease the NFWI into autonomy, but only until 1926. There were other sources of money available, but these were austere times. The Carnegie UK Trust offered £1000 in 1918 to boost the development of rural industries within the WI: principally to make toys, leather gloves and straw or wicker baskets, which could then be sold at profit. The trust also subsidised other occasional and isolated projects. Otherwise, Mrs Auerbach had to rely on the flat 2s personal subscription from the WI's membership (equating to about £3 today).

Increasing that membership, therefore, was crucial. Mrs Auerbach was adamant that the subscription itself should not be raised, in case the Movement priced people out. Instead, she put up the 'affiliation fee' payable to the County and National Federations from each subscription, leaving individual Institutes with only 1s 6d per member per annum (three-quarters of the sub), instead of 1s 10d. The impact of the cut on village Institutes was to drive them to almost manic levels of fund-raising, which might be great fun and productive, or – according to a letter published in *Home and Country* – a damned nuisance:

In the programme which hangs at home there are thirty-seven engagements in six months ... Does an average of over two meetings a week make for 'Home and Country'? Surely you will agree that England is built around its homes. In a little country town the Institute has held a summer fete, a jumble sale, a tombola, and a two-days indoor fete within six months. For each of these the members have begged and are begging and it would surprise Institute workers to know how the Institute is regarded. One person, a shop-keeper, has been asked to give something for each of these efforts; he, among others, wonders if the Women's Institute, with sales and fetes for the sale of often very indifferently made articles, is another competitor with unfair advantages ...

If all these begging stunts and the use of questionable methods such as a tombola [perceived by some as dressed-up gambling] and the taking [of] the woman out of her home are essential to keep the Women's Institute going, then surely the foundation of the movement is rotten, and the hope of building Jerusalem in England's green and pleasant land will not be realised.

I enclose my card and beg to sign myself

A Mere Man.[7]

One 'begging stunt' went horribly wrong, when an Institute in Essex advertised 'an old-fashioned recipe for furniture polish' for sale at an astonishing 5s a tin (equivalent to about £13 today), to help raise money towards building a village hall. A notice in *Home and Country* some time later warned its readers not to use such polish anywhere near a fire: it contained petrol, and 'a young girl of 18 recently lost her life through a similar mixture exploding'.[8]

The Mere Man's wasn't a lone voice in the wilderness of WI-widowers; there was a strong response to his letter from WI members themselves, among whom was Katherine Sturdy, President of the West Dean branch.

It has often surprised me that the husbands of Institute members are so patient, especially when they not only have to get their own tea after a hard day's work, but must put the children to bed and remain in attendance throughout the evening [perhaps the WI was responsible for the birth of the 'new man'?] . . . I have often felt that my duties to the Institute clash with those to my husband and children. If the present low subscription is to be retained the money-making efforts of Institutes have to continue, but must this be so? Is it not time that Women's Institutes consider whether they are really helping the movement by continuously urging their National and County Federations to fresh activities and liabilities, the money for which must in the end be found by the Institutes and through them by the general public? I am a great believer in the Women's Institutes, but I often fear that in our enthusiasm for the movement itself, we are in danger of forgetting the ideals we should strive to attain.[9]

Still Mrs Auerbach and the Executive Committee stood firm, relying on a growth in numbers rather than a hike in the subscription fee to keep the Movement afloat. By 1925, on the eve of the NFWI's final general-purpose grant from the government, membership had risen from 55,015 (when she took over in 1919) to 204,460. The subscription was not raised for another eighteen years, when it went up by 25 per cent to half-a-crown.

There were certain things in the 1920s and 1930s that were common to every WI in the land – are common to them still – and made them immediately recognisable as part of a corporate movement. Mere Man referred to one of them: the concept of the new Jerusalem. But the famous anthem (not, insisted the non-sectarian founders, a hymn) was not always the signature-tune of the WI. Hubert Parry set William Blake's words to music, in 1916, expressly 'to brace the spirit of the nation' in the depths of the First World War. The feminist Millicent Fawcett heard it, and immediately wrote to Parry suggesting it should be adopted as an anthem for the women's suffrage movement: more modern than the slightly dreary 'Shoulder to Shoulder' and less strident than Ethel Smyth's terrifying 'March of the

Women'. When a suffrage rally was held in 1918 to mark the end of the war and the beginning of political enfranchisement for women, 'Jerusalem' was sung by everyone there. The rally was held in the Albert Hall, which – courtesy of WI AGMs and the Proms – soon became 'Jerusalem's' spiritual home.

It was the suffragist Grace Hadow who was responsible for appropriating 'Jerusalem' for the WI. During the first nine years of the WI's existence in Britain, many Institutes sang a hymn or said a prayer at their meetings – 'Glory to Thee My God This Night' as a round, perhaps, or one of Robert Louis Stevenson's 'Prayers Written at Vailima'. But strictly speaking they shouldn't have done so. The non-sectarian rules forbade any overt allegiance to a particular faith, Christianity included. Some Institutes copied the Canadians by reciting 'The Alberta Creed' or the American 'Collect for Club Women', introduced by Madge Watt: 'Keep us, O Lord, from pettiness; let us be large in thought, in word and deed. Let us be done with fault-finding; may we strive to touch and know the great woman's heart common to us all.' It was generally felt, however, that a shared Institute song would be a good thing. It would draw the entire membership together, suggest a sense of belonging, and – if they could find the right one – encapsulate the ethos of this quietly revolutionary new movement.

Grace was at this point a sort of song censor for the WI. Intensely musical, she took on the responsibility of deciding what was suitable for WI members to sing at meetings and concerts, and what wasn't. I don't think it was prurience that made her ban would-be innocent-sounding folk-songs like 'Strawberry Fair' – she was savvy enough to realise that a group of women blithely trilling about having their baskets picked and their cherries plucked was unlikely to do the reputation of the WI any good. When it came to the Institute's anthem, Grace's first idea was to hold a competition for members to compose their own song. It's disappointing that the NFWI Archive doesn't hold the original entries: apparently, they almost made Grace weep in their awfulness. Unable to bring herself to recommend any of them, she looked to her past with the National Union of Women Suffrage Societies and remembered 'Jerusalem'. It was first sung by massed members of the WI in May 1924 at the AGM in the Queen's Hall, London (the first Albert Hall AGM wasn't held until 1931). Though it was never compulsory, almost every Institute in England and Wales has sung it ever since, on special WI occasions or even at ordinary meetings, with or without a piano.

Predictably, not everyone approved of adopting 'Jerusalem'. Complaints soon started rolling in to *Home and Country* (and continue to this day) about the pottiness of people in Dorset or Suffolk singing about 'dark Satanic mills', or the trickiness (and consequent disharmony) of the tune; about stressed accompanists who can only play it at funereal speed, or tone-deaf Institutes who dissolve into quavery chaos every time. One correspondent is fairly sure Jesus never actually visited the Home Counties; another questions, 'What woman nowadays yearns for bows, arrows, spears and chariots of fire?' Besides, everyone knows William Blake was a madman.

Many blamed the singers more than the song:

Every woman who tries to understand 'Jerusalem' will realise that contained in the lines 'I will not cease from mental strife, nor shall my sword sleep in my hand till we have built Jerusalem in *every* green and pleasant land' is the answer of all women to the talk of war, strife and bitterness.

But to a large number of Women's Institute members 'Jerusalem' means nothing ... Perhaps 'Boo-Hoo' or 'Red Sails in the Sunset' would be more appropriate to people whose only objective in belonging to the movement is to spend a pleasant week-day afternoon or evening.[10]

'Jerusalem' survived, though, despite its challenging message and musical score, and the dangerous attraction of the likes of 'Boo-Hoo', which was a wildly popular band tune at the time.[11] The sound of 'Jerusalem' sung by five thousand full-throated women in one building is inspirationally greater than the sum of its parts. Hearing that rendering – as every WI member should try to do – makes up for all those less successful attempts in village halls around the country. Its greatest asset, as far as Grace Hadow was concerned, was to bind the WI together 'in one great, unbreakable sisterhood'.

They formed a strange family, these sisters. Of the seventeen members of the Executive Committee of the NFWI in 1925, three were Ladies, one a Dowager Lady, one a Viscountess, one a Countess, one an Honourable Mrs and one a former Member of Parliament. Several of the WI's most influential officers were graduates and/or former members of suffrage societies. Yet the organisation they administered accommodated hundreds of thousands of rural women across the entire social spectrum. Whole mining villages joined, as the Depression beckoned, and communities of railway workers as well as leisured ladies from the shires. Most Institutes aimed to attract a variety of women to their meetings – otherwise, the Institute was likely to collapse, like Mrs Pickard's at Glynde (see Chapter 3), under the weight of its own exclusivity. As long as twenty-five women were interested in forming a

WI – or, in small villages, twelve – it could, and should, be done.

A membership survey of Ringmer WI in East Sussex for 1920/21 reveals the following class distribution: 11 per cent 'ladies', the same percentage of farmers' wives, 13 per cent tradesmen's wives (or tradeswomen themselves), 8 per cent farm labourers' wives and 2 per cent live-in domestics. There were two teachers and a nurse; the rest included the wives of two publicans, of a headmaster, the vicar (whose daughter was also a member), the village policeman, the sexton, the postmaster, the Parish Council Chairman and the Parish Clerk.[12] The Institute had opened in 1920 with an exhortation, echoing Grace Hadow, from the visiting VCO that all members should consider themselves 'sisters the moment they entered the Institute room whether duchess or sweeper's wife'. By 1922, 43 per cent of the village's womenfolk had joined, happy in the realisation that here – perhaps only here – social hierarchies were obsolete. As a member of another WI in Leicestershire put it, 'What I like about the WIs is that we are all equal. There is no question of Pigeons at one table and Crows at another.'[13]

Other communities were not so lucky in the catholicity or tolerance of their Institutes. There were seldom any issues raised publicly about there being too many workers or tradeswomen in the Movement, except for the odd letter in Tory newspapers claiming that the WI gave 'the lower classes a false sense of their own importance',[14] but plenty of grousing about how top-heavy it was with gentry, especially at county and national level, and how difficult it was, therefore, to get any meaningful work done at meetings. Some of these complaints were flippant and ill-conceived. It helped no one to spread the word, as one malcontent did, that WI meetings offered only death by 'tea and twaddle' and 'a lot of bored women sitting in rows on wooden benches, listening to the Squiress or the Vicaress laying down the law'.[15]

The comments of Helen Wright Brown, an ex-Women's Land Army inspector, were more constructive. Writing in 1925 after a decade of the WI's existence, she noticed that those Institutes whose committees were exclusively composed of efficient and educated women (implying middle- or upper-class origins) rarely flourished. Committees like that only appealed to members 'of the same mentality'; the others tended to distrust them, especially when they insisted on dispensing reams of paperwork sent by NFWI HQ. In a few cases, such Institutes 'kicked over the traces and broke the rules', becoming undemocratic, disloyal and non-cooperative.[16]

The NFWI Executive does appear to have been aware of the dangers of over-organisation, in terms of both bureaucracy and personality. The Movement needed women experienced in administration and management, but ideally only as advisers. The whole idea of the WI was to nurture the skill and confidence involved in public service and self-fulfilment in everyone who joined. Snobbishness and officiousness were bound to get in the way from time to time – but how proud it must have made Trudie Denman, Grace Hadow and the others to hear an ordinary member, when accosted outside an Albert Hall AGM by a man wondering who on earth all these dressed-up women were, declare proudly, shoulders back, that 'we are the backbone of England'.[17]

In order to keep members coming and attract new ones, Grace Hadow maintained it was necessary to appeal to life's 'Marthas' and 'Marys' equally: to those who *did*, in other words, and those who *thought*. The WI must encourage women to value the practical things in life, and take pleasure, as Margaret Wintringham put it, in doing well what they had to do anyway. But this must never be at the expense of a cultural education. Grace's philosophy has underpinned the WI ever since. The Guild of Learners of Homecraft was established in 1920. Crafts were valued for their beauty as well as their workmanship and utility, and regular exhibitions at village, county and national levels were mounted to display the finest examples. These exhibitions were often ceremonially opened by VIPs, from royalty downwards, and were the source of considerable angst as well as pride. When they involved live competitions, when entries from WIs were judged during the exhibition itself and the results publicly announced, the milk of human kindness did not always flow as abundantly as it might. There was once an unholy row over a class for 'a knitted garment without sleeves' for which one enterprising lady entered a skirt she'd made, only for it to be disqualified. Another fracas involved a woman who had spent a long illness making an intricate 'dressing wrap' from old pieces of silk, for a class entitled 'something new out of something old'. The judge appalled her – and many readers of *Home and Country* – by summarily dismissing the entry as 'too showy, and too much work for result obtained'.[18]

A regular bone of contention at handicraft competitions was the inherent prejudice, perceived by working-class women, of the judging system. Whole Institutes were apt to complain if they thought themselves harshly compared with a more prosperous WI:

Why will you not give us classes for the working woman – for the farmer's wife and the cottage woman? How can a cottage woman, her hands stiff from washing, [and] mending thick boiler suits, compete with, for instance, the squire's or the clergyman's wife and daughters, whose fingers are pliable and whose education enables them to be artistic? We may have artistic leanings, but our opportunities to exercise them are few. Our work stands no chance in such company.

Oh, I know all that's ever been said about the best and raise the standard, and all the rest of it; but I contend that, with our opportunities, our best is different from theirs, and can never stand comparison.[19]

Obviously the practice of handicrafts within the WI was never meant to be divisive, but a means – at best – of communicating without words, thus strengthening the Movement's sense of sisterhood while maintaining an important element of Britain's cultural heritage. That's what the Guild of Learners claimed, anyway. Trudie Denman is reputed to have been less than keen on handicrafts – despised them, even – but she was happy enough to show off the fruits of members' labours at exhibitions, and to boast in high places of their skill and creativity.[20]

Music and drama had their own subcommittees at NFWI HQ, and flourished before the Second World War with activities ranging from five-minute monologues at monthly meetings to incredibly elaborate stagings of Peer Gynt, for example, put on by the whole village, or countywide historical pageants of stupendous scope (and presumably stultifying tedium to uninterested members of the audience). Everyone could get involved, from actors and artistes to designers, seamstresses and set-builders: the point of these events was not necessarily (or principally) their artistic merit, but their inclusiveness. Shakespeare was an inevitable favourite at every level, from small afternoon scene-readings to fully staged enactments. In June 1924 one hundred women of Westerham in Kent put on *Henry VIII*, authentically costumed, and directed by Miss Gwen Lally of the Old Vic. All the male parts – in a neat historical inversion – were played by females, as they were in women's colleges at universities before 1945. This sparked off a debate on whether real gentlemen should be invited to take part in similar stagings. The argument ran inconclusively for years through the correspondence columns of *Home and Country* and *The Times*.

Most Institutes appear, like Westerham, to have preferred an all-female cast. It was generally thought that the presence of men at any Institute occasion – except, perhaps, the Christmas party – inhibited the membership. At Hackness in Yorkshire, for instance, when the gents of the village were invited to a meeting in 1930, none of the women spoke at all.[21] Integration was not the point of the WI. The Movement insisted on its own identity, as we have seen, and close guardianship of that identity. This raised suspicions and in some cases resentment, especially when it became part of the constitution in 1923 that men could not be members under any circumstances.

The WI has never been short of detractors. Left-wing politicians labelled it a hotbed of Toryism, while Conservatives claimed it was all part of the Labour propaganda machine. The Primrose League (Tory) and the Mothers' Union (Anglican) doubted its apolitical and non-denominational stance. The Village Clubs Association (founded in 1919) ridiculed its refusal to amalgamate with it because of the VCA's mixed membership, while the Townswomen's Guild (from 1928) and the Women's Citizens' Association (1917–75) hungrily offered an alternative allegiance to those barred from the WI by virtue of 'the 4000 rule', which limited Institutes to settlements of four thousand inhabitants or fewer. These last three organisations were originally inspired, of course, by the WI.

The greatest rivalry between the WI and another women's organisation involved the Women's Voluntary Service during the Second World War, and we shall come to this later on. It was possible, however, to be a WI member *and* a member of the WVS, or of the National Council of Women, as well as of local councils, political parties and religious denominations. So long as no clash of principles or allegiance was involved, nor anything remotely disreputable, WI members were encouraged to take an active part in their communities and individual interests. Lady Denman was careful to oil the wheels of responsible citizenship by creating wide-ranging affiliations between the NFWI and a gamut of other organisations, including the National Union of Women Workers, the National Council of Social Service, the Women's Local Government Society, the Girl Guides, the Young Farmers, the Workers' Educational Association, the League of Nations Union (a particular favourite of Trudie's in the lead-up to the Second World War), the Council for the Preservation of Rural England and the Playing Fields Association. She also elicited testimonials (published in *Home and Country*) from the Archbishop of Canterbury, the Catholic Women's League, the National Council of Evangelical Free Churches, the Chief Rabbi and the Salvation Army. She was a canny woman.

Despite all these opportunities for proactivity and high-profile cooperation, most members of the WI, then and now, went along to their monthly meetings not (just) to save the world but to sit back, relax and be entertained. A varied diet of speakers and demonstrators was at the core of any Institute's programme. Some performers were more successful than others. The pages of *Home and Country* were full of advertisements offering all sorts of subjects, from poultry-rearing, 'Happy Cripples' or seamless knitting ('make a tunic just like Christ's on the cross), to 'The Romance of Forks', 'A New Idea! Whistling Entertainment' and the classic 'How to Be Happy though Educated'. Lady Denman was beset by applications from potential lecturers, some of whom were gladly engaged (not by the NFWI, but by County Federations or individual Institutes), while others – like a gentleman who wanted large audiences guaranteed for his talks on 'Gypsies and Norfolk Life' in dialect, illustrated 'with songs of my own making'[22] – were politely but firmly refused. Terse comments in Institute minute books reveal audiences' critical opinions: 'excellent', or 'rude and poor value'; occasional reviews of speakers imply recommendation or – much as coded job references can do – damn with faint praise. A honeyed piece in *The Landswoman* from Anstye in Sussex in 1918 could be taken either way:

After Mrs Huddart's interesting address, the President called upon Miss H. to sing some Sussex folk-songs, of which Miss H. has recently been making a collection, and some sixty songs is the harvest of only a few weeks' labour. Unfortunately Miss H. did not sing the sixty, but the few with which she did favour her audience left them, like Oliver, asking for more.[23]

A Mr Muddle of Jarvis Brook (also in Sussex) was, perhaps, a better bet: he was repeat-booked. At least his songs were funny.

The speakers were usually made welcome by the Institutes they visited, being met, fed and even accommodated by committee members with generosity and goodwill. Not always, though. An anonymous one, calling herself 'Hungry and Dirty', wrote to *Home and Country* complaining that she was rarely given lunch or high tea or supper before a meeting, nor reimbursed travelling expenses, nor even given the chance of a wash and brush-up before performing. When John Nugent Harris visited an Institute in southern England in the earliest days of the WI, he was put up by a railway porter and his wife and expected to share their double bed (with the porter – the wife slept elsewhere). Another speaker, a woman, arrived at her hostess's home after the meeting to be shown to the attic, 'divided in two by a clothes line on which hung a blanket, a large sheet, and some garments at either end. The hostess said, "My husband and I sleep the other side of the line, and this is your bed here," pointing to a small bed and adding, "My darling sister died in that bed three weeks ago . . ."'[24] A nurse from Wiltshire threatened to take the NFWI to court when she was 'inexplicably' dropped from the Federation's list of speakers; actually, she'd wickedly been using the meetings she addressed to sell Spirella corsets on commission.[25]

The writer E. M. Delafield was a WI member (as Mrs Francis Dashwood) and an experienced speaker. She gives an account of a short tour in her classic *Diary of a Provincial Lady* (1930) which is supposed to be fictional. It does pander to the perennially popular image of a WI being nothing but a bunch of bucolic and endearingly eccentric gentlewomen. But I have to admit that I, too, have been to Chick and Little March . . .

Bus from Chick conveys me to Little March, after successful meeting last night, at which I discourse on Amateur Theatricals, am applauded, thanked by President in the chair . . . and taken home by Assistant Secretary, who is putting me up for the night. We talk about the Movement ... difficulty of thinking out new Programmes for monthly meetings, and really magnificent performance of Chick at recent Folk-dancing Rally, at which Institute members called upon to go through 'Gathering Peas-cods' no less than three times ... We go on to Village Halls, Sir Oswald Mosley, and methods of removing ink-stains from linen ...

Reach Little March, via the bus – which is old, and rattles – in time for lunch. Doctor's sister meets me – elderly lady with dog – and talks about hunting. Meeting takes place at three o'clock, in delightful Hut, and am impressed by business-like and efficient atmosphere. Doctor's sister, in the chair, introduces me – unluckily my name eludes her at eleventh hour, but I hastily supply it and she says, 'Of course, of course' – and I launch out into A Visit to Switzerland. As soon as I have finished, elderly member surges up from front row and says that this has been particularly interesting to *her*, as she once lived in Switzerland for nearly fourteen years and knows every inch of it from end to end. (My own experience confined to six weeks round and about Lucerne, ten years ago.)

We drink cups of tea, eat excellent buns, sing several Community Songs, and Meeting comes to an end. Doctor's sister's two-seater, now altogether home-like, receives me once again, and I congratulate her on Institute. She smiles and talks about hunting.[26]

It was easy in the 1920s, as it is today, to yield to a delicious temptation to caricature people when talking about the Movement as an outsider. Insiders like E. M. Delafield were allowed to tease, however, which they did with affection and admiration. Through everything its membership did, from the bright lights of 26 Eccleston Street to the most remote Institute that timed its monthly meetings by the full moon so its members could find their way home across the fields, the WI tried to make sure that they and their communities were, indeed, 'happy though educated'. It was a lofty ambition, but it worked then, and is still working now.

6

Change the World
in an Afternoon: THE 1930S

Long before women had the right to vote,
they had established a virile parliament of their
own ... This great parliament is, of course,
the Women's Institute.[1]

Gertrude Anson was only twenty-four when she was appointed NFWI Organiser for 'the Northern Counties' in 1920. It was a challenging post, taking the good news of the WI to those who dwelt in the darkness beyond the Midlands, but she was fairly confident of success. She had grown up in the Lake District and still had a house there; she had been to Somerville College, Oxford, and so knew of Grace Hadow, and she burned with evangelistic passion for the young WI. But on her first tour of duty it became very clear, very quickly, that things were not going to be easy. Her first stop was at Amble, in Northumberland. 'I was introduced and began my speech. I looked round the room to see who might appear to be interested but there wasn't one. I might have been talking to a row of cabbages. I tried what I thought were one or two funny stories – not a flicker!' She sat down to sullen silence, and prayed for the meeting to end, when someone mentioned the magic word and suddenly the whole meeting blossomed, like a desert after rain:

> The President said 'Now we'll have tea.' Immediately 40 women sprang to life and started chatting and laughing. I jumped off the platform and sat down by two fat old bodies and asked if I could join them for tea. They said 'yes' with enthusiasm and then one of them said 'Eh that was a good story you told us – fair made me laugh that did.' After that everything cheered up and I went away feeling that I'd got a perfect subject for my next WI talk on what we would today call 'audience participation'.[2]

People who have been geographically and culturally isolated for generations develop an exclusive local identity and self-sufficiency, and feel instinctively threatened when told to change by an outsider. This is exactly what John Nugent Harris and Madge Watt found right at the beginning of the Movement's history in Britain: no matter how good the news, it's the messenger who matters. Miss Anson soon discovered that outside tea-time, Northerners had no patience with 'people from London who imagined they knew what was good for [them]'. So she resigned her mission as Northern Organiser and became resident County Secretary for Cumberland (Cumbria) instead. Now she was in their camp, she could infiltrate the opposition more subtly, with the credibility conferred by being 'one of us'. That's when her real work began.

Before the Second World War no working-class woman who was not a long-term member of the WI would claim any expectation of happiness or education. Happiness was a lucky accident, not something to be pursued. Education happened to other people, who had time and money to waste. A woman's job was to keep the wheels of real life turning, on an often monotonous and rutted road. One of the NFWI organisers' most daunting tasks was to persuade people in the more remote counties of England and Wales not only that things could be better, but that they *should* be.

Lady Denman's genius lay in her recognition, before the organisation became too hierarchical, that the change she so ardently wished in women's lives would only develop organically. Unless members of the WI were convinced they had control over change, and could be persuaded they deserved it and could effect it in partnership with one another, the Movement would mean nothing. That's why the National Executive took such pains to put a definite structure in place, a rigid and secure framework which both contained and supported the growing edifice of the WI. It was a uniform structure which embraced the monthly meeting, local as well as county and national committee meetings, and directed resolutions from the grass roots of the agricultural community to Westminster's highly wrought corridors of power, eventually reaching out to women all over the world.

The WI was also a leveller, whereby women like Grace Hadow and General Secretary Frances Farrer, intellectually sophisticated, were no more important as contributors than the elderly widow described in a letter I came across, written by Monica Money-Kyrle of Wiltshire, in 1934.[3] Mrs Money-Kyrle explains that she has found a mandrake root in her

garden (*Mandragora officinarum*). The mandrake is swathed in
dangerous legend: its root, shaped like a man's body, is said to
scream when it's pulled from the ground, and anyone who
hears that scream is sure to perish within days. Monica takes
it along to her local WI as an amusing curiosity, but is shocked
to be told by an aged member that this is definitely no joke.
The old lady's husband had also dug up a mandrake root, 'in
spite of warnings of the danger', and sure enough had keeled
over, stone dead, soon afterwards. Superstition was still a vital
part of many countrywomen's lives, and can't have sat
comfortably with the NFWI's drive for common sense and
clear-sightedness.

A strong, corporate sense of identity was the key. Every
monthly meeting had (and essentially still has) the same basic
programme – from Anglesey to the Wash, Cornwall to the Scottish borders – and no member, however 'civilised', was exempt
from its requirements. Specific content differed from Institute
to Institute, but according to a programme handbook current
in the 1930s the format remained the same.

There were three main elements: business, educational and
social. Business was usually dealt with first (after a preparatory
committee meeting, probably in a member's home), and
included the reading and signing of the last meeting's minutes,
various communications from 'on high' (county or national
committees), and an update on the progress of current resolutions and mandates via the NFWI's exhaustive *Quarterly Notes
on Public Questions*, published from 1936 to 1971. Announcements
or decisions to be made about Institute events were addressed
at this point. When new committee members were elected, it
would be by secret ballot. If current ones wished to stand down,
they were almost always begged to stay; finding different and

suitable people (with a modicum of modesty as well as efficiency) to stand for office in any voluntary organisation has
never been easy.

The educational section was often more or less palatably disguised as a talk from a visiting speaker, or a demonstration of
some kind – cookery, quilting, first aid, fish-gutting, soldering,
whatever it might be. Possibly it was presented by the members
themselves, asked to split into small groups (to discourage shyness) and debate different subjects among themselves, or take
part in a 'roll-call' whereby a ball was passed from member to
member, and when a bell chimed, whoever was holding the ball
had to say a few words on the day's chosen topic. The handbook
helpfully provides suggestions, including 'How can home and
school co-operate in children's preparation for life?' and 'What
I want to know about Russia'. Closer to home: 'What do we
expect of (a) Our officers and committee? (b) Our members?'
Or even closer: 'What I should do if I caught fire'.[4]

In June or July the Institute's representative delegate reported
her impressions of the recent AGM, either as a business or
an educational exercise. She would have gone to the AGM on
behalf of her own Institute and one other, and ideally a different
member was sent each year. But trips to London or occasionally
elsewhere for AGMs were expensive, potentially disruptive and
often frightening. Many women had never ventured beyond
their county town before. Sometimes two delegates were
allowed to go: the official representative, and a friend to hold her
hand (literally). At more than one Institute it was the station-
master's wife who regularly attended, not so much because she
was considered a woman of the world but because she got
reduced rates on the railway.

It's a mark of members' growing confidence in the value of

their own opinions that their AGM reports grew more critical year by year, at least before the Second World War when the run of annual meetings was inevitably disrupted. Someone who attended at Blackpool in 1930 complained bitterly about the venue: the noise of beasts at the zoo next door drowned out the speakers. Even without the trenchant comments of camels and seals to contend with, hearing what was going on during AGMs was a perennial problem. Some 'Hints to Speakers' issued before the 1937 meeting at the Royal Albert Hall reveal the most common difficulties:

Stand on the place marked on the floor opposite the microphone, and wait a second before you begin to speak.

Do not lean towards the microphone – your voice will carry better if you stand just on the place indicated, and keep as still as you can . . .

You can tell when you are 'on' the microphone as then your voice will suddenly sound louder. Do not attempt to make your speech until you are certain that you are 'on' it.

Do not repeat what other speakers have said. Listen carefully to the speeches before yours and cut out from your speech points which have already been made.

It is easier for those in the gallery to hear speakers who remove their hats.[5]

Members from Buckinghamshire talked of 'terrible discontent' in their report of the last AGM before the Second World War, held at the Empress Hall in Earl's Court. Not only were the speakers poor, but the lack of ladies' lavatories was 'outrageous'. The women of Montgomeryshire considered the sale of ice-cream to be undignified: vendors paraded up and down the aisles like cheap cinema usherettes. Essex ladies said the hall was too dimly lit to see the speakers and (predictably) too cavernous for them to be heard. The most common complaint of all, year on year, was the interminable length of the AGM. From about 3.30 p.m. onwards the audience had usually had enough, and got 'restless and inclined to be irritable'.[6] Changing the world in a couple of hours at the village hall was fine; spending a whole day doing it, far away from home, was just too tiring.

The 1930s programme handbook encouraged Institutes to time their tea-break after the lecture or discussions. The taking of tea, as we have already seen, is a ritual that must never be ignored. As well as enjoying the obvious attraction of a hot drink and perhaps a bun or a couple of biscuits, the wise President made sure her members used the interval to mix with one another (rigorously avoiding cliques), welcome new members, and devise efficient and harmonious rotas for waitressing and washing up. No tea-break should last longer than fifteen minutes – ten was ample – before the President briskly rang her little bell to get things moving again.

The 'social half-hour' followed. This was a versatile period, perhaps involving a competition, a song or two, some charades or other games. In Madge Watt's ideal WI everything was integrated, linked by a 'golden thread' or common theme. This thread wove together a whole year's programmes, and separate items in each month's meetings. The year's theme might be 'Keeping ourselves informed', for instance. Each month's educational and social activities would somehow relate to that. After a roll-call on 'What I most enjoy in the paper' there might be a talk on 'How a newspaper is made', then a competition on 'Most interesting article in a month's newspaper reading'. Next meeting, a 'parade' might be arranged, with each European country represented by a member who must say a few words about it; then there could be a talk on 'Europe today' and a competition (on a postcard) about which European country each member would choose if she could not be British – perish the thought – and why.

This was the ideal. In reality, pre-war meetings tended to be more motley. Joyce Grenfell described her first ever WI meeting, in 1936, in a letter to a friend:

Twenty of us met in the recreation room by the tennis court. Diana Smith is the sec. and an elderly Mrs Serocold from Taplow [Berkshire] is the president. We began with 'Jerusalem' played on a not very well Decca portable and in a key almost beyond human hearing ... Then we did the day's business, the minutes, a report or two, and the formal welcoming of our new member. I stood up, said nothing, and sat down again. Probably not quite adequate.

Mrs Millar from Burnham made a pork pie and some of us took notes and some followed her with their own ingredients at a separate table. This took nearly an hour ... Then we had tea. Buns, brown bread and butter and confectioner's cakes: the sort that look unreal and taste worse ... [*shop-bought* cakes? At the WI?] I've missed some wonderful demonstrations in the past year. 'The use of salads and how to make them' in June, and in August 'Herbs in myth, magic, medicine and meals'. January taught us 'Care of the Feet'.[7]

Miss Grenfell launched her career in show business with a monologue by a gloriously inane WI lecturer on 'Useful and

Acceptable Gifts' (boutonnières made of beechnut husks, wallpapered waste-paper bins and cheeky little Dicky-Bird calendar-holders assembled from India rubbers and a chicken feather). No one could be more mocking of the WI than WI members themselves. In 1928 there was a waspish article in *Home and Country* headed 'Crafts We Do Not Like', which ridicules paper flowers, barbola (modelling in paste), anything involving fishbone, shells or beads; 'and all shams and dust-traps ... Of what use is it to learn how to make a golliwog out of a dish-mop?'[8] The NFWI's Crafts subcommittee tended to agree, admitting that these trivialities might have had their place when the Movement was young, drawing in members who needed distraction from the war and its aftermath. But now it was more mature; its craftswomen were ready to tackle serious projects like wood-turning, upholstery, pottery and bookbinding. *Really* useful and acceptable gifts.

However carefully its agenda was designed, every meeting everywhere closed with notices, and a repeat rendition of 'Jerusalem' or the national anthem. Then members were released, bursting with new ideas, energy and determination to fulfil the WI motto 'to unite in promoting any work which makes for the betterment of our home, the advancement of our people, and the good of our Country'. Or – more likely – they just walked amiably home, wondering what to cook for dinner.

There is no doubt that thanks to the feeling of personal engagement among Institute members, those monthly meetings spawned great things. On a personal level, the WI made friends of strangers, confident speakers of the shy, and skilled craftswomen of haphazard amateurs. The apathetic metamorphosed into informed and active citizens, and the discontented began to cheer up. Grace Hadow was adamant that the WI should never become homogenised into a representative and therefore anonymous mass of women; its strength lay in the fact that it functioned as a movement in which every individual was encouraged to express and if necessary argue her own opinion (while listening thoughtfully to those of others) and then co-operate. This collegiate approach implied a sense of respect that has proven to be one of the WI's most enduring gifts to its membership. It was the whole Movement's 'golden thread', if you like: self-respect, mutual respect, and respect for the environment in its widest sense. Pride isn't always a bad thing; membership of the WI engendered the sort of pride that is almost indistinguishable from love.

More pragmatically, membership was good for you, and not just because it taught you about hygiene and nutrition. Editorials in *Home and Country* identified stress and anxiety as significant mental and physical health hazards for country-women. Friendship and good company were therapeutic, and the Institute did all it could to encourage both. At certain WI 'centres' in England, members were invited to relax completely. They were provided with reading rooms; facilities for leaving parcels, bicycles, even babies; bathrooms with hot water; and little restaurants. These centres tended to be in market towns with, presumably, a fairly prosperous (so less stressed?) membership. There was even a club for WI members visiting London, the Forum, run along the lines of the famous Lyceum and Pioneer Clubs for ladies (the latter associated with the other more sophisticated Women's Institute). The Forum opened in 1919, founded by the NFWI's first Honorary Secretary, Alice Williams, principally for Institute ladies from the shires who had occasion to visit the capital regularly.

The Club Building, which has magnificent views of Hyde
Park Corner and Buckingham Palace Grounds, contains, in
addition to the usual Club rooms . . . a Billiard Room, Bridge
Room, a Salon which may be hired by members for picture
exhibitions and private receptions, a Dark Room for
Photographers, and a fully equipped Hairdressing Room. In
addition to a large number of Bedrooms for Members, there
is accommodation for Members' personal maids.[9]

Perhaps understandably, there was a certain amount of deri-
sion expressed in the correspondence columns of *Home and
Country* whenever the Forum was advertised: whatever had
billiard rooms and maids' accommodation to do with the average WI member? Exclusivity was never the WI's style. The club
was not well patronised.

Home and Country was a considerable asset to WI members.
But despite the strenuous efforts of editorial staff and VCOs
to increase its circulation, even venturing to sell it on the
open market, sadly only a minority of members subscribed
to it before 2007. At that point it was replaced by *WI Life*, and
sent to everyone under the terms of their WI membership, like
it or not. Even now, I'm told, many women put it straight in
the recycling bin, unread. It certainly went through alternating
cycles of dreariness and liveliness over the decades, perhaps
trying to cater to too many different tastes at once, but there
was always something there to relish. It was a little like a WI
meeting in print: business matters came first, then educational
pieces about history, art, local government, astronomy ('Above
our Heads'), and so on. There were book and theatre reviews,
tips on craftwork, and most issues incorporated a knitting
pattern – 'a charming long-sleeved jacket for the not-so-slim' or

a nice woolly bathing suit in stripes. There were competitions for limericks or full-length essays, sections for members' children, a short story or serial, and a vigorous letters page. Aspirational articles appeared on the achievements of women in politics, sciences or the arts, and occasional messages from government ministers reporting on WI campaigns or asking for members' help with surveys.

Recipes were a regular if not conspicuously successful feature. Rabbit brawn popped up fairly regularly, and the odd treat like Turkish Delight or cocoa flapjack, but nothing very imaginative. Perhaps the editor thought WI members were too conservative in the kitchen to try anything more adventurous than macaroni cheese with tomatoes on top. This was not necessarily the case. In February 1932, suggestions for a week's menus were printed. Day one had sausages, tea, bread and margarine and treacle for breakfast, with bread and milk for baby. Lunch was 'Roast flank or clod' (shoulder of beef), sprouts, potatoes and 'economical Yorkshire pudding'; there was bread and margarine *or* jam for tea, with 'dripping cake', and bread and cheese with hot milk for the children. The staples for the next six days were bread and dripping, an occasional 'rasher for father', baked onions, bread pudding, bloaters and a dish of stewed prunes.

The reaction from readers was immediate. Just because money was tight, there was no excuse for recommending such a boring diet, full of fat and starch. 'I must say,' wrote an indignant correspondent, 'that in these times father would expect something more than a rasher.'[10]

Home and Country's advertisements ranged wildly between the quotidian and the exotic. Southall's soluble sanitary towels (very exotic in the 1930s) jostled with Bird's Custard; 'Homes of

Rest' for women suffering from 'Functional Nervous Disorders, Alcoholism and Drug Addiction' with the latest high-heeled ostrich-skin shoes; and the fantastically complicated Vestrol Oil Stove (which looked like the engine-room of a small ship) with 'Black and White Check Knickers with an Inside Fleecy Finish'. Every month top housekeeping tips were contributed by particularly thrifty or imaginative members, such as how to stuff your own mattress, how to make Dorothy bags out of men's top hats (very Grenfellesque), or new bars of soap from the melted-down relics of old ones mixed uncomfortably with silver sand and pumice stone.

The most beguiling bits are the photographs. Jaunty reports of Institute fancy-dress competitions are accompanied by very stiff and solemn ladies, hands clasped tensely in front of them, wearing prize-winning headdresses disguising them extremely imperfectly as, for instance, Toby jugs, birthday cakes or Christmas trees. In one photo six of them stand side by side, looking as though they've crawled into striped paper sleeping-bags head first with only their neat little feet peeping out. They are a catch of mackerel. The Aveley Kings Kazoo Band, dressed in almost matching hats, looks impossibly grim, while eleven mature members of the Herefordshire Federation pose improbably as a human pyramid in their vests and gym knickers. An article on the benefits of a tanning machine for babies, quite terrifying in retrospect, is accompanied by an evil-looking toddler wearing nothing but goggles and a demonic grin, and an advertisement for Mrs Clara E. Slater's Abdominal Belt looks like something out of an S & M manual (if there are such things . . .). There are photographs of children at WI first-aid demonstrations bandaged to within an inch of their lives; and for the magazine's younger readers, a regular children's corner with stories and, on one occasion, a heart-warming picture of 'Two Hedgehogs Eating a Dead Rat'. The WI was never a sentimental body.

Home and Country did a vital job in informing members of Institute failures and successes. Good ideas spread fast, and individual WIs set precedents for many features of community life we now take for granted. Two young mothers died in Barbon, Cumberland, in 1935 after complications during childbirth. Barbon was eighteen miles away from the nearest medical help, so the WI decided to arrange a clinic, with a visiting nurse and doctor, to be held in the village every month. Other WIs campaigned successfully for district nurses, which not only benefited the neighbourhood but highlighted problems which would later be tackled – with the material help of the WI – by the nascent National Health Service. Mrs Walton, a member of Blacko village's WI, was a nurse in Lancashire in the 1930s.[11] She used a communal bicycle to reach her patients, and reported terrible stories of crochet-hook abortions, exhausted mothers who gave birth again and again ('Why not? It's the only thing that's bloody free'), and babies riddled with vermin from the moment they were born. Publicising conditions like these was almost as important as treating them; the WI was a pioneer in helping to do both.

It also agitated for local playing fields because so many members' children were injured or killed by traffic while playing on the streets, even in small settlements. It lobbied for telephone boxes in villages (again, a safety issue), and for public lavatories for charabanc passengers in well known beauty spots. And those public lavatories were much better without the traditional turnstiles, which effectively barred pregnant would-be users as well as the 'not so slim'. It asked for pavements to be demarcated and laid with tarmac, not just to keep pedestrians off the roads but to save wear on the soles of villagers' boots. These are all things that might already have been happening in urban areas, but before the WI spoke up policy-makers seem not to have realised the extent of the countryside's needs and inherent dangers. It helped that, thanks to an urgent summons from the NFWI, an increasing number of politicians on rural and district councils during the 1920s and 30s were women. They knew things men didn't. If (despite their agitation) an organised service was too late in coming or denied altogether by the council, members of the WI sprang into action themselves. They arranged local refuse collection, school lunch provision, the delivery of eggs and freshly cut flowers to hospitals, as well as visiting rotas to the elderly and housebound.

In the Somerset village of East Coker, the WI possessed a chimney-sweeping set which it hired out for a small consideration; Ringmer in East Sussex rather imaginatively had an Institute bath chair available for threepence a day to non-members and a penny to members. But it was almost more trouble than it was worth, and much committee time seems to have been taken up with bath chair ramifications. If two people wanted it on the same day the time was divided, the first applicant having a choice of morning or afternoon. Under no circumstances were children allowed to play on it. After a year or two the bath chair was condemned, worm being found in the wickerwork. But it was soon replaced, and was still going strong years later.

One of the highest-profile enterprises run in communities by the WI was the local weekly market (mentioned earlier), dreamt up in 1916 by the redoubtable Dorothy Drage of Criccieth

WI in North Wales to increase food supplies during the Great War. Although the NFWI declined to support the project when it became clear it was upsetting local tradesmen, in 1919 members in Lewes, Sussex, decided to try again. Other Institutes followed, until by 1932 there were enough markets up and running for the NFWI to apply for another grant from the loyal Carnegie UK Trust, and set up a full-scale cooperative business, which runs (although now officially separated from the NFWI) to this day.

The ethos of the WI market was simple: to sell surplus produce to those who needed it. But the rules and regulations were of Byzantine complexity, with provision for every abstruse eventuality, including what to do with a member's shares if she suddenly became 'insane or lunatic'. Despite the bureaucracy, WI markets flourished everywhere. At best, they brought the whole community together. One Institute held theirs in a pub yard, courtesy of the landlord; goods were measured out on scales lent by a car-dealer; a professional market-gardener provided for any shortfalls, and the big landowner bought up leftovers for the pig club.

Studying the receipt books for Forest Row market during the 1930s is curiously soothing.[12] The Great Depression gripped the nation, and yet here in rural Sussex, week after week, there was fudge and clotted cream for sale, plump rabbits and chickens, ducks' eggs and fresh watercress, lavender bags, butterscotch and potted eggs. Profits were a little down on one occasion because some mice ate the yams and home-made sweets while no one was looking, but generally the turnover was healthy and everyone was happy. Some stalls served coffee, and lonely customers came to rely on a cheerful welcome from the WI ladies, and a chat. To some extent the Depression empowered the WI.

It was generally acknowledged that towns and cities were harder hit by the savage economic downturn than villages, yet unemployment hit agricultural workers worse, their insurance payments were higher, and they suffered terribly. The NFWI's role was to inform rural families about their rights and responsibilities, advise them how to help themselves and each other, and strengthen the Movement's ethos of mutual support.

That said, the NFWI also recognised the countryside might offer opportunities to imaginative and enterprising people not found in industrial areas. So it welcomed economic migrants and did its best to accommodate them. On her own estate at Balcombe Lady Denman built a series of cottages for 'depressed miners', relocated by the government from unproductive collieries to more promising villages with land available for smallholdings. New Institutes were established in mining communities, particularly in Wales and County Durham, and WIs all over the country were urged to 'adopt' unemployed families by sending them hampers of clothes and food, and toys for the children at Christmas.

Things had been different during the 1926 General Strike, when the WI constitution forbade members from taking sides. A memo was circulated in May that year instructing them to help with 'vital services' only if they could do so 'without causing bitterness of feeling within the Institute or the village'.[13] According to Grace Hadow, there were very few 'vital services' safe enough to tackle. In a partially illegible document in the NFWI Archive, she explained her misgivings about strike-breaking: 'The small good we could do in saving food would – I feel – be more than counterbalanced by the probable set-back to the whole Movement if once we were branded on the side of [?the government] against [the] men. The only exception I should make would be [?releasing] animals from suffering or starvation.'[14] There were probably strikers' wives in every Institute, so – as ever – the official WI line must be strict neutrality. But the Depression was less politically divisive than the General Strike; it disadvantaged most people to a greater or lesser degree, and demanded the sort of aid the WI was uniquely qualified to offer. The nation was duly grateful: 'There has never before been a women's organisation of such scope, durability, and power,' gushed *The Times* in 1936. 'One of the greatest merits of the Women's Institutes is that they do not make a fuss.'[15] They just look for what needs doing, and then do it.

Fixing local problems was a job for individual Institutes or County Federations. As long as VCOs and county committee members were happy with what WIs planned to do in their own neighbourhoods, and could be sure there was no hidden political agenda nor any danger of controversy, Institutes were free to act as they wished. National campaigns, however, needed the support of a formal resolution. We have already heard about some of the subjects fearlessly tackled during the first few years of the NFWI, from Mrs Trenow of Epping's crusade for rural state-aided housing in 1918 to another Essex member's concern about maternal mortality in 1925. From 1926 until war broke out in 1939, the ambition and prescience of those resolutions adopted by successive AGMs are staggering. They included campaigns in 1926 for the wholesale improvement of schoolchildren's health, which fed into the Public Health Act of 1936; in 1927 for combating marine pollution, way ahead of its time and referred to in the Water Act of 1935; in 1929 for publicising the work and ideals of the League of Nations, courageously anticipating the Second World War; in 1931 for humane farming and against wearing furs, influencing the Protection of Animals

Act, 1934; and in 1934 for the provision of free school milk, which was finally made a requirement in 1946. In 1936 and 1938 the WI publicly endorsed two important pieces of legislation for which it had been lobbying for some time: the Midwives Act, setting up local authority services, and the Matrimonial Causes Act, which allowed women equal right to a divorce.

Each WI was kept informed of campaign progress in a column in *Home and Country* called 'The Countrywomen's Parliament'. Even if a member's idea for a resolution failed to be adopted at the AGM, *Home and Country* often researched an article on the subject for its readers, which in turn provoked correspondence and discussion on issues as diverse as battery farming, street signage, the treatment of young offenders, the rights of mothers giving birth in prison, and whether or not the 'mentally defective' should be allowed to marry and reproduce.

The national press reported on every single resolution, usually adding a comment on the extraordinary influence of this unlikely band of rural housewives. 'It is not too much to say that [the WI] has created a new spirit in our country life,' claimed one report;[16] another concluded that 'in the village women throughout England, the nation possesses a great and unrealised reservoir of power'.[17] This was demonstrably true. Heady stuff.

The Movement's influence even reached beyond national boundaries. In a series of features under the slightly distasteful banner 'Our Family Estate', *Home and Country* involved its readers in the work of the WI abroad. A sister organisation to the Women's Institute, Associated Country Women of the World (ACWW), was founded by doughty Madge Watt in 1933. Many WIs in Canada and Britain had been affiliated members of the League of Nations since its inception in 1919; some individuals belonged to the International Council of Women; and from 1926 onwards the NFWI's International subcommittee had sent delegates to the women's section of the International Congress of Agriculture, so there had been an awareness of the WI's place in the world from early on. But Madge wanted more: she envisaged a universal network of rural women, committed to goodwill, to learning from each other, and working together to subdue the unquiet planet into peace and mutual understanding.

Lady Denman and the NFWI were a little wary of Madge by this stage: she was still considered a touch autocratic for Institute tastes, and rather too fond of the (now fading) spotlight. Though they supported the ideals of the ACWW – who wouldn't? – they refused to sponsor its formation, and didn't even become corporate members until 1935.[18] Idealism was too expensive a luxury these days: if the WI's interest in international affairs had taught its leadership anything, it was that another war was almost inevitable. It was too late for the global sisterhood of women Madge had dreamt of to soothe the tensions of the modern world. The enemy was already at the gate.

7

Mum's Army:
THE SECOND WORLD WAR

*What could be more satisfying than fiercely stirring
the cauldrons of jam and feeling that every pound took
us one step further towards defeating Hitler?*[1]

The Second World War is the period in the WI's history
which, for good or ill, has defined it ever since. One of the
most abiding images of the Home Front is of an apple-cheeked
wife in her pinny, steadfastly filling jars from dawn till dusk with
ambrosial preserves to feed the nation and spite the Nazis. 'The
land is the mother of us all,' said the Minister of Health Walter
Elliot in 1939, 'but the members of the WI are the mothers of
the land.'[2] They were custodians of England's heritage, the
symbol of home values, and responsible – armed with nothing
more than wooden spoons and a cheerful stoicism – for guard-
ing the gates of civilisation.

Flattering as it is, I haven't yet met any member of the
Women's Institute who isn't heartily sick of this jam and

Jerusalem label. There was so much more to the work of the WI during the war – not to mention all they did before and have done since. According to the government they helped tip the balance between victory and defeat, and you can't do that if your only weapons are a pan full of plums and a song.

Domestic preparations for war started well in advance of its official declaration on 3 September 1939. *Home and Country* had been publishing articles about the state of Europe and the plight of refugees, asking for practical help, since the mid-1930s. Institute delegates attended League of Nations rallies, and Nancy Tennant, as Chairman of the NFWI's International Committee, addressed the World Disarmament Conference in Geneva in 1934. Her report inspired an impassioned correspondence in the magazine about the part the WI might play in holding on to peace.

At this stage, ideology was still thought worth discussing: traditionally (according to one article), men made the effort in international affairs and women the sacrifice; men were active, in other words, and women passive. Now was the time to take a stand by voicing a constructive commitment to peace – otherwise, 'we have only ourselves to blame' when things go horribly wrong. But how did that square with the WI's commitment to non-partisanship and political neutrality? The National Executive was keen, of course, to remind members that they should not sit in judgement over other countries, or our own, for fear of offending or excluding one another. Instead they should pledge themselves to supporting dialogue, diplomacy and non-aggression. Or, as a rather florid correspondent intoned in 1934,

Oh fellow-members who are old enough to remember, let us by our example teach the young that it is what we put *into* life which matters, not what we try to get *out* of it: let us

fan gently but surely the flames of comradeship and united
endeavour in our homes, in our Institutes, in our villages, that
we who live close to the heart of our green and pleasant land
may help to light our country's steps into the path of peace.[3]

Such stodgy sententiousness is almost risible now, but then,
especially to those WI members who were proud of having
kept home fires stoked during the Great War, it was stirring
stuff.

With her usual acumen, Gertrude Denman was able to steer
her members through this emotive quagmire towards a pragmatic patriotism which would benefit them personally, as well
as their country. In February 1936 she called together an NFWI
Conference on International Work. Although this was ostensibly to establish a protocol whereby international affairs could
be discussed in a non-controversial manner at Institute meetings, it turned out to be an apologia for her own belief in the
work of the League of Nations, and the power of truth. In
the conference report speakers at Institute meetings are urged
to be impartial and never censorious, even though 'the challenging nature of the international situation aroused such a different
response in different people'. Talks about the situation in Europe
should be given with courage and an acute sense of justice; they
should make the audience realise that 'it is out of this tangled
mass of threads that the world has to weave for itself peace
and understanding'.[4] The keenest foil to prejudice and belli-
cosity is well informed wisdom. Women, contrary to popular
belief, are inherently wise; wisest of all are countrywomen, who
have learned to compromise and work together – and, crucially,
know what's worth working for.

Come 1938, it was obvious that wisdom was not going to be

enough to stop the war. The Home Secretary Sir Samuel Hoare commissioned Stella, Marchioness of Reading, to establish an organisation to help with air-raid precautions. Lady Reading was a sensible choice, being a former nurse, secretary (and then wife) to the British Viceroy in Delhi, Chairman of the charitable Personal Service League and a magistrate, as well as being at the hub of an influential social network. She formed a committee of representatives from various women's organisations, and in May the Women's Voluntary Service was born.[5] The role of the WVS was to organise evacuees and run canteens and other services to support victims of enemy action in town and country. Conspicuously absent from the advisory committee was anyone from the NFWI, although the General Secretary Frances Farrer was cheekily asked to suggest suitable candidates for the WVS from the ranks of the WI.

Inevitably, there was tension between the two organisations. Lady Denman was clear that the ground rules of the WI prevented it from taking any formal part in civil defence, out of respect for its pacifist Quaker members. But it would have been nice to be asked onto the advisory committee, at least. How would Institutes survive if crowds of members defected to the WVS, seduced by the promise of a smart green uniform or the glamour of a government commission? Besides, the WI had already been asked to help with evacuation and had plenty of experience in running local canteens, dispensing first aid and being 'good neighbours' (which was one of the WVS's mandates), so what was the WVS for?

Lady Denman, reputed not to get on very well with Lady Reading at the best of times, responded to the creation of the WVS with some exasperation. Civil defence, she suggested, should be the responsibility not of a quickly cobbled together hotchpotch of inexperienced ladies, but of us all. Men and women should work together in their local communities to do whatever they could to help each other according to their conscience and ability. Individual members of the WI must decide for themselves whether they wished to defect to the new organisation (or, indeed, serve in both); meanwhile she would continue to urge them to do what the WI did best. Speaking for the Executive Committee in *Home and Country* in July 1938 she made her position clear:

> We feel it to be of greatest importance that Women's Institutes' monthly meetings should maintain their educational and social character, thus providing for the members a centre of tranquillity and cheerfulness in a sadly troubled world.

Let the ladies of the WVS scuttle about and do what they must; the women of the WI would concentrate on keeping alive the spirit of Britain. A devoted WI member who lived in the village where I grew up, and who had been through the war, was clear about the difference between the two organisations. No doubt she was prejudiced, but to her it was a class issue, best illustrated by her favourite Yorkshire saying: 'There are many ways of doing things, as everyone supposes; some folk turn up their sleeves at work, and some turn up their noses.'

Two months later, on Saturday 24 September 1938, the WI suddenly found itself on active service. Frances Farrer was summoned to Lady Reading's London office to be told of the government's urgent instructions to evacuate vulnerable members of the public from London to the countryside.

Neville Chamberlain – brother of a staunch NFWI Executive Committee member,[6] and Prime Minister – was embroiled in the Munich crisis, attempting to appease Herr Hitler, who had just annexed the Sudetenland in Czechoslovakia. If no agreement was reached, Britain would be at war with Germany within the week. The plan was for the WVS to appoint liaison officers in every county due to receive evacuees, to oversee all the local arrangements and report back to London on progress. It was decided that half of those officers should be drawn from the Girl Guide movement, and half from the WI.

The following Monday, Frances and other members of the NFWI resident in London wrote to every County Federation within the evacuation area, and deployed what she called a 'flying squad' of six VCOs to visit each liaison officer and explain the government's instructions in detail. This was done, amazingly, in a matter of days.

Meanwhile the Home Office, close to panic, contacted NFWI headquarters directly on Tuesday 27 September, to ask their help in devising another evacuation plan for children under five years old whose mothers were unable to leave London. This group had somehow slipped through the net; a declaration of war was expected by next Saturday, and there were no gas masks available for infants. Cometh the time, cometh the woman: Miss Farrer, now in her mid-forties, was a Cambridge Economics graduate, the daughter of a senior civil servant and renowned for her bureaucratic efficiency and calmness under administrative fire. Although fully occupied in coordinating the flying squad, she agreed to the Home Office request and immediately set to work. She had four days. 'Every minute was, therefore, precious.'

On the night of the 27th we wrote to 218 infant welfare centres in the London area ... We had an instantaneous and overwhelming response ... The mothers were pathetically anxious to have their younger children transferred. By Wednesday night, the 28th, we had applications on behalf of 7,000 children. Many additional applications came in later ...

We were able to obtain the permission of the Matron of St. Thomas's Hospital to recruit escorts from the Massage Department students. Sixty volunteers thus became available at once. Other escorts were recruited through the clinics, and through Women's Voluntary Services ...

The London Transport Board offered us 100 of their Greenline buses. Women's Voluntary Services had a panel of cars and were prepared to call up many of their volunteers. In addition other kind friends hearing of our need offered help. Altogether by Wednesday we had a fleet of about 200 private cars in addition to the London Transport Board buses ...

Here lay our main difficulty. Though our flying squad of organizers had been asked to beg for help and though we sent immediate telegrams to the liaison officers and County Federations in the evacuation area, their hands were tied by the official arrangements for the evacuation of the school-children and general population. These arrangements were incomplete and behindhand and the additional burden of the younger children was going to prove the last straw ... In spite of this difficulty gallant and successful efforts were made ...[7]

On Wednesday evening another message came through from the Home Office, asking Miss Farrer to hold fire. There was better news than expected from Munich, and it might be that the evacuation plan would not be needed after all. With 'considerable difficulty' she managed to stall everything – apart from a group of sixty infants from Westminster, who left St Thomas's on Thursday morning for Miss Farrer's old Cambridge college, Newnham. They came back next day. Appeasement had prevailed, and Chamberlain had a promise from the Führer. There would be peace in our time, after all.

Naturally, the NFWI Executive was relieved the crisis was over. But the whole episode – dubbed 'Institute War Week' – was disquieting to Gertrude Denman and her fellow officers. The government had left it too late to ask for the WI's concerted help. And the implication was that the WVS had fallen short; it had only been in existence a matter of months, and though it had done all it could to help, the reach and experience of the WI were more effective. Let us hope, said Lady Denman, that the government has learned a lesson from this: ignore the Women's Institute at your peril.

As Chamberlain's smile faded over the next few months, the WI quietly continued to prepare for the worst. A Produce Guild was formed, with a grant from the Ministry of Agriculture, to encourage WI members to reprise their wartime role in food production. The guild appointed its own chief organiser and VCOs and determined the qualifications required of its demonstrators and judges, as well as administering competitions for home-grown produce and the various uses to which it might be put. The need was pressing: of every hundred onions consumed in Britain, for example, only nine came from British gardens, and only 48 per cent of carrots.[8] Linked to the government's Dig for Victory campaign, the Produce Guild was promoted as a solid contribution to the war effort, accessible to almost all the WI's membership.

'Home-grown produce' didn't just mean fruit and vegetables. In what must be one of the most bizarre *Times* headlines ever, readers were encouraged to 'Convert British Bunnies into Bombs' by rearing tame rabbits (those old WI favourites) or trapping wild ones.[9] Their fur could be used for export: the government was asking for a hundred million rabbit and ten million mole skins for the American market. Egg-marketing schemes were encouraged, and more pig clubs; seed-buying cooperatives were bolstered by donations from America and the colonies, and *Home and Country* ran what would formerly have been regarded as impossibly arcane features on soil fertility, the use of sulphur dioxide in the kitchen, and how to be an efficient 'Home Food Controller' (the government's rebranding of the housewife). Institutes were encouraged, as they had been in the last war, to gather herbs for both culinary and medicinal use, and never to waste a single scrap of food. Bones should be boiled two or three times over to extract their goodness for stock; brown onion skins could flavour and colour soup, and grated stale bread was always useful in bulking out minced meat, puddings and sauces.

It was the fear of waste that first inspired the WI's jam-making mission. The summer of 1939, just like 1914, was marked by a glut of plums and blackberries. This was too good a chance to miss for the thrifty organisers of the Produce Guild, who worked with extraordinary vigour to set up 2600 fruit-preserving centres in villages throughout the country, supported by demonstrators in jam-making and fruit-canning like Margaret Leech of Somerset. She was a Rural Domestic Economy instructor, trained in bacon-curing, cheese-making and – by the prestigious Long Ashton Research Station, a government agricultural institute – in the preservation of soft fruit. The WI employed her to teach its members to be businesslike about their jamming and canning. 'The WI audiences were marvellous,' recalled Margaret. 'Nothing like a good war to cheer up the WI.'[10]

Her trickiest task was demonstrating canning, using machines sent from the United States which could be bought by Institutes for £24, or hired by the week. Boiling the fruit and syrup was no problem, nor was decanting it. But immediately after being filled, the cans were meant to be cooled. Often there was no sink in the village hall or hut where she would be demonstrating, so they had to be carried to the village pump and doused there, which might result in nasty burns. 'I remember once I was in a rather remote village and I went outside but couldn't see the pump. I asked a woman where it was and she looked at me and said in some surprise "The pump? It's in the brook." And the brook was in a little ravine and I had to slither down the banks to drop the boiling hot cans in the stream. It was, to say the least, quite primitive.'[11]

Teams of WI members worked flat out during the season to produce literally tons of jam to cheer the hearts of the British people. At one centre in Hawkinge, Kent, just five women managed over fifteen hundred jars between them. So successful was the NFWI scheme during 1939 and 1940 that the Minister of Food, Lord Woolton, wrote to Lady Denman to announce that he was going to model a nationwide government-sponsored enterprise on it. At the outbreak of war, one in three villages in England had a Women's Institute, so it's no surprise that most of Woolton's government centres ended up being run by the WI. Sugar was rationed by now, which made it difficult for independent cooks to make jam at the recommended 60 per cent sugar to 40 per cent fruit ratio; the centres were permitted special supplies of sugar as long as it was used exclusively for cooperative fruit preservation, and they were given advice on distribution and marketing of the finished product.

Anyone with soft fruit in their garden or allotment was instructed to sell it to the local centre, which was always located in some public room (never in a private home); those unlucky enough not to grow their own must scour the hedgerows for elderberries, brambles and bilberries. The whole country must work together to feed its people, via the WI. 'They want more jam,' declared Lord Woolton, 'you women of the country districts can give it to them . . . Good luck to you all for helping in a grand piece of work.'[12]

The regulations governing the official fruit preservation centres were addling but necessary, to avoid the sort of unpleasantness that occurred when one WI member, a Miss Pratt, was discovered by the police to be running a rural black market in Institute sugar. Official logbooks were issued by the Ministry of Food (and sold for 5s each) in which jammers and canners recorded their output; these contained useful tables of weights and measures, boiling times for different fruits, and recommended 'syrup strengths'. They also set down stringent rules for every conceivable aspect of making jam and canning fruit. Sugar had to be applied for via a permit which was only valid for two months. It was to be used solely for jams, jellies, fruit cheeses, chutneys, fruit juices and canned or bottled fruits. It was *not* for marmalade, mincemeat, home-made wines, cider or perry. Such things were clearly unpatriotic.

The fruit must be home-grown, not bought on the open market. Strawberries, blackcurrants and raspberries were only to be used for jam, not for canning. Jams and jellies could be sold at retail prices to shops, market stalls or wholesalers as long as they were judged 'trade standard' (after random visits by Ministry of Agriculture inspectors). Substandard goods were to be sent to schools. Cans went straight to hospitals, army camps, 'charitable institutions' or public canteens at wholesale prices. The Ministry of Food promised to buy any unsold stock.

The canning machine must be carefully oiled twice a day and washed with boiling water. No one should use it without having been trained by someone like Margaret Leech, who knew how to handle these recalcitrant beasts – with the exception of the Queen, who was photographed for *Home and Country* ceremonially (and unconvincingly) sealing a can of WI fruit.

Crofton WI in Devon kept its logbook beautifully, listing 1652 pounds of jam (nearly 750 kilos) produced during 1942 by about ten members, mostly from gooseberries, raspberries, damsons and plums.[13] The jam inspector recorded her comments after each visit: sometimes negative – 'Disappointing to have such a lot of scum' – but usually full of praise. 'A wonderful season's work,' she wrote in the autumn of 1943: 'delightful jam made by a few very hard working helpers. All finished off splendidly.' The pride of Crofton WI is plain to see in its own assessment of the summer's labours: theirs had been judged one of the most successful jam centres in the country, and a special congratulatory visit from the Ministry of Food had convinced them that they 'undoubtedly belong to a very influential organisation'. All hail the 'jam-busters'.

The range of work done by WIs was even wider during the Second World War than in the First. Dorset Federation compiled a record of their contribution to the Home Front, written in 1947 while memories were still fresh and pride ran understandably high.[14] Unique vignettes of rural England at war emerge from its careful calligraphy and detailed illustrations, and there's a strong sense of the spirit of the WI, whose members obviously felt closely engaged with victory. Most of Dorset was relatively safe from air attack; it had been designated a sanctuary for evacuated schools, government departments, colonial servicemen and women on leave, and exhausted survivors of Dunkirk. Winfrith Newburgh, with four hundred inhabitants, absorbed eighty young evacuees from the East End into its small community, while Worth Matravers hosted mysterious scientists and military personnel from the telecommunications research establishment (working on radar) nearby. Several villages lay within the restricted zone during the build-up to D-day, and every WI member found herself expected to billet nervous servicemen. Not just British servicemen: the Americans had arrived, and near the naval base of Portland ten thousand Moroccans and Algerians needed temporary homes. All foreigners were equally exotic; whenever a new contingent landed, the whispers would start at the local Institute: 'Be they white or black this time?'

There were occasional attacks, even in this quietest of counties. At Durweston, a WI member had a spaniel who could recognise enemy aircraft and would caper about barking to warn everyone, in the absence of sirens. Bloxworth women used to gather baskets of unexploded incendiaries, like strange fruit, and found an unexpected bonus in being close to the military camp at Slepe. 'The village always got well scattered with shell fragments from the guns . . . and after raids, German tinfoil in large quantities was often to be gathered, some of which was subsequently used to make button holes to sell in "Salute the Soldier" week.' The foil was used by the Germans to deflect radar; it came in very useful to the WI.

Portland was heavily bombed, and was one of the few places in Dorset where WI rest centres were used to accommodate civilian victims of enemy action. These were set up in every neighbourhood, usually in schools. They were supplied with stores of bedding, food and first-aid boxes, and 'manned' by rotas of trained WI and WVS volunteers. Training was taken extremely seriously. In Netherbury 'the stretcher party of four women practised with such zeal that they could finally carry a sixteen-stone [101 kilo] man half a mile, and over a narrow bridge, while wearing gas masks'. Down the road in Stoke Abbott 'the village women were incited to stab in the back any unlucky German who dared to come within their reach'. With what we are not told.

Elsewhere, WI members were called upon with increasing urgency by government ministries to keep the infrastructure of the countryside intact. 'They wanted us to do it all for them,' grumbled an overworked member from Westmorland. She had a point: a document published soon after the war summarised specific requirements from ten different departments: Agriculture, Air, Food, Health, Information, Supply, the War Office, the Boards of Education and Trade and the Treasury.[15] The Ministry of Information's instructions were perhaps the most daunting: 'There is the probability ... that Hitler will seek to invade Great Britain. People should be encouraged to look forward to that invasion without any apprehension – to prepare for it but not to fear it.'[16] Institutes must meet every month if they possibly can: the Lord Privy Seal himself made that decision, confident (as Lady Denman was) of the WI's talent for raising morale and for cheerfully keeping calm and carrying on.

Further wartime requirements ranged from the distribution of children's cod-liver oil and rosehip syrup to ensuring the welfare of Land Army, Women's Auxiliary Air Force and Auxiliary Transport Service personnel. The WI was responsible for disseminating propaganda in support of diphtheria immunisation, the prevention of sexually transmitted diseases, and making-do-and-mending. Its members were charged with raising thousands of pounds for the National Savings Fund, although Gertrude Denman was adamant that no WI money should be spent on Spitfires – only on ambulances. They were also expected to keep the Home Guard fed and watered while on duty. The pig-club sausage and mash they cooked for night exercises at Shottlegate in Derbyshire was legendary.

There seems to have been a special relationship between the Home Guard and the WI during the war. Many members of each were husband and wife, after all. To Miss Wood of Steeple Aston in Oxfordshire the soldiers of the Home Guard were her heroes. She knitted woolly scarves to keep them warm, and wrote them poems:

> Like Angels you are set to guard the weaker from the foe,
> But Angels get no chilblains, nor feel the frost and snow,
> And that is well, because they have no mother, wife nor kid
> To knit them warm pullovers (with sleeves) if so they did.
>
> Then take this humble muffler, and wind it to your chin,
> To keep your collar snug and warm when cold rain trickles
>   in,
> Not on the helm (as knights of old) but as protective suit
> Our fighters wear the favours of the Women's Institute.[17]

In Dry Sandford in Berkshire (now in Oxfordshire) the relationship was tested to its limits when it was discovered the

Home Guard had sawn the legs off the Institute's grand piano – presumably for firewood – and the poor woman accompanying 'Jerusalem' at meetings had to lie prone on the floor. But the gentlemen were forgiven even that.

WI members were renowned salvage collectors, often to be seen trundling large prams groaning with booty around the villages. Waste paper, scrap metal, rubber, rags and bones were all valuable, plus kitchen refuse for compost and pig-club fodder. *Home and Country* published a table to encourage its 'salvage stewards', explaining that one envelope made fifty cartridge wads; one broken garden fork plus an old bucket made a tommy gun; one ton of mixed rags made 250 battledresses and thirteen army tents, and 'every pound of bones (except fishbones), after cooking, contains enough fat to provide 2oz Glycerine, which makes double its weight of Nitro-glycerine, a very high explosive'.[18] Where did that leave the Quakers? one wonders.

All these were more or less official tasks, but enterprising WIs found extra things to do. Some changed people's lives by offering foster-homes to soldiers' orphaned daughters, or writing weekly letters to British prisoners of war in Germany; others merely made life more bearable, crocheting winter shawls for women in occupied countries, providing a bed for female commercial travellers (deputising for absent men), donating wedding presents of crockery for cash-strapped war brides, or sewing calico bags for foreign refugees to stow their pathetically few possessions. Your WI may have been evicted from the village hall and forced to meet in someone's kitchen or the station waiting-room or the sexton's shed in the local graveyard, but it was hard to be too gloomy if you were enjoying a game of blindfold Pin the Moustache on Hitler or passing round for a penny a sniff a precious lemon someone had been sent from abroad, or sitting with your closest friends in the blackout knitting army socks for other mothers' sons. Chin up, Britain: you've got the WI.

The most significant wartime contribution made by the WI to British society was nothing to do with jam. Jerusalem, maybe: it was a small booklet published in 1940, based on an NFWI evacuation survey, called *Town Children through Country Eyes*. The week war was declared, at the beginning of September 1939, Operation Pied Piper swung into action. Three million people were shifted from vulnerable cities to the supposed shelter of the countryside, many of them destined for the doorsteps of the WI. Gertrude Denman asked the government to send only certain types of evacuees to her members: she had evidence – presumably from Institute discussions – that there was 'very strong feeling' among countrywomen against indiscriminate billeting 'whereby householders would be compelled to take in any type of adult refugee without safeguards against disease and dishonesty'.[19] She didn't fancy expectant or nursing mothers either, nor children from two to five, or schoolchildren – which didn't, in fact, leave much else.

There was obviously a great deal of apprehension in village Institutes about evacuees. The authorities were kept well occupied in rural areas checking the validity of all the applications for exemption, which flooded in from manors, rectories, farmhouses and cottages during 1939. This was an alien invasion almost as unwelcome as the one expected any moment from Nazi Germany, and, as one elderly member told me sternly, 'we didn't hold with it'. Why was the WI so afraid – and why did Lady Denman indulge their fears? The burden of the WI's stated ethos for the previous quarter-century had been all about inclusion, justice and human rights on a global as well as a local scale. Yet not for 'townies', it appears. Townies were diseased and dishonest, and lacked the inherent decency of country people.

One wonders if Lady Denman was influenced by a lingering interest in eugenics, still fashionable in certain highly respectable circles: she was not a prejudiced woman nor the slightest bit xenophobic, and remarkably clear-minded in most other aspects of her work. She was not alone in her belief that British society could be engineered by judicious breeding. In their time, such luminaries as H. G. Wells, George Bernard Shaw, John Maynard Keynes, and Sidney and Beatrice Webb had all advocated 'artificial selection'. So had Winston Churchill, years ago. He had co-chaired the first International Eugenics Conference in London in 1912, warning then that 'the multiplication of the feeble-minded . . . is a very terrible danger to the race'.[20]

The government had neither the time nor the inclination to satisfy all the WI's demands about evacuation. Members took what they were given, and – like everyone else – got on with it. There are many stories of successful placements where warm and lasting relationships developed, and these were celebrated with pride and gratitude. But there were some terrible experiences, too. The most distressing were chronicled in *Town Children through Country Eyes*,

In December 1939, Frances Farrer sent a letter to all the WI secretaries in the country. It accompanied a questionnaire to be filled in by any members who were looking after evacuated children and, in some cases, their mothers. Aware of the general predisposition against evacuees, Miss Farrer warned that the survey was not to be undertaken 'in a spirit of grievance, but as a definite contribution to the welfare of our fellow citizens'.[21] It wasn't a long questionnaire: it just asked how many children there were in the house, where they came from, and whether they suffered from head lice, skin disease or bed-wetting and 'other similar insanitary habits'. If the children's mothers were with them, WI members were asked if there were any 'who lacked the knowledge or will to train their children in good habits'.

One thousand seven hundred Institutes replied, and their response was shocking. Children were repeatedly described as filthy, sometimes verminous; so much so that evacuation reception areas had to be fumigated after they left. Of 849 children who arrived at Dorchester WI in Dorset, 229 had lice, 19 had skin diseases and 43 habitually wet the bed. One distraught WI member reported a family from Bethnal Green (whose mother was present) climbing onto the bed to urinate and defecate; another had to cut her charges free of the ragged clothes into which they had been stitched who knows how long ago. Many mothers had no notion of discipline and behaved so badly themselves that at one Institute in the Isle of Wight, for instance, a clean sweep of WI husbands was driven from home to the pub, and householders in Buckinghamshire chose to abandon their homes altogether rather than endure their evacuees' dreadful company. 'One bad case [from Rotherhithe was] a mother with 7 children under 10 who seemed to think she had done her part in bringing them into the world and that there her responsibility ended. The children were nice little things, but utterly out of control.'[22] The staple diet of impoverished city children appeared to be bread, or fish and chips, and they were appalled or else completely bemused by the thought of eating fruit and vegetables. Some had scabies, and several had 'dirty septic sores all over their bodies'.

The news wasn't all bad. Occasionally WI members would report 'a nice class of child', and talk about the pleasure of having 'war visitors' around. And things could get better very quickly: two children in Norfolk put on half a stone in one week, and mothers were learning to cook and sew for the first time in their lives. It was a joy to watch children visibly growing healthy and happy in the countryside. But overall, the picture presented by the WI questionnaire's results was a grim one, and revealed the state of Britain's urban slums with uncompromising clarity. William Beveridge, commissioned by the government to write a report into social reconstruction after the war, took careful note.

So did the social reformer Margaret Bondfield. She had served as Britain's first female Cabinet minister (for Labour) under Ramsay MacDonald in 1929, and was heavily involved with the Women's Group on Public Welfare. *Town Children through Country Eyes* inspired a book she prefaced in 1943, published by Oxford University Press under the title *Our Towns: A Close-up* in association with the National Council of Social Service and the Hygiene Committee of the Women's Group on Public Welfare. *Our Towns* had a wider remit than *Town Children*, sourcing information from other organisations as well as the WI, and presenting it to anyone with a social conscience, a 'stout stomach' and 'an appetite for facts, including the unpleasant'.[23] It recommended economic and educational reforms (including child allowances and state education from the ages of two to sixteen) and acknowledged its debt to the WI, whose members were arguably the first to open Britain's eyes to the desperate need for a nationwide Welfare State.

The NFWI abandoned its London headquarters during the

Britain as a haven of traditional virtues, the paradigm of [ur]ban enlightenment and rural idyll. Now was not the [time to] undermine that image.

Home and Country bought into the illusion, month after [month,] choosing nostalgic front covers with charming country [scenes], sturdy English oaks, and acres of rolling fields quilted [alo]ng hedgerows. Within those covers, however, were stern [articles] on the still squalid state of those very cottages, and the [serio]us lack of piped water and sewerage systems in villages [up and] down the land. The results of surveys and questionnaires [were pu]blished, revealing just under a third of rural parishes in [Englan]d and Wales to be without piped water supplies, and [over] a half without sewerage systems. Fewer than 10 per cent [of agri]cultural workers' homes had electricity.[27] All of these [were c]onsidered 'essential services' in towns and cities.

[One] WI member speaking at an AGM after the war boasted [that in] her village she was known as the 'Queen of Sewage' for [her rep]eated attempts to get something done about the state of [the d]rainage. Children paddled in the effluent, she said, and [played] with 'solid fluid'.[28] Another member wrote to *The Times* [to rep]ort that her son, a soldier fighting in North Africa, had [use]d far more sophisticated systems in the desert than at [home] in England, and readers frequently complained in *Home [and C]ountry* that temporary army camps, set up close to villages [which] had been campaigning for water and drainage for years, [were] always mysteriously provided with every possible amenity [withi]n weeks.

[Th]e WI mounted a major campaign immediately after the [war fo]r grants towards the refurbishment of cottages. Not just [p]atching up old and decrepit buildings, but redesigning [them] in the local idiom for comfortable and efficient modern

Blitz of 1940, and decamped first to Frances Farrer's brother's farm in Hertfordshire and then to her parents' home at Abinger Hall near Dorking, Surrey. Its only Annual General Meeting during the war was bravely held, in June 1943, at the Royal Albert Hall. Three thousand delegates came, and just as the meeting was about to begin, a surprise visitor was announced. Thrillingly, it turned out to be Queen Elizabeth, who delivered a long speech thanking the WI for defending 'those values for which we are fighting' and for helping to win the war (not yet actually won, of course). After her departure the meeting addressed a long list of resolutions, most of which looked forward to a fairer and more supportive postwar society designed by architects like Beveridge, who was given the WI's explicit support. Perhaps the most whimsical resolution was proposed by a lady from Bures WI in West Suffolk: 'That men and women should receive equal pay for equal work'. Dream on.

Lady Churchill was a guest at the AGM: she came to thank the WI for supplying rabbit skins to Russian refugees. The Oxford academic Sir Richard Livingstone was also a speaker. He made a startling suggestion during a discussion of further education. 'Why shouldn't WIs, who have shown such remarkable common sense in their educational questionnaires, fill the Adult Education gap and provide a People's College?'[24] This marked the conception of what became the WI's most precious possession, Denman College. How Grace Hadow would have applauded, had she been there; sadly, she died in January 1940 of pneumonia and was mourned with genuine affection throughout the WI. One member of her home WI in Headington, Oxford, said her death was 'worse than the war'. 'How shall we ever do without her?' asked a desolate Gertrude Denman.

They must try their best. It was Miss Hadow's indomitable positiveness that inspired this anonymous member to write to *Home and Country* with a vision: 'Perhaps after the rush and tension of these last years, these days may bring us single-mindedness, an acceptance of life and death, and inward peace ... The common lot of men binds us to each other, and if we will, we may pluck virtue from tragedy.'[25] Prime Minister Winston Churchill had the same idea. He spoke at a National Conference of Women convened by the Minister of Labour Ernest Bevin in September 1943, thanking them for their sensitivity and solidarity and assuring them of a new and vital role in postwar society. Dorothy Elliott was a delegate there, on behalf of the Trades Union Congress; when she responded to the Prime Minister she was speaking for the WI too:

> For many years your voice has called us to heights we never believed we could attain. You have taken us into your confidence and set the seal on the status of women in the war effort ... We women hate war and we shall find our fullest opportunity for service in the peace, for if you cannot win the war without women, neither can you win the peace.[26]

The WI had been arming itself to win the peace for some time. Long before VE and VJ day were celebrated in 1945 (virtually ignored in *Home and Country*, to spare the anguish of bereaved wives and mothers), the National Executive preoccupied itself with preparations for a brave new Britain. Sensing the political opportunities offered by this natural caesura in the nation's history, Gertrude Denman and her colleagues worked relentlessly throughout the war to impress on WI members the

importance of contributing – as a m[...] to reshaping their world.

Lady Denman was heavily involve[...] tee, formed in 1941 to investigate the [...] agriculture and land use in rural areas. [...] the Scott Report stressed the part W[...] cohesion and cooperation. She urge[...] countrywomen. They should be treate[...] local and national government about th[...] *Children through Country Eyes* – and sug[...] only to their own lives but to those of [...]

The zeal of the NFWI in this regard[...] questionnaires and memos fluttering do[...] headquarters in Surrey like that Germ[...] skies – except rather less useful. Institute[...] choked with directives and harried by re[...] in the short term they cursed the powers[...] be left alone to cope with their own war. [...] this new vision of the Movement's lea[...] revolutionary.

Two of the commonest subjects under [...] immediately after the war were those old[...] housing and public sanitation. Despite its [...] Merrie England, the Ministry of Reconstru[...] previous war, had not delivered. The impro[...] by WI members like Mrs Trenow of Eppin[...] fast enough. There were reasons for this. T[...] then the darkening shadow of war, had go[...] progress. Come 1939, everyone was otherwi[...] NFWI realised that part of the government[...] ing up morale and bolstering pride for the[...]

living, with indoor WCs and wide windows to let the healing
sunshine in. Northamptonshire Federation held an architects'
competition for a pair of family cottages; *Home and Country*
commissioned an article about women in the building industry, and then canvassed the entire membership to design a
fantasy 'WI House' for the 1951 Ideal Home Exhibition in
London. The winning entry, the cost of turning it into bricks
and mortar sponsored by the *Daily Mail*, was beautiful and
entirely practical, with three bedrooms, an upstairs bathroom,
large kitchen, and a separate laundry with a washing machine
and clothes airer. There was no lawn in the garden, but six neat
little apple trees, several blackcurrant and gooseberry bushes,
a potato patch, rows of vegetables and a chicken run. *This* was
the WI's rural idyll. Raising living standards for its membership
was all part of a greater cause being fought by the Movement
during the 1940s and 1950s: feminism. Not the blood-and-thunder feminism of the young Edith Rigby or even Grace Hadow,
but a more down-to-earth brand, to do with self-respect and
just reward. The writer Renée Haynes produced an article for
Home and Country in 1942 entitled 'The Nation's Cinderella'. It's
about the dignity of domestic work and the unfairness of
housewives' dependence on their husbands. It is not right that
wives should have to take their husband's nationality on marriage, argues Miss Haynes: during wartime it made 'aliens' of
old friends. Why aren't women working at home allowed to
contribute to and benefit from health insurance schemes? They
never have a penny to call their own – and 'being able to call
pennies your own is very necessary to self-respect'.[29] Their
work is more vital than almost anyone else's: it keeps people
alive and makes them happy. Yet because it's unpaid it goes
largely unnoticed, and wholly unacknowledged. Housewives

are not even properly compensated for taking in evacuees.
What an insult!

When wives and mothers are taken seriously as skilled pro-
fessionals, continues Miss Haynes, their opinions – about
housing, sanitation, health, childcare, animal welfare and so
on – will count far more than they do now. She credits the WI
with giving this forgotten workforce pride in their skills and
traditions, as well as some cheering companionship. But they
deserve more, and are quite right to campaign for it. Encouragement was not long coming. The Family Allowances Act of 1945
made child benefit payable to mothers from 1946 onwards. The
National Health Act followed in 1948. After three decades of
hard work by the NFWI and hundreds of thousands of its members, from small village discussions to what one overawed AGM
delegate called 'the Revolutions at the Halibut Hall', the Welfare
State was on its way.[30] The Women's Institute had helped raise
the status of housewives as skilled workers, and mothers as professional carers; it encouraged its members to change what they
could to make their neighbourhoods safer and fairer, and to
campaign for what they couldn't change. Because of its organisers' political connections and the calm reliability of surveys
like *Town Children through Country Eyes*, the government tended
to listen to, and trust, its collective voice. 'I think that countrywomen are the salt of the earth,' said a proud Lady Denman. 'I
do not think they get a fair deal, and I have always thought that
if we got together we could do something about it; and it has
been extraordinarily satisfactory to me because we *have* been
able to do something about it. It has given me the very greatest
happiness.'[31]

At this stage, the WI's brand of feminism didn't extend too
far beyond the kitchen sink. Someone responded to 'The

Blitz of 1940, and decamped first to Frances Farrer's brother's farm in Hertfordshire and then to her parents' home at Abinger Hall near Dorking, Surrey. Its only Annual General Meeting during the war was bravely held, in June 1943, at the Royal Albert Hall. Three thousand delegates came, and just as the meeting was about to begin, a surprise visitor was announced. Thrillingly, it turned out to be Queen Elizabeth, who delivered a long speech thanking the WI for defending 'those values for which we are fighting' and for helping to win the war (not yet actually won, of course). After her departure the meeting addressed a long list of resolutions, most of which looked forward to a fairer and more supportive postwar society designed by architects like Beveridge, who was given the WI's explicit support. Perhaps the most whimsical resolution was proposed by a lady from Bures WI in West Suffolk: 'That men and women should receive equal pay for equal work'. Dream on.

Lady Churchill was a guest at the AGM: she came to thank the WI for supplying rabbit skins to Russian refugees. The Oxford academic Sir Richard Livingstone was also a speaker. He made a startling suggestion during a discussion of further education. 'Why shouldn't WIs, who have shown such remarkable common sense in their educational questionnaires, fill the Adult Education gap and provide a People's College?'[24] This marked the conception of what became the WI's most precious possession, Denman College. How Grace Hadow would have applauded, had she been there; sadly, she died in January 1940 of pneumonia and was mourned with genuine affection throughout the WI. One member of her home WI in Headington, Oxford, said her death was 'worse than the war'. 'How shall we ever do without her?' asked a desolate Gertrude Denman.

They must try their best. It was Miss Hadow's indomitable positiveness that inspired this anonymous member to write to *Home and Country* with a vision: 'Perhaps after the rush and tension of these last years, these days may bring us single-mindedness, an acceptance of life and death, and inward peace ... The common lot of men binds us to each other, and if we will, we may pluck virtue from tragedy.'[25] Prime Minister Winston Churchill had the same idea. He spoke at a National Conference of Women convened by the Minister of Labour Ernest Bevin in September 1943, thanking them for their sensitivity and solidarity and assuring them of a new and vital role in postwar society. Dorothy Elliott was a delegate there, on behalf of the Trades Union Congress; when she responded to the Prime Minister she was speaking for the WI too:

> For many years your voice has called us to heights we never believed we could attain. You have taken us into your confidence and set the seal on the status of women in the war effort ... We women hate war and we shall find our fullest opportunity for service in the peace, for if you cannot win the war without women, neither can you win the peace.[26]

The WI had been arming itself to win the peace for some time. Long before VE and VJ day were celebrated in 1945 (virtually ignored in *Home and Country*, to spare the anguish of bereaved wives and mothers), the National Executive preoccupied itself with preparations for a brave new Britain. Sensing the political opportunities offered by this natural caesura in the nation's history, Gertrude Denman and her colleagues worked relentlessly throughout the war to impress on WI members the

importance of contributing – as a movement and individually –
to reshaping their world.

Lady Denman was heavily involved with the Scott Committee, formed in 1941 to investigate the possibilities for postwar
agriculture and land use in rural areas. Thanks to her influence,
the Scott Report stressed the part WIs played in community
cohesion and cooperation. She urged higher expectations of
countrywomen. They should be treated as a resource, to inform
local and national government about the status quo – as in *Town
Children through Country Eyes* – and suggest improvements not
only to their own lives but to those of every British citizen.

The zeal of the NFWI in this regard resulted in a shower of
questionnaires and memos fluttering down from the temporary
headquarters in Surrey like that German tinfoil from Dorset
skies – except rather less useful. Institutes complained of being
choked with directives and harried by requests for information;
in the short term they cursed the powers that be and longed to
be left alone to cope with their own war. Long-term, however,
this new vision of the Movement's leadership was to prove
revolutionary.

Two of the commonest subjects under discussion during and
immediately after the war were those old WI chestnuts, rural
housing and public sanitation. Despite its promise of a modern
Merrie England, the Ministry of Reconstruction, set up after the
previous war, had not delivered. The improvements demanded
by WI members like Mrs Trenow of Epping didn't materialise
fast enough. There were reasons for this. The Depression, and
then the darkening shadow of war, had got in the way of real
progress. Come 1939, everyone was otherwise engaged, and the
NFWI realised that part of the government's strategy in keeping up morale and bolstering pride for the duration was to

market Britain as a haven of traditional virtues, the paradigm of both urban enlightenment and rural idyll. Now was not the time to undermine that image.

Even *Home and Country* bought into the illusion, month after month choosing nostalgic front covers with charming country cottages, sturdy English oaks, and acres of rolling fields quilted by singing hedgerows. Within those covers, however, were stern editorials on the still squalid state of those very cottages, and the dangerous lack of piped water and sewerage systems in villages up and down the land. The results of surveys and questionnaires were published, revealing just under a third of rural parishes in England and Wales to be without piped water supplies, and almost a half without sewerage systems. Fewer than 10 per cent of agricultural workers' homes had electricity.[27] All of these were considered 'essential services' in towns and cities.

One WI member speaking at an AGM after the war boasted that in her village she was known as the 'Queen of Sewage' for her repeated attempts to get something done about the state of local drainage. Children paddled in the effluent, she said, and played with 'solid fluid'.[28] Another member wrote to *The Times* to report that her son, a soldier fighting in North Africa, had noticed far more sophisticated systems in the desert than at home in England, and readers frequently complained in *Home and Country* that temporary army camps, set up close to villages which had been campaigning for water and drainage for years, were always mysteriously provided with every possible amenity within weeks.

The WI mounted a major campaign immediately after the war for grants towards the refurbishment of cottages. Not just for patching up old and decrepit buildings, but redesigning them in the local idiom for comfortable and efficient modern living, with indoor WCs and wide windows to let the healing sunshine in. Northamptonshire Federation held an architects' competition for a pair of family cottages; *Home and Country* commissioned an article about women in the building industry, and then canvassed the entire membership to design a fantasy 'WI House' for the 1951 Ideal Home Exhibition in London. The winning entry, the cost of turning it into bricks and mortar sponsored by the *Daily Mail*, was beautiful and entirely practical, with three bedrooms, an upstairs bathroom, large kitchen, and a separate laundry with a washing machine and clothes airer. There was no lawn in the garden, but six neat little apple trees, several blackcurrant and gooseberry bushes, a potato patch, rows of vegetables and a chicken run. *This* was the WI's rural idyll. Raising living standards for its membership was all part of a greater cause being fought by the Movement during the 1940s and 1950s: feminism. Not the blood-and-thunder feminism of the young Edith Rigby or even Grace Hadow, but a more down-to-earth brand, to do with self-respect and just reward. The writer Renée Haynes produced an article for *Home and Country* in 1942 entitled 'The Nation's Cinderella'. It's about the dignity of domestic work and the unfairness of housewives' dependence on their husbands. It is not right that wives should have to take their husband's nationality on marriage, argues Miss Haynes: during wartime it made 'aliens' of old friends. Why aren't women working at home allowed to contribute to and benefit from health insurance schemes? They never have a penny to call their own – and 'being able to call pennies your own is very necessary to self-respect'.[29] Their work is more vital than almost anyone else's: it keeps people alive and makes them happy. Yet because it's unpaid it goes largely unnoticed, and wholly unacknowledged. Housewives

are not even properly compensated for taking in evacuees.
What an insult!

When wives and mothers are taken seriously as skilled pro-
fessionals, continues Miss Haynes, their opinions – about
housing, sanitation, health, childcare, animal welfare and so
on – will count far more than they do now. She credits the WI
with giving this forgotten workforce pride in their skills and
traditions, as well as some cheering companionship. But they
deserve more, and are quite right to campaign for it. Encouragement was not long coming. The Family Allowances Act of 1945
made child benefit payable to mothers from 1946 onwards. The
National Health Act followed in 1948. After three decades of
hard work by the NFWI and hundreds of thousands of its members, from small village discussions to what one overawed AGM
delegate called 'the Revolutions at the Halibut Hall', the Welfare
State was on its way.[30] The Women's Institute had helped raise
the status of housewives as skilled workers, and mothers as professional carers; it encouraged its members to change what they
could to make their neighbourhoods safer and fairer, and to
campaign for what they couldn't change. Because of its organisers' political connections and the calm reliability of surveys
like *Town Children through Country Eyes*, the government tended
to listen to, and trust, its collective voice. 'I think that countrywomen are the salt of the earth,' said a proud Lady Denman. 'I
do not think they get a fair deal, and I have always thought that
if we got together we could do something about it; and it has
been extraordinarily satisfactory to me because we *have* been
able to do something about it. It has given me the very greatest
happiness.'[31]

At this stage, the WI's brand of feminism didn't extend too
far beyond the kitchen sink. Someone responded to 'The

Nation's Cinderella' article by suggesting that it might be a good idea if married women whose children were at nursery or school went out to work part-time. This was a step too far – one of the resolutions at the 1950 AGM stated: 'This meeting deplores the efforts being made to attract mothers of young children back to industry'. *Home and Country* began a series of features at the end of 1946 highlighting 'careers for girls' – that is, unmarried women – and declaring its support for equal pay for men and women. But none of those careers is particularly ambitious. There's the odd unusual suggestion, like slaughter-house assistant, accountant or dietitian; what's left is nursing, secretarial work, veterinary nursing and gardening. Good jobs, all of them, but hardly radical.

The WI's most significant contribution to feminism remained, and remains still, what it had been from the very beginning: to equip women with the confidence to think and speak for themselves, and to make well informed decisions for their own good and for the benefit of their families and the wider community.

8

Halibut Hall and the Revolutions: 1945–1960

Our old country is in trouble, and the whole world
is watching to see how we get out of it.[1]

Meanwhile, in the background to this ideological battle between different notions of feminism, real life in postwar Britain trundled on. Once again, austerity was the watchword, and the NFWI did all it could to encourage its members to support one another emotionally as well as materially. A psychologist was commissioned to write an article in *Home and Country* in 1944 to prepare women for the difficulties that would almost certainly arise when their husbands were demobbed. Remember, it warned, that those on active service have lived far more exciting lives than is possible in peacetime, and they're likely to get bored and irritable with the old routine. They will have met strange people and tasted adventure; don't take their complaints at the tedium of normal life as criticism. Try not to be too worried or offended if they seem restless, or fail to appreciate how hard you've been working in their absence. Be prepared for them to have changed – as you probably have – and begin your courtship again. And if you must complain, do it to your friends at the WI, not your husband.

An interesting meal might perk things up. Rationing was still in force – and would remain in Britain until the mid-1950s – but that was no excuse for lack of imagination in the kitchen. 'Have you ever thought of deep-fried whale-meat pasties?' asked *Home and Country*'s increasingly desperate cookery columnist. How about making kebabs out of '1 raw kipper, 1 cauliflower, and 1lb of Brussels sprouts', or trying a vegetarian menu (described in a feature irresistibly entitled 'Going Gay without Meat')? Her *pièce de résistance*, bound to win any husband's heart, was this recipe combining traditional English cuisine with a touch of the exotic:

Brains and Pineapple
1lb calves' brains
1 small tin pineapple pieces

Batter for Fritter	*Marinade for Brains*
4 oz flour	2 tablespoons best vinegar
Big pinch salt	2 tablespoons olive oil
¼ pint water	1 teaspoon chopped parsley
1 teaspoon oil	Salt & pepper
White of 1 egg	

Soak the brains for 3 or 4 hours changing the water so as to take away the blood. Take off the skin. Put them in a saucepan with enough tepid water to cover them, a teaspoon of

salt and a tablespoon of vinegar. Poach for 15 minutes ...
Take out and drain, then cover with the marinade and spoon
it over the brains from time to time. They should stay in the
marinade for an hour. Turn out the pineapple and drain it
(use the juice for a sauce or jelly). Drain the brains also and
put both pineapple and brains in the batter. Fry in spoonfuls
in deep fat.[2]

Enjoy.

If any housewife happened to have a tin of pineapple in her
larder, it was probably courtesy of the Australians, who shipped
food parcels to Britain to help tide the Mother Country over
the leanest years directly after the war. Even jam was in short
supply: Queensland sent pounds and pounds of it home to the
shires. Food shortages were everyone's most immediate problem now, and it became a matter of national pride that Britain
should be seen to cope with them in the same defiant spirit
that had got her through the war. So at the end of 1947, fresh
from the success of the Produce Guild, the NFWI sprang into
action again, this time with 'Operation Produce'. The premise
was simple: every single WI member in the land – over 379,000
of them – should be encouraged to produce an extra ten pounds
(five kilos) of food during the coming year. Institutes with
participating members were to keep logbooks of their efforts;
not the official printed logbooks of the fruit-preserving centres,
but individual ones organised to display the unique achievements of each Institute.

Eighty-five thousand members responded, and 404 logbooks
were submitted to County Federations at the end of 1948 to be
judged and admired. None can have been more impressive than
Bacton and District's, an Institute in East Suffolk with sixty-one

members.[3] There, the Institute secretary, a Mrs Muscroft, considered record-keeping a work of art. In the true spirit of the WI, Bacton and District's beautiful book also reveals a great deal of hard, constructive work tempered with good humour and a sense of celebration. It opens in March 1947, when each member was given six seed potatoes to plant. There was a competition to see who could coax the highest yield from the Suffolk soil:

> To mention some may seem invidious
> But the digging fever was insidious;
> Most of them dug, and we encore them,
> The rest got their husbands to do it for them.

Meanwhile, another competition opened, this one for the best Ode to a Potato. The prize, of gladioli bulbs, went to a rhapsodic composition by a modestly anonymous poet:

> Lovers may dream of eyes of blue,
> But I dream only, Spud, of you,
> Whose eyes aren't limited to two,
> Sweet eyes of brown
> Which match your gown
> And are so full of promise, too.
>
> Though somewhat bulky round the hips,
> Your figure's praised, even by Cripps;
> I yearn to claim you with my lips,
> Baked, mashed or boiled,
> Roasted or broiled,
> Or even (if there's fat), as chips . . .

'Cripps' refers to Sir Stafford Cripps, Britain's stern new Chancellor of the Exchequer.

To reach their target of ten pounds of food each, most members diversified from potatoes. There are pages in the logbook – each with utterly beguiling illustrations – about a dedicated band of tomato growers, and people keeping bees (with varying degrees of success during what appears to have been a particularly bad year for honey). Cabbages, carrots and salad vegetables were all successful, as long as the soil was friable enough. Worms were the answer, if not. ('Has any member got a superabundance of these little heroes to spare? If so, I would like to do a deal. I have one elderly rabbit and a neighbour's hen, who find much pleasure in my young greens ... ') There are pages of 'Egg Activities', about parent chickens, geese, ducks and turkeys. Apparently Mrs Church's hens 'took a new lease of life, thanks to a lazy one of their number coming to an untimely end'. The 'Rabbit Recreation' page reports an *amazing* amount of rabbit re-creation, while my favourite page deals with 'News from the Sties', in which it's noted that 'Mrs T. Gooderham is attempting to fatten a pig but it has grown, not only in girth, but also in charm, and has become a Pet ... '. There's a sketch of said pig, very portly, sitting on Miss Gooderham's lap in an armchair.

Three members of the Institute bought a portable canning machine between them – it's still there in the village – and continued the soft fruit preservation at which they had become so expert during the war. Others made dandelion or cowslip wine, and further afield in Suffolk people bottled walnuts and almonds, pickles and lard.

In August, the results of the spud competition were announced. They were staggering. The winner, Mrs Manning, managed to produce fifty-nine pounds of potatoes from her original six little tubers. The average yield was thirty: from the two pounds of seed-potatoes shared among them in March they conjured up a total of 1414 pounds. That took Bacton and District WI way beyond the ten-pound target, without counting all the other stuff they grew or nurtured between them.

Following a diary of every member's Operation Produce activities, signed by the women themselves, Mrs Muscroft closed the logbook with a short apologia for her own absence in the roster of producers:

After reading this book, Gentle Judge, you may think
'Twas a sheer waste of energy – even of ink,
'How much better employed the compiler might be
In coercing a cabbage or coaxing a bee . . .'
In this, O my Critic, I beg of your pardon,
For I am a menace in anyone's garden,
Much worse than greenfly, or the pestilent slug . . .
So it's best to have written, and not to have dug.

Bacton and District's logbook was submitted, as required, to the county authorities at the end of 1948, no doubt with a good deal of confidence. The best from around the country were due to be sent to the United States, to thank the American people for supplying so many seeds to the WI. Surely Bacton's would be hard to beat? But Mrs Muscroft reckoned without the adamantine seam of bureaucratic pedantry running through the edifice of the NFWI: Bacton and District had been a little too free in its record-keeping, and a little too unnecessary in its presentation. A terse note came back with the logbook: 'Book used not according to schedule, but otherwise excellent.' We should be grateful it was never sent to America. It's a treasure.

To mark the success of Operation Produce, the NFWI held an exhibition in the New Horticultural Hall in London from 9 to 12 October 1948. This was not a fund-raising exercise: it cost over £2000 to mount, and the entrance fees helped it break even, but no more. Its real value to the Movement was as a public relations exercise. Thousands of visitors came, both Londoners and travellers from Federations around the country, to wander around what was essentially a microcosm of the WI world. There were stalls for literature and general information; an exhibition about Denman College (which we shall come to in the next chapter); cookery displays, including samples of both traditional and international cuisine; demonstrations on preservation, handicrafts, flowers, gardening and bee-keeping; a live WI market; and – most people's favourite – a series of 'shop windows' selling herbs, dairy goods, sweets, wine, pig-club products, honey and general groceries. This is what the WI had been doing to save 'our old country' in its latest hour of need, and the results proved surprisingly popular. Between 1948 and 1949, membership of the Movement leapt by over forty thousand.

More high-profile exhibitions and festivals followed. For a national singing festival in 1950 the NFWI commissioned perhaps the most eminent British composer at the time, Ralph Vaughan Williams, who was a friend of General Secretary Frances Farrer, to compose a WI cantata, *Folk Songs for the Four Seasons*. Over a thousand WI choirs rehearsed the music for almost a year; the best were chosen to perform it at the Royal Albert Hall, conducted by Sir Adrian Boult and accompanied by the London Symphony Orchestra. The iconic Festival of Britain in 1951 included a 'Mural of the Country Wife' worked not exclusively by WI members, but given to them afterwards as an act of homage to their work. Institutes were also asked to compile village scrapbooks for the year. The Victoria and Albert Museum held a WI craft exhibition in 1952, to showcase a newly completed wall-hanging on which WI members had been busy since 1947. Called *The Work of Women in Wartime*, it is now deep in storage at the Imperial War Museum at Duxford.[4] At the time of the Victoria and Albert exhibition this massive and intricate piece of work – some five metres by three – was hailed as a modern-day Bayeux Tapestry. It was sewn cooperatively, in tent-stitched moth-proof wool on hemp canvas, after a design by a Hampshire artist, Sybil Blunt; three needlework schools were held in Winchester to kick off the tapestry, and then four hundred embroiderers around the country were chosen to work on the separate panels, which were later imperceptibly joined to make a panorama of WI members at their wartime occupations. It is exquisitely worked in soft, earthy colours from specially developed vegetable dyes, and skilfully displays the very virtues it was made to celebrate: imagination, application, expertise and teamwork.

The panels illustrate little cameos of WI members' lives. Some come as no surprise: women making jam, for instance, queuing for shopping or running a canteen. Others show how versatile the wartime experiences of individual members could be: one woman is in a sailor's uniform, busy waving signals from a clifftop, one is working in an industrial plant of some kind, while another's a railway porter. A banner runs across the whole thing, wittily quoting from Shakespeare's *Henry VIII* (Act I, Scene 1): 'the madams too, Not used to toil, did almost sweat to bear The pride upon them, that their very labour Was to them as a painting'. The hanging went on tour after the London exhibition, travelling through England to Edinburgh at the invitation of the Scottish Women's Rural Institutes, and then to the WI's equivalent organisation in Australia. It came to rest back in London at the Imperial War Museum, the NFWI having proudly presented it to the nation. It was occasionally displayed there, but gradually disappeared from view as the decades went by.

Home and Country was a comforting constant throughout the war and during the difficult years that followed: it remained in most respects resolutely traditional, chronicling the work and achievements of the WI at national and local level, offering its readers recipes and knitting patterns, the occasional story, puzzles and pictures for the children, and edifying features on history, art and public affairs. Reading old copies of the magazine is a treat. Sometimes it takes itself terribly seriously – appropriate, of course, when discussing the circumstances of war refugees, the evil influence of violent films on children, or breast cancer awareness. But one wonders how many members were really as rapt as they were expected to be about procedural problems at monthly meetings (there was a special column for those), about the minutiae of the NFWI's constitution or the ins and outs of town planning.

Reflecting the miscellaneous nature of the WI's membership, the postwar *Home and Country* was a slightly confused publication. Jaunty and genuinely interesting articles about the problems of setting up a WI in British Malaya (to quell the influence of the Communists), or on how to develop a sense of fashion and 'personal style', vie for attention with tedious explanations of European foreign relations or the most scientific method of washing up. On one page you'll find instructions for knitting a vest and knickers from tickly Shetland wool; on the next, a discussion of myxomatosis; and on the next a heartbreaking appeal from a WI mother whose eight-year-old daughter has recently died and who's looking for a similarly aged girl to adopt. Surprisingly modern issues like oil-polluted beaches, pesticides on verges and the export of live cattle for slaughter are interspersed with drearily old-fashioned tips on wart-charming and keeping hubby happy.

This bizarre pot-pourri mirrored what was obviously a period of change within the Movement, as well as in the world outside. Operation Produce was a triumph. More people took part in it than had joined the Produce Guild (because of the latter's membership fee), and it was gratifying for everyone that it did so well. The exhibitions and festivals held to cheer the country up after the war opened doors for countless WI musicians, actresses and craftswomen, giving them confidence and credibility. But not everything in the WI's carefully composted garden during the late 1940s and 1950s was rosy. Letters to *Home and Country*, always impartially edited, began to smack of resentment and disaffection. Why were members given such stupendously inane competitions to enter – like the best boiled potato, eating jelly with knitting needles, or – cop-out of cop-outs – the cleverest idea for next month's competition? New members, like Peggy Downs of South Ruislip, complained bitterly that there was nothing meaningful for them to contribute to society through the WI. She felt compelled to resign, 'sadly disappointed in the range of appeal'.[5] She found that the official ban on controversial discussions involving party politics or matters of religious belief denied intelligent young women like her a voice. Their elders, meanwhile, harrumphed that the

WI didn't need members of Mrs Downs's age. Youth had 'nothing in common with the older woman', according to Mabel Bristow of Topsham in Devon, and any attempt to mix the two, she warned darkly, 'would not make for a happy Institute'.[6]

In May 1953, there was a spat between a Suffolk WI and the National British Women's Total Abstinence Union over a decision to toast the Queen's health on Coronation Day with port or sherry. This was strictly against the letter of the law, since the Institute in question had not applied for a licence, and besides, it set a louche example to the community. Someone shopped the WI to the Temperance ladies, the National Executive, and the press. 'Women Break Rules,' screamed an article about the incident in the *Daily Telegraph*; nonsense, retorted the Institute members. If the rules can't be relaxed on Coronation Day, then it's a poor do. The National Executive's uncompromising response was to uphold the rules, and thereby humiliate the local WI.

It was decisions like this which alienated the more progressive members of the Movement, who now – thanks to the WI – had the courage of their convictions and the confidence to speak out. The annual Devon Institutes' carol service in Exeter Cathedral was a popular tradition, but in 1950 an Institute secretary wrote to the Federation headquarters to complain that Roman Catholic members of her Institute had been forbidden by their bishop to attend, due to the fact that Anglican prayers were read during the ceremony. So, because a handful of members were barred from it, the NFWI decreed – according to its non-sectarian rules – that the carol service must be cancelled. This caused outrage. 'We all looked forward every Christmas to this inspiring gathering, which is absolutely crammed, and many people have to be turned away. Carols are both international and non-sectarian. What are we coming to? Is not the spirit more important than these frustrating rules?'[7] A similar furore erupted in 1957 when Frances Farrer informed a journalist at *The Times* that prayers were to be banned at WI meetings – even though, it transpired, many Institutes had been opening proceedings with a short prayer for years, quite happily. The correspondence following this edict, which had always been current but perhaps never enforced quite so energetically, was poisonous. It ran in the national press as well as in the columns of *Home and Country*. Perhaps the WI was growing too numerous to be bound by its leaders' inflexible regulations, however well meant they were. Maybe the leaders themselves were getting out of touch.

In a way it was gratifying that the press was still interested in the WI. In fact the WI's relationship with the media flourished during the 1950s, before the Movement was eclipsed by its tearaway young niece, the Women's Liberation Movement. Lady Denman and other Executive Committee members had occasionally been asked by the BBC before the war to speak bracingly to 'countrywomen' on the air, and the Gaumont-British film studios had made four films of WI members demonstrating handicrafts in 1939. Now newspapers regularly ran features and even leaders based on the Institutes' work and campaigns, and the BBC commissioned members to give talks or take part in 'expert' panel shows. Films still did the rounds of Institute meetings, sent by outside agencies to educate the membership in something new, like hoovering (did you know a carpet holds its own weight in dirt?), and popular magazines were glad to include women's pages, like mini-*Home and Countrys*, for their many WI readers.

Best of all, *The Archers* began. Originally piloted for a week in the Midlands on the BBC's Regional Home Service in 1950, it was regularly broadcast on the Light Programme five evenings a week from 1 January 1951. This 'everyday story of country folk' was created in collaboration with the Ministry of Agriculture to raise farmers' morale (with that of their wives) and make their industry fashionable – and so more productive. The WI loomed large from the very beginning, with prominent characters regularly attending meetings, chairing them, and even visiting AGMs. In 1959, *The Times* noted that many WIs had changed the hour of their meetings so that no one would miss the evening's episode, and in the NFWI Archive there are boxes dating back to 1956 full of correspondence between the National Executive and BBC producers discussing likely subjects, requesting the inclusion of specific WI events or simply that they get the facts right.

A letter from the NFWI to the BBC dated 28 July 1959 is rather sadly prophetic: 'We are not entirely pre-occupied,' it sighs, 'with making jam and knitting depressing pullovers . . . '[8] But on the whole, the WI enjoyed the exposure and benefited from it. The year 1954 was the Movement's most successful ever in terms of membership: 467,000. It has been downhill, more or less, ever since. But now that there's a new generation of young WI members in Ambridge, who knows what the future might hold?

Most of the media attention focused inevitably on AGMs and resolutions. The implication of most press coverage during this postwar era is polite surprise that all these thousands of matrons turning up at the Albert Hall every year should be capable of producing such feisty and well informed campaigns.

(In fact, the novelty of 'massed women' having something sensible to say still doesn't seem to have worn off, even now.) It *would* be remarkable if every one of those delegates really had been the little Boudicca that journalists imagined her to be. But AGMs were not entirely peopled by village viragos in fancy hats intent on changing the world. Ruth Audis was a Derbyshire housewife, sent from her Institute in the village of Palterton to the 1958 AGM in London. To her, this was not some sort of political rally, just a huge adventure.[9]

Setting off from home on the ten-to-eleven bus on Wednesday 4 June, Ruth travelled to Chesterfield station to meet a friend from the neighbouring Institute; together they caught the train to London, spending the three-and-a-half-hour journey talking excitedly all the way. After checking into their hotel near Oxford Circus, the two women went sightseeing, covering all the usual highlights from Trafalgar Square to Buckingham Palace, Downing Street to Scotland Yard. By 10.30 that night they were exhausted. 'We then went back to our hotel nearly crawling upstairs as there was 82 stairs to our room, but it was very comfortable and we sat chatting together while [*sic*] about 11.30.'

Next morning after breakfast – where they couldn't get used to being waited on at table – Ruth and her companion walked across Hyde Park to the Albert Hall in time for the morning's programme. Their seats were up on the third tier. It was a marvellous sight to look down on the packed arena of women 'dressed in lovely summer dresses and suits of nearly every different colour'. The Chairman's opening comments were not some soul-stirring call-to-arms, but a polite request that ladies sitting on the balcony should take care not to shake crumbs on those below during lunch, and that no one should faint. 'If you felt like fainting, go out before you did.'

The meeting opened at 10.45 with a rousing rendition of 'Jerusalem'. Various reports followed, including an exhaustive one from the Treasurer (during which Ruth admitted getting 'a bit mixed up'). When it was time to elect the Executive Committee, each candidate was invited to step forward and be introduced. According to the bedazzled Ruth, it was like a mannequin parade, with everyone dressed so elegantly. Voting was a haphazard affair, since no one could possibly be expected to know enough about each candidate to make a meaningful choice – in this instance, democracy had its drawbacks. Debating the resolutions came next. Ruth tried to take notes, but this part of the meeting got a bit boring. Eventually it was decided that (among other things) housing authorities should be urged to consider repairing rather than demolishing old cottages wholesale; that the government be lobbied to impose more severe penalties on those who committed sexual assault; and that 'the appropriate Ministries' should take immediate action to prevent the pollution of rivers and seashores with sewage.

A ballet dancer then came on stage to give a talk about her career; a delegate had a fit and had to be carried out (which put Ruth 'off my stroke'); and after they had all roared out the national anthem the meeting closed in time for Ruth and her friend to catch the train home. She wrote a report of the meeting, as she was required to do, and conscientiously presented it at the next meeting of Palterton's WI. She had had a wonderful time.

The Chairman at Ruth's AGM was not Gertrude Denman. She had resigned at the 1946 AGM, after nearly thirty years at the Movement's helm. Her contribution to the quality of rural life in Britain, and to social reform, was incalculable. The Queen said as much during a visit to the meeting. When Trudie's decision was announced, a gasp of shock echoed round the Albert Hall, followed by a rampant ovation. She confessed to the delegates that she'd often tried to resign before, believing strongly in the refreshing benefits of new blood, but the Executive had never allowed her. She was sixty-one now, a little tired, and determined to go. Her successor was Diana Keppel, Countess of Albemarle. She was a glamorous figure in her late thirties, with an impressive pedigree in public service with the WI and the WVS, and as a trustee (with Trudie) of the Carnegie UK Trust and an adviser on youth and community development. She was an inspired choice to follow Trudie: sufficiently different to be judged on her own terms, but astute and sensitive enough not to rock the boat too much. In fact the WI was more a stately galleon than a boat, but it was still gathering speed at this stage.

Lady Albemarle stayed for five years; after her came a beautiful and highly charismatic former actress, Elizabeth Brunner. Lady Brunner was chatelaine of Greys Court, now a National Trust property, in Oxfordshire. She was the granddaughter of thespian Sir Henry Irving, wife of a distinguished industrialist, mother of three boys – and entirely her own person. Her belief in the power of the WI was unshakeable, and she had a knack of charming into action people across all strata of society. She was the spirit behind Denman College, the WI's adult education centre, and behind the famous Keep Britain Tidy campaign adopted by the WI in 1954 (and then by the whole country). She too stayed in post for five years.

In 1956, the WI's fourth aristocratic Chairman was appointed. Barbara, Lady Dyer, was a Justice of the Peace like Elizabeth Brunner; her strengths were in administration and local government. She joined the WI in the first place only because her cook had wanted someone to go with her to meetings ... It was a sign of the times that Lady Dyer's successor in 1961 was the first 'non-Lady' Chairman in the forty-six-year history of the NFWI.

All change at the top, then – and an even more significant transformation was happening behind the scenes. Grace Hadow had died in 1940, and between 1948 and 1957 almost every other pioneer of the NFWI left the stage. The indomitable Madge Watt succumbed to a heart attack back home in Canada in 1948, aged eighty. In 1952 Lil Nugent Harris died, two years before her husband John. Trudie Denman underwent major surgery in June 1954 – just at the time of the AGM – to rectify a problem which had been simmering ever since a tricky appendectomy eighteen years previously. Everything seemed to be fine at first, but the day after the operation she fell unconscious and, while six thousand women were singing 'Jerusalem' in the Albert Hall, she died. She was sixty-nine. Next year, in 1955, the Institute's doughty MP Margaret Winteringham passed away; Dame Meriel 'Slasher' Talbot followed in 1956, and in 1957 the Movement's first General Secretary and editor of *Home and Country*, Alice Williams, died at the age of ninety-four.

Two years later, Frances Farrer resigned – the last of what she affectionately called the old battleaxes. A whole generation of leaders was suddenly gone, and when the new one looked to the future it was with a mixture of pride and real trepidation.

9

How to Be Happy though Educated: DENMAN COLLEGE

*My wife seems to be growing brighter,
and no wonder!*[1]

It is rarely advisable for authors to admit to complacency, but there's a point in the life of most books when a sly little moment of self-satisfaction creeps in. It's when the long process of research appears to be over; all the facts are neatly collated, the seeds of ideas are germinating nicely, and anything – even a minor masterpiece – seems possible. My moment was interrupted by an unexpected email. It came from Canada, and informed me that the writer's mother (who didn't do the Internet) had heard about my project and wondered if I'd like to go and visit her in Leicestershire. The mother was called Rachel Root; she had been a member of the WI for most of her life and had recently compiled a history of her family's involvement with the Movement from 1922 onwards. In eleven volumes.

Despite a slightly desperate hope that by now I had all I needed to get down to work, after a year spent in libraries, archives and record offices and examining local collections around the country, I couldn't ignore eleven volumes. With bad grace I postponed Chapter 1, and set off up the motorway.

It was the right decision. The first thing I saw when Rachel opened the door to welcome me was a decorated wellington boot overflowing with flowers, standing in the hall. Very WI. She'd been helping her grandson plant it up for school. A roaring fire burned in a sitting-room gleaming with embroidery and brightly quilted cushions; a table was laid ready for me with a neat pile of ring-binders, carefully labelled, a steaming cup of coffee and a plate heaped high with biscuits. Just by the table, hanging from hooks on the wall, were little crocheted bags from which, at various points during my visit, Rachel extracted dowsing crystals to help her consider questions or make decisions. This lent a strangely measured pace to the day, as if we were being patiently directed in a play from offstage. Beyond the window was a spectacular garden, and a greenhouse still full, in early October, of cabochon tomatoes in glowing red and yellow. She had made some into chutney, and we had it with our lunch.

Rachel herself was quick, articulate, curious about my work and confident about her own. The eleven volumes contained beautifully written records of one family's public and personal involvement with a movement that had influenced them all. Rachel was obviously proud of her relatives' (both ancestors' and descendants') involvement in the WI – not just in Leicestershire but back in Ontario, where her great-aunt emigrated in 1912 to Whitby, the home of the world's second Women's Institute. She was just as proud of the WI itself, marking historical and political milestones in her archive and commenting on the Institute's significance with scholarly reflection. I wondered if perhaps she'd done a history degree?

No, replied Rachel – she had been to Denman College.

Denman, the WI's own adult education centre, opened shortly after the Second World War: a women's college for *real* women, not slips of girls from grammar schools. It was a long time coming. Education had always been one of the Movement's raisons d'être from the earliest days, when Adelaide Hoodless campaigned for instruction in food preparation and home hygiene. Madge Watt, herself a university graduate, tempered Adelaide's pragmatism by encouraging WI members to regard their monthly meetings as leisure time – a complete novelty – and to exercise their minds by cultivating non-essential skills like art appreciation and political awareness, which needed teaching too. By the time the WI came to Britain in 1915 its dual purpose – practical and cerebral – was already well established and was met more or less successfully, given there was a war on, through the ordinary programmes of speakers' visits, handicraft classes, occasional choral concerts or plays, and the pages of *Home and Country*.

Higher education for women hit the news headlines in 1920 when, following the Sex Disqualification Removal Act, Oxford University decided to allow its female students to graduate, like those of almost every other university in the country. The first of the women's colleges at Oxford had opened its doors over forty years before, but not until now were its students admitted to full membership of the university, which meant granting them the right to wear academic dress and have their final exam results acknowledged by the formal award of a degree. Cambridge University couldn't quite bring itself to match Oxford: it allowed its 'undergraduettes' to list the appropriate letters after their names when they had finished their studies and passed their exams after 1920, but declined to give them degrees until 1948 – the year Denman College opened.

Thanks no doubt to its resident academic Grace Hadow, the NFWI made sure to report these laggard breakthroughs in *Home and Country*, as part of its policy to encourage scholarship among its members alongside creativity. Grace's home Institute in Headington Quarry, Oxford, was reported in *The Times* as being an outstanding example of the 'ennobling' qualities of adult education: members there had completed a village history (a project undertaken by several WIs from the mid-1920s onwards) which was so well researched and presented that Oxford University Press was going to publish it.[2] The newspaper pontificated that intellectual discipline like this turned WI members into 'bigger people' and put them 'on a footing of equality with the best of humanity'. It also noted, with virtuosic chauvinism, that for village women such a project was

as rational and dignified a hobby as any other, and the contributors, if the functions and uses of history are explained to them, need not be ashamed to chronicle their small beer as faithfully as they can. In the heart of most Englishmen, even long after they and theirs have left the ancestral village, lurks the villager, a primitive being who has never grown wholly reconciled to urban life and perhaps never will. It will be his interests as well as their own these village historians will be serving.[3]

Never mind all that; Grace and the members of the WI just enjoyed the challenge.

'Brains Trusts' were remarkably popular village entertainments during the Second World War, consisting of panels of experts – or opinionated local worthies – who discussed questions from the audience in turn. They were based on the BBC radio programme of the same name, which broadcast regularly from 1942 onwards (later transferring to television) and became the precursor of today's *Any Questions?*. WIs were usually expected to field a panellist – if not the entire panel – at village Brains Trusts, and sessions were always well supported. Home-grown intellectualism was becoming fashionable, and as ever the WI was quick to take advantage of the spirit of the times. Here was a movement being encouraged by its own Executive and by the government, in the pioneering spirit of postwar reconstruction, to take rural Britain by the careworn hand and lead it towards enlightenment. How better to do that than through education?

Despite the rhetoric, there wasn't a great deal of material help from the government at this stage. The Ministry of Agriculture did offer scholarships to sons and daughters of farm workers to attend farm institutes, agricultural colleges or, occasionally, universities, but made no provision for freely accessible adult education. There were opportunities elsewhere, however. The Women's Co-operative Guild had been running classes for women – much as Mechanics' Institutes did for working men – since the 1880s. These tended to be based in industrial areas, and didn't offer many opportunities to rural women. The Workers' Educational Association, founded in 1903 and still flourishing as the WEA, had a wider reach. WI members were also encouraged to attend 'extension lectures' available from their local university (what we would now call outreach programmes) and to join or form reading circles. Respectable correspondence courses could be subscribed to and benefited from, and some establishments advertised residential courses for temporary students.

Hillcroft College for Working Women in Surbiton was one of these. Founded in 1920 by the Educational Charity for Women, it offers residential courses of varying lengths for those who wish to catch up on lost qualifications, or prepare for university as mature students. Its motto, when it first opened, was 'By Rough Ways to the Stars', which sounds rather less inspiring than the equivalent Latin tag *Per Ardua ad Astra*. In the early 1930s a WI member called Miss Bezzant joined a course at Hillcroft and found it so stimulating that she went on to win a scholarship to Ruskin College, Oxford, where she read Agricultural Economics. The NFWI was very proud of her.

Newnham College in Cambridge ran women's summer schools for the public from 1934 onwards, which were heavily oversubscribed. They offered a varied but stodgy menu of courses, including Physiology, Current Affairs and Geographical Backgrounds, and the History of the British Empire. One year, six hundred women applied for twenty-five places. Of the successful candidates, 'some were middle-aged housewives,' reported *Home and Country*, 'one was a land girl ex-kennel maid, one a supervisor in an aircraft factory, another a garage hand'.[4] And four were WI members. The quest for self-improvement came as no surprise to champions of the WI like the Oxford classicist and celebrity intellectual Sir Gilbert Murray: he recognised in the Movement 'a great and unrealised reservoir of power' ready to be tapped through

used to Toil, did

almost Sweat t...

One of the panels from the immense 'Women in Wartime' tapestry worked by Institute members, to show the variety of tasks they accomplished during the war. Here they are using semaphore flags, probably home-sewn.

NEWS
THE

Miss Gooderham is fattening two pigs on household refuse.

Mrs T. Gooderham is attempting to fatten a pig, but it has grown, not only in girth, but also in charm, and has become a Pet...........

Mrs Welham has been fattening a pig— Killed in October.

Mrs Jackson has been feeding pigs.

FROM STIES

Mrs Ash is fattening one pig, which is allocated for Christmas Consumption; and six others, to be sold when they are too fat for their stye.

DON'T FORGET! Have contributed to PROGRESS REPORT Page 19

Mrs Alderton: 12 lbs Marmalade, 12 lbs Rhubarb, 8 lbs Gooseberry, 10 lbs Gooseberry & Rhubarb, 16 lbs Black Currant, 4 lbs Strawberry, 10 lbs Black Currant & Rhubarb, 2 lbs Raspberry.
Total: 155 lbs of Jam. (See details under Individual Report.)
78 lbs of Bottled Fruit.
(Plus — in September — 4 lbs Blackberry jam & 10 lbs Bottled)
Mrs. Meadows: Total of 32 lbs. Jam, + Blackberry Jam.
and 30 lbs. Bottled Fruit. + Blackberries.
Mrs. Manning: Total of 66 lbs. of Jam and Marmalade.
16 lbs of Bottled Gooseberries and Apples.
Mrs. Webb: 6 Extra Jars of Bottled Gooseberries.
Also Bottled: Blackcurrants, Greengages, Plums.
And made: Blackcurrant, Greengage and Victoria Plum Jam.
Mrs. Culley: About 40 lbs. of different Jams.
30 lbs. of Bottled Fruit.
Mrs. G. Finbow: 20 lbs. Jam, 10 lbs. Blackberry Jelly
30 Bottles of Fruit.

PRODUCE

The TOMATO Plants were issued from the Parish Room on May 18th at the rate of 3d each, having been purchased from Mr. Murton.

Each Member received three.

All from 3d bit!

Bacton and District WI's 'Operation Produce' Logbook is full of postwar joie de vivre. It depicts the Suffolk villagers' attempts – ultimately triumphant – to help increase the country's stocks of fresh meat, vegetables, bottled fruit and (of course) jam.

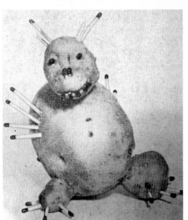

WI activities between the 1920s and 1950s were remarkably varied. Here members around the country are strenuously doing gymnastics, playing 'human whist', blowing kazoos and taking part in a head-dress contest. The deeply disturbing potato is a result of another competition. Less adventurous members could knit the tickly underwear ensemble or help keep Britain tidy.

PLEASE TAKE LITTER HOME

Denman College, the WI's centre of learning near Abingdon, Oxfordshire.

Sam was the college's first co-warden. His fame, like his smell, went
before him.

'Baker's Half-Dozen': six of the original Calendar Girls, still raising huge amounts of money every year for Leukaemia and Lymphoma research.

WI members at Westminster, campaigning against the patchy provision for women victims of violence, with their hand-sewn British 'map of gaps'.

A poster advertising forthcoming events at the Shoreditch Sisters WI in London.

education. He tried to call the WI to arms at the 1932 AGM,
rallying delegates at the Albert Hall to listen to the radio, read
books, teach and learn from one another; that way a little bit
of education might go a very long way. A cartoon in *Punch*
added its pennyworth, showing an imperious, hook-nosed
woman looming over a rather wet-looking young man, with
the caption, '"I hear your dear wife is to give our Women's
Institute a lecture." "My dear lady, it's no use appealing to me.
I can't stop her."'[5]

Gradually, the NFWI became more confident in demand-
ing opportunities for higher education for its members and
their communities. The first step was to appoint Cicely
McCall its Education Organiser. She was an intriguing character: not easy to work with, but passionate, imaginative and
supremely confident. She should have had an easy life: her
father was a barrister, and Cicely was a clever girl. It was her
ambition to go to Somerville College – she had once visited a
family friend who had been there, and was so struck by her
pink crêpe de Chine blouse that she appointed her as chief
role model on the spot. But there was no money: her father
was declared bankrupt before Cicely made it to Oxford, and as
St Hugh's College had offered her a scholarship she went there
instead.

Cicely was not a model student. She was rusticated, or
suspended, after staying out too late on the river one evening,
and though she was allowed back after a term the episode
seems to have knocked the stuffing out of her, and she failed
her subsequent exams. This meant she must leave. It was
clear that she faced the prospect of earning her own living,
and she managed to secure a post as English teacher to the
children of a Polish prince immediately after Oxford. In 1926

she found herself in Cairo working for the International Bureau for the Suppression of Traffic in Women and Children, a Victorian foundation working for the abolition of prostitution, which sparked off an interest in social and welfare work. Back in England, she acted as a prison visitor before her appointment as assistant housemistress at Aylesbury Girls' Borstal. Then she moved to Exeter as headmistress of an approved school, and trained in psychiatric social work.

It was in Devon that Cicely met the writer and NFWI Executive Committee member Elizabeth Dashwood, alias E. M. Delafield, who recommended her to Lady Denman as a potential Education Organiser. Cicely was always a careful businesswoman: she demanded a higher salary than the other national organisers – and got it, after a trial-by-luncheon interview with Gertrude Denman that might have terrorised many a lesser woman but worried Cicely not a jot.

One of Cicely's first tasks in her new job was to travel through the counties of England and Wales to introduce the idea of adult education to WI members. She asked what they wanted in the way of provision for themselves and their children, tried to raise awareness of what the government's postwar plans were, and to advise how the WI might influence those plans. The NFWI was sent a questionnaire in 1942, inviting comments from members before the government issued its White Paper on Educational Reconstruction the following year (which would materialise as the Education Act of 1944). Cicely was pleased to note the emphasis on wide-reaching adult education in the White Paper, and must have been gratified (ostensibly, at least) when the chairman of an international conference on education held in London in

1943, Esther Neville-Smith, was announced as another Executive Committee member. Cicely attended that conference with the NFWI's Education subcommittee chairman, Adeline Vernon; it's where the idea of a WI college was born, during a discussion after a lecture on adult education in Denmark.

The NFWI began to administer residential courses during the 1940s, soon after Cicely's appointment. It had always run in-house training schools, ever since Madge Watt's first one for VCOs in 1918, and provided opportunities for craftswomen and artists to work together on particular projects; but from 1940 onwards it started holding 'Speaker Parties' in different counties, teaching WI members to address an audience confidently and usefully at meetings. In September 1943 the NFWI invited students to a much more ambitious four-day course under the general heading of 'Questions of the Day'. It was held at Radbrook College in Shrewsbury. Fifty WI members attended, from twenty-six counties, and the highlight of the occasion was a speech by the academic and educationalist Sir Richard Livingstone, President of Corpus Christi College, Oxford, and later the university's Vice-Chancellor.

Livingstone was one of the country's most outspoken advocates of adult education. His theme for Radbrook students was 'Education for Life'. It was scandalous, he said, that 80 per cent of the population had no education at all after fourteen. The nation's mind had grown sleepy for lack of exercise, and stagnant. The vast majority of Britons were mentally old at forty and senile at fifty. This didn't happen in Scandinavia: there they had 'People's Colleges' where 'common' men and women could go to study for months at a time. Why not have the same thing here?

Such Colleges would give education, but education in the right sense of the word. Dismiss from your mind schools or examinations. Think instead of a chance to find new interests or pursue old ones, to study religion, politics, conduct, learn something of the meaning and power of science, to understand life and its activities better and so to make more of them, to escape from the daily routine and have leisure to think and learn. This has been hitherto the privilege of the few; adult education, properly organised, would make it possible for all.[6]

Few can have been more supportive of this suggestion – confidently aimed by Sir Richard at the WI – than Cicely McCall (who had mentioned it to him in the first place) and her colleagues Betty Christmas and Lady Elizabeth Brunner. None of these three women was a university graduate (although Cicely had come close) nor an academic, yet each was wholeheartedly passionate about the cause of adult education. They were striking women, all three, and lively, charismatic characters: just the right evangelists for Denman College.

Betty had joined the WI in 1925 at the age of fifteen, when her mother, who was already a member, had mentioned a play the Institute was putting on. Betty fancied a part. She was immediately and happily gathered to the generous bosom of the WI. Her first job was at a Post Office counter; then she joined the staff at the Buckinghamshire Federation before moving to a clerical post at NFWI headquarters. By dint of sheer enthusiasm and a particularly engaging personality, she soon rose to become General Organiser. Everyone liked her – even Cicely, who was naturally suspicious of rivals – and admired her lack of 'side'. Betty treated all she met with the same easy familiarity and respect. She was a joyful person who recognised in Sir Richard's proposal a unique opportunity for 'ordinary girls', as she had been, to transform their lives.

Elizabeth Brunner was also much loved. A former actress, as mentioned earlier, she was witty, highly attractive, full of fun and utterly devoted to the idea of bringing culture to Institute members. She was easily convinced there should indeed be a People's College, and the first People's College of all must belong to the WI.

With the full support of Gertrude Denman, Cicely, Betty and Elizabeth put forward a resolution at the 1945 AGM to establish a Women's Institute college. Elizabeth proposed it, as a member of the Oxfordshire Federation, in a masterly eight-minute speech. It must have been the most significant stage performance of her life, given the influence Denman has had on so many thousands of people.

The omens were not good. The platform at the Albert Hall looked particularly drab that year: all the Executive Committee members were in austere black, grey or navy blue. There had just been a tedious discussion and a recount over a vote to raise the WI subscription fee, and the five thousand delegates – exhausted by five years' duty on the Home Front – were feeling somewhat deflated. Then Lady Brunner stepped to the microphone. She had daringly decided not to wear a hat, and looked radiant as she beamed at the crowd and asked in a deliciously clear voice whether everyone could hear her. She had already noticed that the delegate from Cambridgeshire who was due to second her resolution was unaccountably wearing her gardening boots. This would have to be good, or else no one would take the resolution seriously and the whole idea might evaporate.

First, she tried to scotch the concept – as Sir Richard had done – of a dry and academic place full of grim-looking blue-stockings and dominated by exams. Imagine instead a welcoming home from home, free of the responsibilities and distractions of usual life. You could choose what to learn – whether you'd prefer 'useful practical crafts' or a course about current affairs, history or politics – and at what pace. Our college, she promised, would be a real community, where students shared a common interest already and where everyone contributed to each other's comfort. No one would begrudge an hour's washing-up or bed-making in the mornings, and individual Federations could make the furnishings and pictures for different rooms, showing off their craftsmanship while celebrating the heritage of their own little corners of Britain. An enterprise like this would attract younger members to the Movement, drawing on the new spirit of adventure among women after the war. For older members it would be the best kind of holiday: the sort of change that's as good as a rest. A real tonic. Elizabeth summed up:

It must provide fun and relaxation as well as instruction. It must not be a place where only our most forceful intellectuals vie with each other in solving the world's problems. What we teach must be related to the everyday practical things that make up our members' lives. In addition, there must be inspiration and a vision of wider horizons, so that life and the living of it becomes more important and worthwhile.

I beg to move.[7]

Mrs Hopkinson from Cambridgeshire squelched onto the stage, mortified, in the boots she'd forgotten to change, and valiantly suggested that the college might be enhanced by a nursery in the grounds so that young mothers could bring their children along, and that the cost of travelling to the college from different parts of the UK might be averaged out (so that as few members as possible would be deterred from attending). But the audience was not convinced. The whole idea was rather overwhelming. Too few members would be able to take advantage of it, argued a lady from East Kent: there were three hundred thousand WI members, of whom only about three thousand, she estimated, would benefit from a residential college. A Warwickshire delegate was greeted with a storm of applause when she claimed that only a 'certain class' of WI member would be able to afford the time and childcare to attend courses, and someone from the Shropshire Federation was similarly cheered when she implied it was fundamentally unfair to expect every WI member to contribute money (as would surely be the case) to a hare-brained scheme from which the majority would get no benefit at all. The opposition centred on the incontrovertible facts that there wasn't enough money around at the moment to finance an inessential service like this, and that mothers should be concentrating on their children's education, not indulging in their own.

Lady Brunner's supporters were immediately carried away by the idea, however, undeterred by the inevitable financial implications of finding a suitable building, equipping it for use and maintaining it. The WI had always been good at raising money: this would be a challenge, and – when the target was met – the Movement's greatest achievement. A member from Surrey was excited at the thought that the college would belong to, and enhance, the whole rural community. 'We could all help to make it, even if it's a few stitches, or a pot of jam, and afterwards, we and our sons and daughters would have it, to share and enjoy.'[8] Another member declared her support because she believed quite simply that if housewives had been better informed, the two world wars would never have happened.

Esther Neville-Smith – like Betty Christmas – was also struck by the less tangible promise of a WI college. She was a friend of Benjamin Britten and Peter Pears, a public schoolmaster's wife who witnessed at first hand the heights to which education could raise the human spirit. A liberal place of learning like this, she said, could enrich beyond measure the lives of members who had been forced to leave school at twelve or thirteen, who would no sooner think of attending somewhere formal like Hillcroft, or a university summer school, than fly. But they might come here with a friend, explore familiar skills, learn to talk about what really matters to them, and perhaps gradually discover 'the confidence and knowledge to take a responsible position in the community'.[9]

The resolution was carried, with an amendment urging the NFWI to proceed with arrangements as quickly as possible. Betty Christmas and Elizabeth Brunner were jubilant, recognising this as one of the most important moments in the history of the Women's Institute. No doubt Cicely would have been gratified, too, had she not been sacked by Lady Denman the previous month. Her story continues later.

Another residential school was held soon after the AGM in the summer of 1945, this time at Grace Hadow's old Oxford college, Somerville. It ran for a full week, with twice as many students as Radbrook had been able to accommodate, on the theme 'The Future of the Village'. By then, however, the Institute's own college was already – and feverishly – being planned. A dedicated committee was set up with Lady Brunner at its head, Esther Neville-Smith as a member and Sir Richard Livingstone as a consultant. A suitable house was identified in Marcham Park, near Abingdon in Oxfordshire. It was a honey-stoned Georgian mansion, with a lake and several cottages, requisitioned by the RAF during the war and then put up for sale in the autumn of 1945 for £16,000. The committee reckoned it would take another £45,000 or thereabouts to adapt the building and set up an endowment fund to help keep the college going. That was a crippling amount of money – equivalent to £1.5 million today – and no one knew quite where to find it.

The government refused to help. This was a private enterprise, insisted the Minister for Education (ironically the post's first woman, Ellen Wilkinson, who came into Parliament from a working-class background via the University of Manchester). It would not attract a subsidy. I suppose this was fair enough: the NFWI had strenuously avoided being financially beholden to the government all its life. It couldn't have it both ways. The Carnegie UK Trust, yet again, rode to the rescue by offering the WI a grant of £20,000. In addition, each WI was asked to contribute £10 annually over several years (a different kind of Operation Produce), with the result that by 1953, when the college appeal closed, the total of funds raised stood at £66,000.

The committee's next task was to find a suitable name for the college. When Gertrude Denman announced her resignation as NFWI Chairman in 1946 after thirty years, the choice was obvious. 'Thank you,' she replied with uncharacteristic demureness when the suggestion was made by her successor. 'I think that is a lovely idea.'

Denman College – usually just called 'Denman' – opened the doors to its first students in September 1948. Chattering coach-loads of members had already been to look around, to whet their appetites, on summer outings from Institutes all over the country. Work parties had camped out there to prepare the bedrooms and reception rooms, and gifts poured in, of clocks, blankets, paintings, books and improbably large pieces of furniture, plus plants for the garden, to help get the place ready for action. The WI in Ontario thoughtfully sent sheets and pillow-cases as a gesture of support. Betty Christmas moved into a cottage in the grounds as Warden, with her beloved black Labrador Sam, a gift from Elizabeth Brunner. According to Cicely McCall, it was Sam who believed himself to be in charge, not Betty. 'He was there to welcome new arrivals, he had free range of the college and he slept on any upholstered chair and on any quilted bed if the bedroom door had been left open.'[10]

On 24 September Sir Richard Livingstone was invited formally to open Denman College for business. Guests of honour were Lady Denman, the current Chairman Countess Albemarle, Lady Brunner and of course Sam, who always looked utterly appealing but unfortunately stank to high heaven. Only Betty was immune to his fragrance, which for hundreds of early visitors became one of their most pungent memories of Denman.

Betty was as much a success at Denman as she had been throughout her career at the NFWI. She greeted every student, helped them settle in, and introduced them to the dog (who wore a label with 'Don't feed me' round his neck and an expression pleading the opposite). Students were – and still are – funded by bursaries, raised by their individual Institutes and drawn by lot, often at Christmas. Or they could pay the fees themselves. It cost £1 to attend a five-day course in 1958, and about £400 for four days today. Students shared rooms more than they do now, and though the experience of being away from home and friends was initially daunting, they gradually relaxed. Mealtimes were perhaps the greatest novelty: most conscientious housewives endured a period of discomfiture at being waited on by other women – but it didn't last long.

The courses offered during the first few years were usually lively and, in some cases, surprisingly weighty. A 'Country Housewives' course ran from the very first season, with sessions on cookery, housekeeping, domestic design and laundry. This was a safe choice for timid students, but hardly very inspiring. Braver souls chose to learn about social or industrial history, 'Feeding a Hungry World', 'TV for the Family', 'The Problems of Race' or 'Science and Ordinary People'. Lord Beveridge, whose wife Jessy was a WI member, chaired a discussion on social legislation; Patrick Moore spoke about astronomy; David Gentleman taught art; and Dame Kathleen Lonsdale shared her passion for crystallography. Here at last was a worthwhile foil to what some may have considered the useless crafts, asinine games and dismal competitions with which WIs had been grappling for years. 'Better a dusty house than a dusty mind,' wrote a *Home and Country* correspondent in 1954; at Denman, you could burnish them both till they shone.

All appeared to be well. But there was a constant undercurrent, which still moves subtly beneath the surface of the place. In many unreconstructed British families, WI meetings were known more or less affectionately as 'Mother's afternoon out'.

Courses at Denman weren't always so charitably described: they became a selfish 'Mother's fling'. Getting away from home for a while was all very well – but, deep down, was this really what a good wife and mother should be doing with her time? Even now, there can be a frisson of guilt at booking a four-day session on chocolate, self-discovery, or something else equally solipsistic. It feels faintly wicked, abandoning home commitments to stay in a beautiful house in sumptuous grounds, being fed three or four times a day, going to the bar and buying your own drinks before dinner, laughing with strangers till the tears flow.

The founders tried to sell the idea of adult education as our right as working women, and even our duty. A favourite Denman embroidery tutor used to nag her students to 'get the kids off to school, leave the dishes in the sink, and stitch your way to heaven'.[11] In reality, for those of a certain age, 'me time' still smacks of self-indulgence. But that's our problem, not Denman's.

Betty Christmas was diagnosed with cancer in 1951, and spent the next few years in and out of hospital. She refused to leave her post at Denman. When she died at the age of forty-four in 1956, there was a short period of interregnum during which the NFWI racked its brains to find a successor, until the Chairman Lady Dyer briskly wrote to invite Cicely McCall back into the fold. Cicely had summarily been given her notice in 1945 following her decision to stand as a Labour candidate in that summer's general election. Presumably this was a pragmatic rather than a party-political act on the part of the NFWI, given the precedent set by Liberal MP Margaret Wintringham. It was considered Cicely would not have the time both to campaign and to run Denman efficiently. When she failed to win a seat, she retired from politics to Norfolk. She had a responsible post in a hospital, with a house, two poodles, three geese and a vigorous garden, and belonged to her local WI: she was well content. On the other hand she was one of Denman's pioneers: it all began with her. She assumed a move to the college now would mean a job and a home for life (she was in her mid-fifties) so she accepted, and moved in. She wasn't given Betty's old cottage, but a darker, damper one in a corner of the grounds where mildew crept into her books and under picture frames, and she could never get warm. No matter: that could be sorted out later. Now, she was too busy.

The moment she arrived, Cicely got to work with a clinical series of 'reforms'. She changed the booking system, which before had relied on 'the Bursar's secret list of elderly WI members who were lonely or lived by themselves ... regardless of their suitability for the course, or indeed for residential accommodation. One, I found out, lovable and slightly confused, was incontinent, for example, though I was assured she was such a dear old thing that she couldn't be refused. The staff were deeply shocked when I suggested a waterproof sheet.'[12] Cicely was the first Warden to open the college at weekends and holiday periods, and she welcomed WI members who wished to look around at any time, as long as they gave a little notice. She made the college more accessible, expanding Betty's idea of allowing husbands to accompany their wives on certain courses (which incensed some students), and running sessions for mothers with young children. She increased the profile of Mrs Flanders, an alarmingly efficient German woman married to an Oxford don, to whom some students with sour wartime memories had taken exception, and – worst of all – she got rid of Sam. First he was taken to the vet for some obscure procedure to rid him of his stench, and then she persuaded the Bursar (with whom she was not on good terms) to take the dog home and keep him there.

Denman missed 'dear Betty' under Cicely's bracing regime, and this was not one of the college's happiest periods. The relationship between Cicely and the NFWI had suffered in 1945 – just as Denman was getting off the ground – when Cicely was dismissed. Tempting her back as Warden twelve years later might not have been the NFWI's wisest decision: Cicely appears to have been rather good at grudges, and her autobiography reveals that she felt resentful towards the Executive Committee. She only stayed in post for a year: in 1958 she was sacked again – ostensibly for being 'a square peg in a round hole', for 'hopeless administration' and for causing a 'staff crisis'. In fact the sudden termination of her contract seems to have been based on allegations by Sam's new mother, the Bursar, and on a lack of confidence in the improvements she had tried to make at Denman.

Reeling from her dismissal, Cicely admitted that perhaps she had tried to change too much too quickly, but she had halved the college deficit and doubled its student intake during her short tenure as Warden. She never forgave the NFWI for treating her (in her opinion) so shabbily. She received twelve days' notice to leave and instructions not to set foot inside the grounds again; she had no home, no job, and precious little pension. 'If I had defrauded the college,' she wrote bitterly, 'or been found in bed with the gardener, the terms of the dismissal could hardly have been more insulting.'[13] She fled to Norfolk, where the Federation had always been supportive of her, and carried on with psychiatric social work. She was awarded an MBE and died at a great age, locally much admired.

Denman College has never been an easy place to run, and crises of finance and personnel have recurred throughout its life. Things looked particularly bleak during the mid-1980s, when high inflation conspired with the need for urgent repairs to threaten the college's future. The Open University had opened in 1969 and evening classes were growing in popularity throughout the country, so Denman had stiffer competition now than ever before. A survey revealed that only 2 per cent of the WI's membership (which totalled about 350,000 by then) attended courses each year, and their fees were not bringing in enough money to keep the college open – or keep it upright, even. An appeal for £1 million was launched, and despite much chuntering from those WI members who didn't plan ever to go there, the target was reached and Denman survived.

A glance at the programme for 2011–12 is reassuring: Denman expects about ten thousand students – members of the public as well as the WI – to attend either residential courses or day schools throughout the year (the accommodation and facilities having expanded hugely since the old days). It will offer them some five hundred subjects to choose from, from sessions practising crafts that were traditional when the WI began in 1915 – smocking, willow-weaving, poultry-keeping and wood-carving – to seminars on Shakespeare's women, eBay expertise and ancient Iraq. My friend from Leicestershire, Rachel Root, will be there.

Rachel is surely the ideal Denman student; just the sort of woman Sir Richard Livingstone had in mind when he suggested the idea of a 'People's College' back in 1943. She left school with no qualifications, and married a railwayman. They thought it right and proper that Rachel should stay at home to bring up their two daughters – which meant they must live, financially, from week to week. She is highly intelligent and must always have been instinctively proactive, but until discovering Denman she had neither the confidence nor the education to direct her formidable energy.

She had already been a member of the WI for twenty-five years when she first went to Denman, but would never have thought of signing up had it not been for an episode over the pick-and-mix counter at Woolworths one day in 1983. She was with her daughters, choosing sweets for a friend, and got chatting with the lady at the till, explaining who the sweets were for. Her girls, full of teenage hauteur and embarrassment, were mortified that their mother should choose to have a personal conversation with an unknown Woolworths lady. Their attitude shocked Rachel into making a vow: from now on she would damn well speak to anyone she liked, and show her family that in future she intended to live life on her own terms, not theirs.[14]

Visiting Denman was a statement. The fact that she enjoyed the course (on 'Discovering your Neighbourhood') was a bonus. She stayed in a bedroom sponsored by the Nottinghamshire Federation, and the exquisite workmanship of the lace bedspread and cushions – 'all the co-ordination' – stunned her. She sensed pride in everything she saw. The students were obviously proud of where they came from and of the work they did, be it ever so humble: even housework was an art here. They were supportive, understood each other, got to know each other without distractions, and learned just what Rachel had wished to learn: to trust their own judgement. 'I realise it was the first time I had ever in my whole 40-odd years been allowed to be myself – in fact I didn't realise there was a "me" inside'.

That first visit was nearly thirty years ago. Since then, Rachel has been back to Denman *seventy* times. She worries about its future: they're thinking of stopping people paying with cheques. What will that mean to elderly students who can't manage the faff of pin-numbers and electronic transfers? They might be phasing out the traditional 'College Chairmen', a pair of WI members, different ones for each course, who attend as Betty Christmas substitutes to welcome students, make them feel comfortable and deal with any problems. They want to install night porters instead. And they've changed the entrance hall so it looks less like some impressive but friendly family home and more like a hotel foyer. But the spirit of Denman, which is the spirit of people like Grace Hadow, Cicely McCall, Betty Christmas and Elizabeth Brunner, will live on lustily, as long as people like Rachel can keep going there.

10

Not According to Schedule:
1960–1999

*I do beg of you to live more dangerously, not recklessly,
but to accept the challenge and tackle it.*[1]

I grew up during the so-called permissive age, in a rural community dominated by the WI. I was reasonably politically aware as a teenager, but I have no memory at all of anything remotely progressive going on in our particular Institute. The single most important event of the year in our neighbourhood, as far as I can recall, was the Village Show. You could hardly get more traditional than the Show. It was a competitive horticultural and agricultural exhibition, for which the WI was partly responsible and which included an Institute tent – shimmering on Show day with pride, rivalry and fierce indignation in equal measure. My mother was the Show organiser. It was the most harrowing job she ever had. Something kept her at it for several years – a blind sense of duty, perhaps, to the WI – but the memory of the Show, even years later, made her shudder.

The first job of the year – running from just after the last Show (in mid-July) to just before the next – was compiling the Schedule. This was a complete list of classes, covering everything from gymkhana ponies to cattle to budgerigars to ginger loaf to dahlias to model animals made out of vegetables to matchstick models to patchwork quilts. And rabbits. The rules for each class were stated with the utmost explicitness, so that there was no room for misinterpretation or fudging. Prize money had to be arranged, with rosettes for the first three in each class and trophies wrested back from last year's winners, even though many of the victors would no doubt be taking them straight home again. For certain families produced dynasties of prize-winners, so that their victories became a matter of divine right. This produced much muttering among those who tried and lost, year after year. Innocent judges were terror-stricken at the thought of choosing someone new.

My mother had a stout sense of justice, but a thin skin. It was Deidre Thimble who finally did for her.[2] Mrs Thimble was an ancient and immovable part of the WI furniture. She made my mother's life a nightmare, come Show time. One could picture her in other members' gardens, angrily lifting carrots before their time or spreading rumours of cheating and conspiracy. If she ever won a cup, it was rarely returned. She scorned those classes she couldn't enter, and those competitors who beat her. Once she came storming to our door wielding a brolly like a broadsword, accusing my broken-spirited mother of corruption. That was the final straw: Mum left the WI soon afterwards.

Tricia Stewart, one of the original 'Calendar Girls', has similar memories of North Yorkshire Shows, especially concerning the mythic importance of the Schedule. Some people prepare their class entries for months; Tricia tended to leave everything until the evening before, doing an all-nighter to get them finished. It took her eight hours to make a gingerbread house one year – an exquisite gingerbread house it was, with unimaginable detail. Also, she fiddled for ages with tweezers, scissors and glue to construct 'my favourite room in a shoebox', and knitted her whole soul into a cardigan. On the morning of the Show every competitor made their way to the WI tent, with their class entries either borne aloft in front of them or swathed somewhat apologetically in tea-towels. Some WI members turned up hours early to bag prominent display positions at the front of the table (and so arrest the judges' attention straight away). Others – like our Mrs Thimble – would follow on a little later, then rearrange the exhibits so *theirs* were at the front. A third group, like Tricia, slipped in at the last minute, to hide their offerings behind other people's.

At about 11 a.m. the tent was officially declared out of bounds, so the judges, all behatted and bearing clipboards, could begin their esoteric business. The tent didn't open again until two, after a judges' lunch in a special little satellite tent decorated with fresh flower arrangements, with glasses set out for sherry in place of the beakers of saccharine lukewarm orange-and-pineapple squash enjoyed by organisers like my mother, and ham salad instead of cress-and-meat-paste rolls. By then there would be a queue of competitors at the main tent, waiting impatiently to rush – or stroll not quite nonchalantly – to see who had won what. Each cake had a neat little triangle nicked in its rim, scones were sliced and shortbread crumbled, and a teaspoonful of jam was deposited on a saucer next to its jar to see whether it stayed where it was in jellied splendour, or oozed embarrassingly.

Most of the entries were decorated with a written adjudication on a slip of paper. Often it was patently obvious who had won, and why. But sometimes, the results depended on an impossibly abstruse interpretation of the Schedule. When Tricia Stewart's cardigan was damned with the terse comment, 'Would have been better if the buttons had fit the buttonholes', it was disappointing, but fair enough. The 'favourite room in a shoebox' failed because the cushions on the floor of her yoga studio were stuck down – everyone knows that cushions should never be stuck down on a model of a yoga studio in a shoebox. But the disqualification of her beautiful gingerbread house was the hardest to take. The architecture was good, no doubt about it, and the décor very original, but what had Tricia been thinking of, siting a door in the gable end? *Nul points*.

Occasions like this didn't have much to do with the outside world, as far as the WI was concerned. They may have showcased traditional talents and encouraged members to take advantage of handicraft and cookery training during the year, but in reality they were all about competition: the thrill of success or, in Tricia's case, the wonderful barminess of failure. There was nothing missionary about taking part in a Show. They were – still are – celebrations of the WI itself.

Away from the oasis that was Denman College, and the ritualistic convention of occasions like Show Day, the political dynamism of the postwar period was changing the Women's Institute. It was no longer symbolised by the comfortable, homely face of the farmer's wife. It wasn't even an organisation exclusively for countrywomen any more. If the modern WI member hadn't quite burned her bra, she was definitely assertive, perhaps even a little abrasive. She was as fearless in her choice of AGM resolutions as her predecessors had been, tackling drug abuse, AIDS, conditions in psychiatric hospitals and the reform of the Divorce Bill. But now, that fearlessness was in danger of being identified by the public, and by more orthodox WI members, with the militant stridency of that unlovely creature, the 'women's libber'.

The public recognised an almost comic mismatch within the WI, between the radicals and the traditionalists. At the time of the Greenham Common peace camp and Erin Pizzey's crusade for battered wives – both of which were heartily supported by Institute members – a smug cartoon appeared in a national newspaper featuring two middle-aged WI ladies. One looks haughty, well upholstered in twinset and tweeds; the other, called Marjorie, is decidedly grubby, with sagging breasts and trousers. 'Move with modern society if you wish, Marjorie,' runs the caption, 'but that's no reason not to behave like a lady.'[3]

There was a disconnection between the Movement's visionaries and those ordinary members whose intentions were good but whose scope was traditionally small. It would be easy to think of this in generational terms, but it's more complicated than that. Grannies can be far more radical than young mothers. What lay at the root of the Movement's difficulties during the last three or four decades of the twentieth century was its image. Every massed-membership organisation suffers from stereotyping; when it's an organisation of massed women, as we have seen, stereotype tends towards caricature. This encourages solidarity when outsiders are the culprits, but the trouble with the WI was that its own members caricatured each other. To many of them the National Executive appeared petty bureaucrats, obsessed with procedural administration. All activists were shrieking feminists. Committee members were busybodies, and those who enjoyed tootling along to meetings month after month, just for the company, were hopelessly old-fashioned and sad.

There was a further problem. When the Movement was first established it aimed explicitly to make confident citizens of isolated provincial women, by encouraging constructive political awareness and a sense of responsibility. Now, to Marjorie and her progressive sisters – including the new generation at 39 Eccleston Street, where the NFWI HQ moved in 1926 – awareness was not enough. Nor were 'fun and friendship'. They saw themselves principally as a protest group, rather than a social network with practical ideals. They forgot the original reason for the WI.

These were exciting but risky times. In the early days, with a strong and controlling leadership, members were biddable enough to remain cohesive. Cohesion was inevitable during the two world wars, given the nature of the WI's work. But in the permissive postwar era the Movement threatened to split laterally, with a dazzling caucus of action-women on top, the tip of an iceberg, and the bulk of the membership, feeling leaden and unremarked, lumbering along below. At the same time, numbers were falling (467,000 in 1954 to 272,503 in 1995). Complaints streamed into Head Office about recalcitrant committee members and wrong-headed policies. Many of those who had lived through the war and kept their communities going by making do and mending, keeping calm and carrying on, felt affronted and ignored. The shared sense of purpose that had given the Movement direction since 1915 began to falter. The novelty of the WI was wearing off.

As ever, artless *Home and Country* gave the game away. The magazine's mission was to be all things to all people, and strenuously fair-minded. The danger of that approach is obvious. From the late 1950s onwards it presented to its dwindling readership a confusing mélange, strangely detached from real life and surreal in its scope. The Suez crisis came and went almost without comment; so did the axing of over two thousand of Britain's railway stations by Dr Beeching after 1963, profoundly affecting the quality of rural life at a stroke; the Pill; the election of Margaret Thatcher as Britain's first female Prime Minister; the Falklands War; the miners' strike of 1984; and the poll-tax riots of 1990. Instead, *Home and Country* published news about a WI in Hampshire regularly gate-crashed by a dear little white cat and a New Forest pony. It continued to suggest tips on wart-charming and 'adventurous jams' (including banana or tomato flavours). Whenever it mentioned individual WI members it began by describing them physically – 'fair and forty', 'slim and pretty', or 'with a cloud of dark hair'. And the covers plumbed new depths of frumpiness.

All this would be easy to rationalise, were the magazine aiming itself at the older cohort of WI members. But tucked among the crochet and knitting patterns is a young black woman, in 1982, modelling a natty shirt-waister. Next to a feature on how to enjoy retirement there's a stark examination of 'artificial insemination for women'. Dreary recipes involving kippers or rabbits (both stalwarts of WI cookery columns) sit alongside the clearest article on teenagers and drug abuse that I have ever read.

This confusion was mirrored at Institutes all over England and Wales. Some continued in the traditional spirit of Lady

Denman, Grace Hadow and even Madge Watt, with varied programmes to suit rural housewives, encouraging engagement with local communities and self-education – at Denman College if they could get there; otherwise, by listening to speakers at monthly meetings. Wraysbury in Berkshire was a splendid example of this traditional ethic. Its President, Peggy Willatts, compiled a record of all the meetings from 1942 to 1979: nothing much changes throughout those thirty-seven years. This is Peggy's summary of 1963, the year of President Kennedy's assassination and the Cuban missile crisis which brought the superpowers to the brink of nuclear war.

Jan.   The January meeting had to be cancelled owing to the severe weather.

Feb.   The social half-hour has been re-introduced and two members read a short extract from books of their choice.

Mar.   The talk was given this month by a gentleman from the Milk Marketing Board and his name was Mr Bull!

Apr.   A decision has been made this month to re-start the Produce Stall.

May   Outings to Ascott House Musical Party and to Waddesdon Manor have been arranged. Mrs Satterthwaite gave an interesting report on the resolutions passed at the Council meeting.

June   A letter had been sent to the Parish Council complaining about the bad state of the chairs in the Village Hall. Two members had had accidents. It was stated that £9 had been made on the Stall at the Village Fair.

July   A Whist Drive will be held in July and it was

suggested that we should vote on increasing the cost
of tea from 4d to 6d in September.

[No meeting in August.]

Sep.   The Whist Drive made a profit of £4. 6s. 1d. And it
was suggested that members might like an outing to
Windsor Theatre, also to the Tommy Steel show.

Oct.   Members were invited to attend a WVS
demonstration on the protection of the home in a
nuclear explosion.

Nov.   It was explained to members that by an oversight
invitations had not been sent to other Institutes for
our party.

Dec.   The speaker gave a very interesting talk on the work
of the Associated Countrywomen of the World and
the social half hour consisted of the singing of carols
by Mrs Goodfellow, Mrs Satterthwaite and Mrs
Wyld.[4]

(Incidentally, it appears to have taken a decade – and how
many terrible seating accidents? – to get those chairs fixed.) Ten
years later, the routine is much the same:

Mar. [1973]   Mrs Hope, who is our representative on the
Village Hall Committee, and who had attended a
meeting as our delegate, gave a glowing report of the
new hall and one of the new chairs was on view.[5]

. . . . .

Apr. [1974]   It was announced, with regret, that Miss
Hannah Whitelaw, a founder member, had died at
the age of 98. A few moments' silence was observed.
Mrs Willatts offered to dispose of waste paper. If

       members would bring it to her house she would sell
       it in aid of the Windsor and District Dog Rescue
       Society.

May Our charity this year was for the Wraysbury ward at
       Wexham Hospital. Some members attended the
       presentation to the ward of a model of the ear, nose
       and throat for demonstration purposes.

July Another mystery outing. Miss Brookes guessed the
       destination . . .[6]

One thing everybody in the WI has always enjoyed, and which has bound the Movement together since the earliest days, is its love of celebrations. Not necessarily national celebrations like the coming of peace after war, but certainly internal ones. Anniversaries are marked meticulously, often commemorated with a special publication of some kind, and each Institute is urged to celebrate its own 'formation' birthday. When the Movement reached its Golden Jubilee in 1965, Chairman Gabrielle Pike picked up the phone to ask a fellow WI member if they could hold a party in her garden. She happily agreed, and on 31 May that year nine thousand women representing every WI in England and Wales duly arrived at Buckingham Palace for the 'do'. They had been selected by ballot, and were asked to remember as much of the occasion as they could, to share with all the others at their June meetings. There were allegedly only two men present: the Duke of Edinburgh and a newspaper reporter. What the Duke felt about this invasion of rural ladies is unrecorded. Their massed hats threw the entire garden into shade, apparently, and – because of the crowds – made movement among the guests almost impossible. Like Tony Blair thirty-five years later, the journalist declared himself quite terrified. 'They'll make jam of me,' he whimpered, with a wink.[7]

The Poet Laureate, Cecil Day Lewis, was commissioned to produce a piece about the Jubilee which, though read at the 1965 AGM, was not published in *Home and Country* until 1981. I imagine it must have left its audience slightly nonplussed, with its evocation of WI members 'scolding the children, scalding the cream' and generally doing 'what is needfullest to womankind'.[8]

Village scrapbooks compiled by WI members commemorated the Jubilee in a more meaningful way. Thousands of them still survive in County Record Offices or private hands, and the best are very moving. Members who excelled at needlework stitched and embroidered the scrapbooks' covers (Waddesdon's, in Buckinghamshire, looks as though it's wearing its own little quilted smoking-jacket). Calligraphers drew maps and captions with grace and skill; artists did sketches of local landscapes and characters, and writers described the history and significance of their homes with great sensitivity.

North Kilworth's scrapbook goes beyond merely recording information: its editor takes this high-profile opportunity to discuss the nature and future of the WI itself, both at home in Leicestershire and nationally. Her main preoccupation is a lack of new members. 'Why can't we attract young people?' she wonders. 'Where have we gone wrong?' She thinks older members find it hard to change their attitudes and dislike sharing with younger, more progressive women (like her). Programmes are dull – too many talks on 'ghosts, horse-brasses and gardening'.[9] Perhaps there should be a bit more on babies and children, fashion and make-up. Committee business should not be as ponderous as it is, and meetings should be more light-hearted. Not frivolous, but tempered by a little joie de vivre.

Here is another mismatch within the WI. The whole Movement was becoming a little like *Home and Country*: a slightly baffling mixture of banality and ground-breaking ambition. On the one hand you had your petty Schedules and silly competitions and stultifying talks on cycling holidays and spring bulbs, your older members complaining about the disrespectful young, and 'incomers' losing patience with stick-in-the-mud recalcitrance. But you also had Denman College and moments of sheer inspiration, when lives were changed not only here at home but right across the world. Several of those moments happened on Gabrielle Pike's watch.

Mrs Pike ('tall and elegant'), the woman at the helm of the WI during the Jubilee celebrations, was remarkable on several counts. She was the Movement's fifth Chairman, elected in 1961 in her mid-forties, and the first 'commoner' to hold the post. After a mildly rebellious childhood as a daughter of the Bishop of Lichfield, she worked for the War Office (one source has her at MI5),[10] and then ran Cothill House School with her husband, near Denman College. Her involvement with the WI developed through public speaking, at which she excelled, and her commitment to it grew with the realisation that despite its party neutrality this was a deeply political movement. 'The thing about the WI,' she pointed out, 'is that it has always been one step ahead ... [We were] the first people to bully the government about getting women policemen, the first ... to say that we must have telephone kiosks in villages. And gradually these things collected and we began to get a reputation for being the sound-box of what women wanted.'[11]

During her five-year tenure at 39 Eccleston Street Mrs Pike

supervised not only the Golden Jubilee, but several high-profile campaigns as well. The most successful of these was the national Freedom from Hunger crusade, which ran from 1962 to 1967. Back in 1933 Madge Watt had founded the Associated Country Women of the World, to raise funds from every WI in England and Wales for rural women all over the globe. This was all very well, but to most WI members the Country Women of the World were distant figures who existed only in the pages of *Home and Country*. One gave them charity, or 'pennies for friendship', but they weren't really friends. The Freedom from Hunger campaign brought the international reach of the WI home to almost every member in England and Wales; whether she raised money through knitting blankets, singing in a village concert or baking a cake for a fête, her contribution was desperately needed, and made a fundamental difference to others' lives. Members raised an immense total of £185,000 (about £2 million today) to fund – among other things – a farm institute in Uganda, a cooperative trading store in Botswana, equipment for a university farm in Trinidad, buffalo for some farmers in Sarawak, and two bulls and a rotavator for Tristan da Cunha. This link between the women of rural England and their less privileged sisters overseas was direct. The campaign marked the beginning of the WI's conception of the global village, which came into its own when, between 1972 and 1974, members welcomed over twenty thousand Asian refugees from Idi Amin's Uganda, with practical help, unquestioning generosity and love. Some of these refugees became WI, members themselves.

At the same time as the Freedom from Hunger campaign was getting under way, Mrs Pike accepted a supposedly unsolicited and unexpected invitation from the Kremlin, in the midst of the

Cold War, to visit Moscow and talk with ordinary Russian women there about their lives and ambitions. This was a different sort of outreach, but no less interesting to her. Closer to home, the NFWI's first national art competition was opened by John Betjeman in 1963, and various festivals of drama, food and country life were celebrated with vigour and imagination. Perhaps the most elaborate of them all was a staging of Malcolm Williamson's *The Brilliant and the Dark*, with a libretto by Ursula Vaughan Williams (Ralph's widow). The piece was a musical treatment of 'the woman's view of our history'; specially commissioned by the NFWI, it involved three years' preparation, and soloists, choirs, orchestras, actors, dancers and designers from all over the country. Its world première was held at the Albert Hall in 1969, to much acclaim.

Another significant development during the 1960s and 1970s was the establishment of 'Special' WIs across England and Wales. In 1957, following a resolution from Devon that Institutes should make more effort to support the mentally ill, a local WI was set up within Fulbourn Psychiatric Hospital in Cambridgeshire. It was the first of many, engaging long- and short-term psychiatric patients and those with learning difficulties. Visiting WI members helped with organisation, and although this mission may have originated in a blithe lady-bountiful sort of way – 'they love it when the ladies come!' – it developed into a mutually enriching exercise. Patients at Royal Earlswood Hospital in Surrey – originally 'the Royal Earlswood Asylum for Idiots' – even proposed a resolution, which was passed, that all scrapped refrigerators should have their doors removed. A child had been found dead, trapped inside a dumped fridge, and the news had broken a patient's heart. At last, the Movement had a chance to rid itself of its hackneyed attitude to the 'mentally defective', as well as its (largely naive) preoccupation with eugenics.

More unconventional WIs began to spring up, in Cheshire Homes for the physically disabled, RAF and United States Air Force bases, army camps and Royal Naval establishments, with the result that although the roll of WI members declined steadily from the mid-1950s, the number of Institutes did not reach a peak – at 9333 – until 1974. In 1965 the '4000 rule', limiting the formation of new Institutes to villages of four thousand inhabitants or fewer, was abandoned. This meant the WI could compete for new members on the same turf as Townswomen's Guilds, though sometimes with unhappy results, as in Harrow, when the Institute was accused by the Guild of poaching: 'The WI is trespassing and ought to go back to the woods.'[12] One WI had rather different concerns: its maverick committee turned down a potential member from a council estate for being an unsuitable sort of person. Readers of *Home and Country*, when this was publicised, were appalled. Surely the Movement should be nothing if not welcoming.

Competition worked the other way, too. Women's Institute members could choose to become Townswomen's Guild members instead, as long as they lived close enough to the town in question. The National Housewives' Register was set up in 1960 after a letter from a Mrs Maureen Nicol in the *Guardian* proposed the idea of building a contact list of 'housebound housewives with liberal interests and a desire to remain individuals'. The University of the Third Age got going in the early 1980s, and while none of these outfits threatened to replace the WI they did erode its membership.

In Wales a home-grown alternative to the Movement evolved. The NFWI has always been well aware of its Welsh heritage; *Home and Country* often included (and still includes) articles in Welsh – much to the annoyance of Anglocentric readers. But after 1967 it refused to allow the minutes and other official business of its Welsh-speaking Institutes to be recorded in their native language, which led to disaffection and accusations of discrimination. Merched y Wawr, or 'Daughters of the Dawn', was founded the same year, in direct competition to the Women's Institute. It conducted its business entirely in Welsh, and within a couple of decades had some ten thousand members: not all of them ex-WI, but surely a good proportion. It's still going strong.

After the triumph of the Freedom from Hunger campaign, the modern WI got a taste for jumping onto national bandwagons. It helped that the constitution was altered in 1971 to reinterpret the sacred non-party-political and non-sectarian rules. The requirement to avoid discussing potentially controversial subjects at meetings and at county and national level was rescinded, 'provided the Movement is never used for party-political or sectarian propaganda'.[13] In 1972, a resolution was passed at the AGM urging the government to provide a full and free family-planning service now that the Pill was a fact of life. Lady Denman, who had been chair of the Family Planning Association – but strenuously kept that interest separate from her role in the NFWI – must have danced in her grave. The WI merrily joined in the 'I'm Backing Britain' campaign in 1968, to boost home trade, and banged the drum during 'Women's Year' in 1975 (the year of the Sex Discrimination Act) by organising a high-profile conference on equality, with guest speakers including the writer and counsellor Claire Rayner, Baroness Seear (later leader of the Liberal Party), the Chairman of the TUC

Marie Patterson and Shirley Summerskill MP (a doctor and a Labour politician).

One wonders whether Margaret Thatcher was invited. She was Secretary of State for Education and Science at the time, but seems to have cultivated a distant relationship with the WI, regarding them – as Tony Blair still does – as good-enough matrons but not terribly important. Mrs Thatcher lost the sympathy of the WI, assuming she ever had it in the first place, when she abolished the free provision of school milk for primary school children in 1970. The WI had worked hard to win that provision; its significance harked back to the old Adelaide Hoodless days. It was a sad, sad day when it went.

Many of the resolutions brought to AGMs – and, after the NFWI became incorporated as a charitable company in 1990, to intermediate and triennial general meetings – reflect the preoccupations of a liberal age with which some members were finding it hard to grapple. Institutes worried about nuclear testing (1962), difficulties faced by single mothers (1966), about the closure of sub-Post Offices (1971), the coordinated recycling of rubbish (1974), alternative energy sources (1977), the provision of hospice care (1983) and the spread of AIDS (1986). With the Movement's customary prescience, these were all matters that would go on to absorb the attention of the general public – but not until several years after each resolution was passed. Mrs Pike was right: this was an organisation astonishingly ahead of its time. In 1987 the WI's main concern was a matter that is still consuming us today: 'to bring under control the aggressive and indiscriminate sale of credit, and to give more publicity to the hazards of borrowing money'. In 1995 it called for detailed food-labelling, and four years later for a proper examination of genetically modified foods.

Until 1990, the NFWI's Public Affairs Committee must have been one of the best-informed pressure groups in the country. It comprised eleven WI members, representatives from the Departments of the Environment, Transport, Health and Social Security, Agriculture, and the Home Office; also, advisers from the National Council for Voluntary Organisations, the BBC, the Independent Broadcasting Authority and the Inland Revenue. Organisations with guest WI representation on their own committees were many and diverse; they included the Towns-women's Guild (warily), the Girl Guides, the National Trust, the Red Cross, the Dairy Trade Federation, the Campaign for Freedom of Information, the National Association for Mental Health, the British Federation of University Women and – bizarrely – the Royal Artillery Association.

There was a huge amount of positive work being done by the WI throughout the forty-year period I'm talking about in this chapter. Most of it was the consequence of members looking out at a world they wished to influence or change. Perhaps that's the very reason for the constant discontent rumbling away in the background. Ordinary, conventional members felt neglected and redundant. And none of the high-powered activity at national level seems to have affected places like Wraysbury or my mother's Institute in Yorkshire. If members were aware of it, they don't appear to have realised its relevance. The WI has always inspired loyalty. Its members feel proprietorial about the organisation. In the early decades this feeling was essential to its survival. Now, it was becoming increasingly obvious to many members that 'my' WI was not necessarily the same as 'hers'.

People were pulling in different directions, and it mattered. Traditionalists were perceived to be compromising the activists, and the activists betraying the traditionalists. Incomers, whether from council estates down the road (if they could get in) or relocating from towns for a taste of the rural idyll and a part in a real-life Aga saga, were more likely to turn long-serving members into reactionaries than to invigorate the local Institute. National Executive bigwigs were resented by the ordinary membership for travelling too much, spending an extravagant amount of money on administration, being out of touch, over-dogmatic and addicted to red tape.[14] Conversely, the grass-roots membership, at times, drove the National Executive to despair.

There's a file of correspondence in the NFWI Archive stuffed – groaning – with grievances. Behind each page is a barely hidden agenda of jealousy and resentment. A member from Newport on the Isle of Wight sends a letter in 1971 which must have taken courage to write. I reproduce it unedited:

> I wonder if you would be so kind as to settle an argument that have arisen in our Institute in which I have been a member for 33 years, is there a rule where by a new member can be appointed or Elected on the committee I have my own views but would like to hear it from Head quarters. Maybe rules have changed since I first joined and I am wrong, but I say a new Member cannot know suficiant about an Institute in two or three meeting. I would like you to treat this letter confidently but it would Put my Mind easy to get your Reply. I have been extremely Happy in Past but I'm afraid at Moment things are not quite the same.[15]

The answer from 39 Eccleston Street is that she's wrong: the new member is indeed eligible for election. The rules, freely available, are unequivocal.

A lady from Caernarvonshire asks what sort of offence is enough to terminate someone's membership of the WI. 'I assume conviction of any misdemeanour or crime would be sufficient grounds, but what else? It is a delicate matter, fraught with difficulties.' Breaking the Institute rules, bringing it into disrepute or causing dissension are all reasonable grounds, comes the reply, but 'it is better to try and keep within the Institute a defaulter than to cast her out'.

A Buckinghamshire WI finds itself in dangerously murky waters when it expels its President for speaking at a monthly meeting about the divorce of another member. The President then brings an action against the WI for defamation of character.

The heftiest wad of correspondence concerns a woman from a village in Huntingdonshire who claims she was told, when applying to join the local WI, that it was full: there was no room for her. Subsequently, the woman has discovered this is untrue. In fact they are actively recruiting new members. They just don't want *her*, and she demands to know why. She sends Alison King, the then General Secretary, a sort of curriculum vitae to prove her suitability. She considers her highest recommendation to be the fact that she's married to a lieutenant commander in the Royal Navy, and has six children. Her eldest sons are away at prep school, so she has some time on her hands. She takes an active part in community life; at present she's busy trying to organise a better refuse-collection service, 'because we have lots of rats'. She presents the prizes every year at the village cricket club, and is involved with the Darby and Joan Club and the Church. A little pathetically, she assures NFWI HQ that she is 'clean in habits, reasonably well groomed and [I] have no political preferences ... I do my own cooking, make my own jams and chutneys, knit, sew and garden, and paint a bit . . . If you can tell me the reason why I have been black-balled I really would be grateful, it's a hurtful thing to have happen.'[16]

Her final paragraph is ominous. The WI President's husband is apparently the Chair of the local Parish Council, and the writer has had 'a few battles with him concerning local affairs' in the past. No doubt heaving an exasperated sigh, Miss King conscientiously picks up the phone and speaks to a committee member at the village concerned. She is immediately subjected to a torrent of detailed information about how many people this woman has irritated or alienated during her five years in the village. So she writes a tactful reply (after many draft attempts) explaining that, unfortunately, no stated reason is required for refusal of membership. Privately, she notes: 'If her friends want her to join they will put her up for nomination, if they don't want her they won't and there's nothing she can do. I'm not surprised they are not keen . . . '[17]

In an attempt to avoid the tedious aftermath of situations like this and defuse some of the anxiety they caused, *Home and Country* published a piece by a WI member in Ulster entitled 'A Dozen Ways to Kill an Institute'. These included 'Never accept office, as it is easier to grouse than to do things. Nevertheless, get cross if you are not elected to the Committee: but if you are, do not attend Committee meetings. If asked by the President to give your opinion on some important matter, tell her you have nothing to say. After the meeting tell everyone how things ought to be done.'[18] There isn't much evidence that anyone took any notice. The magazine also published statistics on how many new Institutes were formed each month, and how many closed. Between 1974 and 2000 the total number of WIs in England and Wales dropped by nearly a third.

It is not surprising, therefore, that most of the NFWI's in-house campaigns during the decades leading up to the millennium (as opposed to national efforts like Freedom from Hunger) were to do with improving the Movement's image, making it more relevant to modern women – while keeping the traditionalists on board, of course – and pushing up the membership rolls. The subscription was doubled in 1976 from 50p to £1; it's a measure of the hyperinflationary age that within ten years it went up to £3.75, and by 1994 to £11.60. Everyone was suffering from the devaluation of the pound; the National Executive could hardly expect to extort money from its members, however politely, to keep it going. It was the same problem that Treasurer Helena Auerbach had faced in the 1920s: if we can't have higher subscriptions, we'll need more of them instead. Somehow the NFWI kept financially afloat, mostly by asking outright for extra donations from loyal Institutes, and managed to limp along from crisis to crisis.

Some of the WI's publicity campaigns were gratifyingly successful. A *Life and Leisure* exhibition at Olympia in 1984, which involved commercial sponsors and was opened by the Queen, harked back (but with a modern twist) to the old Caxton Hall and Westminster exhibitions of craftwork and community involvement so popular in the 1920s and 1930s. It inspired a 'Women in the Community' bus, painted with clouds, trees and a church steeple, which toured the country, luring in potential members by offering them a baking session in the tiny fitted kitchen inside, a crochet lesson, information about music and drama, and campaign literature.

The 'Year of Promotion' of 1984 followed a report commissioned from Strathclyde University on the profile and public perception of the WI. The 'Towards 2000' project, also initiated in the 1980s, involved thousands of questionnaires encouraging members to articulate what it was they needed from the Movement, and where they thought its future lay. Regional conferences were held on the same subject. The results were somewhat predictable, and impossible to analyse constructively. Some people wanted a more traditional image, others a more modern one; some were in favour of younger members, or a warmer welcome for the elderly; greater influence on national issues, or a focus on local affairs; less committee business or more committee involvement. Possibly the only thing to unite everyone was a shared hatred of questionnaires.

When a book about the WI was published in 1977, its title – *Jam and Jerusalem* – was understandably controversial. The idea was, of course, that Jam stood for creativity and Jerusalem for public service, but there was the obvious risk that the general public would take it as an endorsement of that most enduring of all caricatures, the mumsy, quavery-voiced, middle-aged gossip who doesn't have enough of a life *not* to be in the WI. To counter this perception, it was arranged that a panel of WI members should appear on what was arguably television's most popular news programme at the time, *Nationwide*, to show how lively and current the Movement was. A letter of complaint to NFWI HQ reveals what a disaster that dalliance with TV was: 'To show an elderly lady who did not appear to be quite aware of what was happening and a young president who wasted valuable media seconds by quibbling about her exact age ... was a waste of a great opportunity to present the WI as a forward-looking organisation ... I, for one, felt ashamed.'[19]

A few years later the NFWI commissioned a pop song and accompanying video celebrating the modern spirit of the organisation. In hindsight it strikes me as excruciating, and though a few staunch delegates were dancing in the aisles at the AGM when it was launched, most members just squirmed. 'Prospects are Sky High (at the WI),' goes the first line. And the chorus: 'At the WI there's a guaranteed greeting/ For different ideas at every meeting/ At work or leisure we've got it together/ Knowing we're growing for ever and ever.'[20]

Never mind 'for ever and ever': something drastic had to happen, and happen soon, if this organisation was going to grow at all 'towards 2000' and beyond.

Cue the Calendar Girls.

11

Bloody Marvellous:
1999 ONWARDS

*WI Ladies Tour the World in Search
of the Perfect Brothel.*[1]

It was a good old-fashioned sense of fun that saved the Women's Institute. That, and eleven women of a certain age from a remote WI in North Yorkshire not wearing anything. It's slightly ironic that the Calendar Girls actually operated outside the WI: as a charity, it can't raise money for another charity. That's why the original was an 'alternative' WI calendar: with special permission from the Board of Trustees the girls were allowed to publicise themselves as members, but not to market the calendar through the WI. Yet they have raised awareness of the Movement like nothing else – *almost* nothing else – thanks not just to the calendar itself (and its annual successors) but to the film that followed in 2003 and the stage play still going strong.

The story of how the Calendar Girls conquered the world is

well known. Briefly, it all began when Tricia Stewart, a member of Rylestone and District WI since 1978, tried to think of an imaginative way to raise funds for leukaemia research in honour of a sister WI member's husband, John Baker, recently diagnosed with non-Hodgkin's lymphoma. This was in 1998. Tricia and Angela, John's wife, had done the usual sponsored walk – for which John was no doubt grateful, but it didn't really turn him on. They needed to think of something to distract him from his illness and at the same time catch the public's attention: something different.

Some time earlier Tricia had mentioned to Lynda Logan, an artist friend of hers (also in the WI), a vague ambition to be painted in the nude. Tricia thought it would be fun if a group of friends got together as subjects for Lynda. It would be a new experience for them all. The idea was soon forgotten, but it resurfaced when, shortly after John's diagnosis, a request came through at a WI meeting for photographs to be sent in to the County Federation for possible inclusion in the 1999 calendar. They were after the usual things: a local snowscape for January, spring lambs for March, some pots of jam and sprays of elderflower on a gingham tablecloth for July, and so on.

Tricia suddenly remembered her nude painting idea, and more to amuse John than anything else she suggested to him that Rylestone and District WI should submit some Pirelli-like poses instead, with different members modelling for each month. John loved sunflowers: they could preserve their modesty with a well placed bloom or three and shake up everyone (certain WI members included) who thought the Women's Institute was nothing but a collection of old biddies who liked knitting and complaining.

John loved the idea. Everyone else thought it was just a joke. But when John died, only five months after his diagnosis, Tricia and Angela vowed to go ahead with it, if only in tribute to a gentle spirit and a wicked sense of humour. An alternative calendar, with naked WI members on every page, would be fun – like a sort of rural *Full Monty* – and it might even raise some money for medical research.

Lynda Logan's husband Terry, also an artist, was commissioned to take the photographs. Only ten members of Rylestone and District WI were brave enough to volunteer as models, so Tricia managed to persuade a friend who ran the local café, Ros Fawcett, to enlist as number 11 (that's one person per month, with a group photo for December). 'More scary for Ros than the thought of taking her clothes off was that she would now have to join the WI,' remembers Tricia. Ros was 'Miss November, 2000'; the others – aged from forty-four to sixty-five – were Beryl Bamforth (January), Angela Baker (February) and so on, in the shape of Lynne Knowles, Leni Pickles, Moyra Livesey, Sandra Sayers, Lynda, Rita Turner, Christine Clancy and Tricia herself.

Somewhat ambitiously, they decided to print three thousand of the calendars and hold an official launch at their local, the Devonshire Arms, in April 1999. The brewery who owned the pub offered to help with the party and, initially, with distributing the orders. The media reacted instantly, and by June twenty-three thousand copies had been sold. The girls were instant celebrities. This took its toll: Tricia's marriage barely survived the arrival of 'that fucking calendar', as her husband called it (although their subsequent separation was only temporary). Some people associated with the calendar resented the publicity inexorably flooding into their homes and community; even the girls themselves could not agree on how to handle it best, and now, even though the calendar is still issued each year, just six of the original models are involved. They call themselves 'Baker's Half-dozen', in memory of John.

The frenzy only increased when the film was released, starring Helen Mirren as the character based on Tricia and Julie Walters as Angela; and though there's no shock value to be had from it any more, the cheerful idea of naked WI members posing behind strategically placed cherry buns continues to raise money (some £3 million to date) for Leukaemia and Lymphoma Research, as well as awareness of the Women's Institute. Behind the entertainment value of the whole Calendar Girls phenomenon lie all those things a WI should stand for: mutual support, cooperation, practical idealism, courage, loyalty – and fun.

The reaction of the national press when the calendar was first launched was predictable in tone, if not in volume. The Calendar Girls themselves were relying on the clash between the hackneyed public image of the WI (irrelevant, old-fashioned, buttoned-up and tweedy) and a new reality – a powerful cocktail of feistiness, sexuality and humour – to sell their product. They knew better than anyone what a joke the whole thing was, but also how important was the message behind that joke. They look radiant, these middle-aged women with middle-aged spread or varicose veins or wrinkles: their confidence makes them so. They're obviously not aggressive, but they are certainly witty, brave and completely committed. The media and the public loved them.

Closer to home, in the correspondence columns of *Home and Country*, opinions were a little more mixed. Proud supporters wrote how grateful they were to Tricia and her friends for shattering the stuffy old stereotypes and revitalising the WI. Goodbye jam and Jerusalem, at last. The women of Rylestone and District were described as refreshingly broad-minded, innovative, full of fun, 'bloody marvellous'. Not everyone approved of their antics, however. Tricia was once told she was little better than a prostitute, who had sold her body for profit. A WI President from the Home Counties was appalled by the whole exercise:

The ladies who bared their bosoms in the name of leukaemia fundraising were using publicity in the worst possible taste. Their activities not only debase the many skills domestic, artistic and scientific that we possess, but one of the finest hymns we know, 'Jerusalem'. Presumably nobody concerned realised how offensive the many snide remarks would be that were made to members of every age suggesting that this type of calendar should be produced in their local area.[2]

Home and Country itself celebrated by publishing a photo of two young male employees at NFWI Head Office, stark naked, each clutching a sunflower and wearing an expression like a rabbit caught in the headlights.

The NFWI was never less than supportive of the Calendar Girls, and often much more than that. Helen Carey, elected Chairman in 1999, has always been their staunchest ally. She decided to invite them to the *Woman 2000* exhibition accompanying the AGM at Wembley Arena, to take part in a fashion show. That fashion show should have been a highlight; even the keynote speaker referred to it, by congratulating himself on being dressed at all.

*

Even now, no one seems to be absolutely certain how Tony Blair found himself on the platform at that same AGM. Whether he was asked to come, as Downing Street has always insisted, or whether he invited himself, the result was a public relations disaster. It is true that a few of the points he made in the course of his speech drew widespread applause. He spoke about fathers taking responsibility for their children's upbringing; about supporting stay-at-home mothers; and ensuring equal pay for men and women doing the same job. He embraced the old-fashioned values of his parents' generation in terms of respect, good manners and courtesy. Recalling that particular passage later, he professed complete bewilderment: how courteous was the WI, virtually to boo him off the stage?

It wasn't quite as bad as that. But this was patently the wrong audience for a rambling and partisan speech incorporating a list of government initiatives, plans for NHS reform and a discussion of interest rates. And he went on far too long. He made the dangerous assumption that these ten thousand women would support him simply because of who he was, and that they would allow him to use them as a political conduit because they were unsophisticated. That was his greatest mistake.

Media reaction to the speech was divided on party lines. The *Daily Mirror*, under the headline 'Handbagged!', declared the whole thing was a set-up by Blair's political opponents, implying the WI was an accessory in some dark Tory conspiracy. It labelled the AGM delegates an unsavoury mixture of 'expensive hair-do fusiliers' and – less imaginatively – 'little old ladies'. The *Daily Record* called the event an 'ordeal by battleaxe', while the *Daily Sport* reported gleefully that the Women's Institute 'gave Tony Blair the clap'.

The broadsheets were more thoughtful, debating how seriously Blair and his administration had been damaged by this
horribly public display of hubris and/or political naivety. They
agreed that this was a highly significant event in New Labour's
history. Jackie Ashley wrote a piece for the *New Statesman* which
came closest to understanding where Blair had gone wrong.
Members of the WI, she argued, were 'the backbone of the
nation, formidably hard to fool and, above all, they hate to be
talked down to'. She understood that they were 'unimpressed
by ingratiating smiles [or what Alastair Campbell called Blair's
'Bambi look'], fashion, rhetoric or the latest thing. They are
coldly impervious to spin.' She also recognised what a chastened
Downing Street was only just cottoning on to: that the audience
at the AGM had represented 'the people who dominate opinion
in many a village, church circle and small town ... compulsive
doers and voters'.[3]

Tricia Stewart and the rest of the Calendar Girls decided not
to listen to Tony Blair's speech; in preparation for their fashion
show they were enjoying a reflexology session elsewhere in the
Wembley complex. So they missed all the fun on the day the WI
made history.

The adventures of the Calendar Girls and the Tony Blair episode
invigorated the WI, though strangely, membership didn't start
increasing until 2008, after dipping to the lowest number,
201,663, since 1924. But seventy-five years of gradual decline is
a difficult thing to arrest, and even harder to reverse; though the
Movement had been hurled into the public eye in 1999 and 2000,
building constructively on that exposure took time.

Thanks to its soaring profile, opinion about the Women's
Institute was highly polarised at the beginning of the twenty-first

century. It was variously labelled a trade union for housewives, a reactionary outfit intent on destabilising the government (a sort of monstrous regiment of blue-rinsed women), a band of frustrated attention-seekers rather pathetically offering themselves up for sexual exploitation, 'a cantankerous, humourless, colourless mob of old hags';[4] a depressing anachronism, and the last refuge of the British frump. Every new article or feature about the WI unerringly relied for impact on the contrast between the stereotype in her twin-set and pearls and the surprisingly radical things she was suddenly doing. It got a bit wearing, and distracted from the real story.

The NFWI took most of this media fantasising in good part. It had had enough practice in turning the other cheek, after all. But when Matt Lucas and David Walliams portrayed a couple of Institute members in a *Little Britain* sketch on the BBC in 2004, the Board's patience snapped. Under a large banner emblazoned with the WI logo, 'Judy' and 'Maggie' were judging a jam-making class at the local village Show. They chatted happily with passing Conservative MPs, and cheerfully unleashed copious streams of projectile vomit every time a non-white or non-heterosexual person was mentioned in conversation. More gouts of sick followed when they realised they had just tasted some raspberry preserve made by someone who was married to a black man; still more when they faced a pot of marmalade apparently produced by one 'Sanjana Patel'.

It was intolerable to the NFWI that its members should be portrayed as racist, homophobic and rabidly right-wing. It doesn't collect data about the ethnicity of its membership, but ever since the Ugandan refugees were welcomed so warmly in the 1970s, women of every background – social, cultural, religious and political – have been encouraged to join their local Institute. Diversity of all kinds is a matter of fact in the modern WI. A formal complaint was made to the BBC, with a solicitor's letter mentioning infringement of copyright (regarding the WI logo) and the possibility of libel action. The logo was dropped, but Judy and Maggie survived. No such action was taken when Dawn French, Jennifer Saunders and Joanna Lumley created the satirical BBC sitcom *Jam and Jerusalem* the following year. Their 'Women's Guild' was unmistakably the WI, but not explicitly so. It wasn't as overtly offensive as *Little Britain*, either, but nevertheless managed to make an awful lot of WI members extremely angry – even those who claimed to possess a perfectly healthy sense of humour.

In 2005 a new WI formed at Leeming, located, like Rylestone, in North Yorkshire. Its founders (average age thirty-three) called it the Wythit WI, and it hit the headlines when it organised an Institute outing to a lap-dancing club, to inspire a course of 'pole-dancing pilates' sessions. The attention this drew from the press marked the beginning of a series of news stories which gradually changed in tone over a number of years from disingenuous admiration (barely disguised ridicule, in other words) to real appreciation.

The founding of the Whey Aye WI in Newcastle and the Jam Free Institute in Surrey both attracted attention in 2006, principally because their members looked unusually young and glamorous. Then, when Bramley Lite WI was set up in 2008, journalists were beside themselves with delight. The original Institute in this Hampshire village had been toddling along since 1919; it had twenty members, a seventy-year-old President and a very traditional programme. Its 'rival' was an alternative for women keen to push the boundaries of the WI. Bramley Lite opened with some sixty members when its provocative President, Emma Cunningham, was only thirty-five. Its first Institute trip was to the play *The Puppetry of the Penis*. Its members enjoyed a bracing variety of demonstration sessions, from burlesque dancing to life-drawing with a nude male model. Predictably enough, not many column inches were wasted on the other, more public, work of either WI. It's hard to blame the papers too much, and the NFWI was happy its constitution embraced alternative approaches to the work of the WI, even within a single village, and here was free publicity aimed at an energetic new generation of potential members.

Only half a dozen WI's now have 'Lite' in their name, but the youthful sparkiness of the pioneering Bramley is no longer a novelty within the Movement. Another innovation, the workplace WI, reached even further. For the first time, working women were able to join a local Institute without having to leave their homes to turn out – exhausted – for an evening meeting. If their employers agreed, the members of an in-house Institute could take an extended lunch break once a month to hold their own meetings. Employers did tend to agree: a WI gave the workforce a feeling of belonging and community, and that engendered loyalty.

The first workplace Institute was formed at the headquarters of the Cheshire Fire and Rescue Service at Winsford in January 2005. The former NFWI Chairman Helen Carey suggested the idea in conversation with the Chief Fire Officer: she was keen to widen access to the WI, and this seemed an imaginative way of doing it. At first, there were worries that the inevitable hierarchies of the workplace would permeate these WIs, and members would feel inhibited. A robust explanation of the egalitarian ethos of the Movement was usually enough to counteract any undue illusions of grandeur, and reassure the timid.

More workplace Institutes followed Winsford's – at Taylors and Bettys famous tea-rooms in Harrogate, for example, called the Fondant Fancies WI – and gradually the emphasis began to shift in the public's perception of the Women's Institute from affectionate (or cruel) caricature to frank interest. This dear old national treasure was somehow transforming itself into a novel and fresh-faced phenomenon. It's a tribute to the open-mindedness of the Board of Trustees at the time that the WI was encouraged to be so adaptable and accommodating. But the original founders are the ones who really deserve the credit for revitalisation: Meriel Talbot, the Nugent Harrises, Grace Hadow, Lady Denman, Alice Williams – they all recognised that for the Movement to evolve and develop in the future, its constitutional objectives must be simple, unequivocal and unassailably inclusive. In 1916, the Agricultural Organisation Society published a pamphlet about the part Institutes should play in postwar reconstruction, and advising WIs how to maximise their influence on society:

The success of an Institute must depend on the inclusion of women of all ranks in its scope. Their aim of mutual help and combined effort can only be achieved by a better understanding of each other's needs and interests and the points of view from which those are regarded.[5]

This is as relevant now as it ever was, and there's still plenty of room for pioneers.

Despite all the innovations of the past decade, at the core of every WI in the country is still the spirit of cooperation and mutual support (fuelled by a good cup of tea) that drove the Movement forward in its earliest days. No doubt today's sex-therapy sessions are enlightening, along with belly-dancing, strip-tease lessons, parachuting, abseiling and so on. But these are diversions, however welcome. Time and time again, when I ask modern members what is the most important thing about their WI, they say friendship. They joined as newcomers to the village – or, nowadays, the town and city – because a kind neighbour took them along to a meeting, to make friends. There they found sympathetic (if not necessarily like-minded) women of all ages and backgrounds with whom they could relax and be not mothers or wives, nor workers, but themselves. A friendly, non-judgemental atmosphere gave them the confidence to trust their own judgement, keep an open mind and stand up to be counted on issues they believed in. Courage is a gift of friendship, too. Nothing's changed about that since the day Stoney Creek, Ontario, was founded in the early spring of 1897.

I spoke to one woman who said that it was the WI that kept her going when her first and then her second husband died: she reminded me of the First World War widows who relied on their Institutes for the strength to carry on. Another reported the recent achievement of a degree in Quantum Mechanics, inspired by trips to Denman College with similarly inquisitive friends. A young mother explained how, when her baby was in hospital for a month, WI members delivered her and her husband an evening meal every night for the whole four weeks. In the agricultural community, the WI's spiritual home, you won't hear a bad word said against members: they have fought for increases from supermarkets to the milk price paid to farmers, supported farmers and their families through the BSE and foot-and-mouth crises, and staunchly attempted to hold back the tide of asinine bureaucracy galloping in from Europe.

In 2001, the NFWI surveyed a thousand Institutes to find out how much volunteer work members did. The result was 3,477,312 hours a year. At that time there were some seven thousand WIs in England and Wales, which factors up to over twenty-four million hours of freely given involvement in the community. And some people think the Big Society is something new.

A healthy sense of public spiritedness is not the only thing to have survived the vicissitudes of time, age and changing fashion within the WI. Still glowing with admiration for the Imperial War Museum's tapestry worked by Women's Institute members and completed in the late 1940s – *The Work of Women in Wartime* – I recently made an appointment to view another large-scale piece of needlework, stitched cooperatively like the first one, and of deep personal significance to those who created it.

In 2007, the Diamond Light Source in Oxfordshire went operational. It is the UK's national synchrotron, producing intense, precise beams of X-ray, ultraviolet and infrared light which can be focused on the molecules and atoms that build our world. The previous year, Science Oxford and the Wellcome Trust funded *Designs for Life*, an imaginative and somewhat unlikely project involving the Oxfordshire Federation of Women's Institutes. The idea was to invite local members of the WI to the brand-new synchrotron (which looks like a vast chrome doughnut, 235 metres in diameter) to meet Diamond Light scientists. The WI women asked the scientists questions about operational and technical details, and about the impact of their work on everyday life. In turn, the scientists asked the WI for their opinions on the ethics of this kind of research, and the social significance of scientific experimentation. To consummate this relationship between cutting-edge physics and the rural community, an art installation was commissioned for display in the foyer of the Diamond Light Source when it opened.

Anne Griffiths, a textile artist and member of Filkins and Broughton WI, was asked to supervise the design and creation of the installation. *Designs for Life* comprises thirty panels, each half a metre square and worked in different techniques with fabrics, embroidery silks, wools, wire, sequins and other haberdashery. The basis for each panel's design was a magnified image of something likely to be examined through the synchrotron – the HIV virus, for example, or a DNA fingerprint. Students at Oxford and Cherwell Valley College helped translate the images into artistic terms; Anne suggested the materials and techniques, and every WI member in Oxfordshire – as well as every scientist at the Diamond Light Source – contributed at least one stitch to the result.

The panels are beautiful, and inexplicably moving. Their colours and textures sing with energy, but sometimes it's a poignant song. A WI member who worked on the panel representing CJD (Creutzfeldt-Jakob Disease) chose to do so because her husband suffered from Alzheimer's, and research suggests the two diseases affect the brain in similar ways. She felt it brought her closer to understanding – almost befriending – her husband's enemy. Two of the panels, worked in exuberant pinks and greens, are of breast cancer cells. Another shows the confused scribble of threads and spaces behind osteoporosis. A nurse working with vulnerable elderly patients chose the flu virus (lime-green and menacing). My favourite panel looks like a display of adorable little rainbow-coloured caterpillars, each one knitted and wiggly, like a toddler's toys. They are cancer chromosomes.

Like the war-work tapestry, *Designs for Life* is so much more than the sum of its parts. It was born of a desire for acknowledgement and understanding between two sections of society whose work was mutually unfamiliar; it is stunningly accomplished and works both as a composite piece and as a series of separate works of art; yet one never forgets that, on a micro level, it's been created from thousands upon thousands of single stitches, like atoms, by hundreds of different people in cooperation.

The installation went on tour soon after it was finished – again, like the war-work tapestry – but is now permanently on display at its proper home, an uplifting fusion of traditional domestic craft and the edgiest of scientific innovation. The art is just as awesome as the science.

The year 2008 was something of an *annus mirabilis* for the WI, for several reasons. Its membership felt united in adversity, after a hugely unpopular decision to raise the annual subscription from £22 to £26 and to make *WI Life* (a reinvented version of *Home and Country*) a compulsory element of that subscription. This meant sending it not to the local WI for distribution, but straight to members' homes. They complained bitterly not just at the price increase, but at having *WI Life* foisted on them willy-nilly and being compelled to provide their home addresses, which would presumably be entered onto a central database and – who knows? – perhaps sold to all and sundry. They felt they had not been consulted enough about this new departure, and resented it.

Fortunately, the resentment did not result in mass resignations. Instead, WI members at grass-roots level were inspired to make the WI what *they* wanted it to be, and the media – now allies again, as in the old days – supported them. At the invitation of the WI, Sky TV announced a campaign, at the 2008 AGM in Liverpool, to find a modern 'W-Icon' to present a series of online lifestyle guides (including one, inevitably, on sex tips for the over-fifties). The billboard advertising the campaign was enormous – six metres by three – and was entirely knitted. It took four WI members 250 hours to make it, using fifty miles of wool. In the end two 'icons' were chosen: the young Emma Cunningham, founder of Bramley Lite WI, and Valerie Wood-Gaiger (sixty-seven) of Carmarthenshire.

A YouTube video on masturbation, pragmatically delivered by the WI, also caught plenty of attention in 2008, as did a serious investigation launched by Jean Johnson (sixty-two) and Shirley Landels (seventy-three) of the Hampshire Federation. They were moved by the victims of the so-called Suffolk Strangler Steve Wright, who murdered five prostitutes in the winter of 2006. Jean felt they should have been protected:

These girls were from all stratas of society. They were somebody's daughters, somebody's grand-daughters and somebody's sisters. If it could happen to them, it could happen to anyone. My concern was that if women were to work as prostitutes – and there will always be prostitution – then they should be able to do so in safety. I wanted to get prostitutes off the streets, where they have no protection. My fellow members agreed with me.[6]

With the backing of a Channel 4 film crew, Jean and Shirley planned a fact-finding mission to discover 'the perfect brothel'. They interviewed sex workers in Amsterdam (where 'men must wear condoms, which makes sense, and girls are regularly tested for infection'). They felt uncomfortable, however, that girls were expected to advertise themselves by posing at street windows. At the Moonlite Bunny Ranch in Nevada, 'the girls were standing in line like we used to at school for selection in the hockey or football team. Apparently men came from all over the world, they've even got a helicopter pad ... All in all, it really wasn't something we would want in Hampshire.'[7] New Zealand came out best, where the girls worked from 10 a.m. to 7 p.m. five days a week, and cooperatively owned their own brothel.

Sadly, Shirley died in October 2008, but Jean continued her campaign for safer conditions for sex workers, with the full support of her Federation and the gratitude of the English Collective of Prostitutes.

All this activity paid dividends in spreading the word about the WI. Membership numbers steadily increased from 2007 onwards. Some of the most enthusiastic members of all were those from brand-new Institutes. More and more were opening in urban neighbourhoods, including Manchester, Leeds, Sheffield and Birmingham, and in London at Fulham, Shoreditch (the 'Shoreditch Sisters') and Borough (the 'Borough Belles'). They often meet in pubs, just as many of the earliest WIs did in the 1920s, and concentrate on traditional crafts like knitting and cookery to attract their clientele.

In 2009 the first university-based WI opened, at Goldsmith's College in New Cross, London. I've met four of the founder members – now veterans at twenty-one or twenty-two – and their loyalty to the Movement is fierce. With the help of their WI Adviser (what used to be the VCO) Goldsmith's WI does everything a WI should in terms of administration: they organise speaker meetings, demonstrations, outings and parties; they support one another through emotional or academic crises; and they feel utterly committed to the ethos of the Movement, with which they are happy to comply. They appreciate its feminist heritage (several have grandmothers who are members – and one persuaded her non-member granny to join), and they value the inspiration and mutual support to be found in the WI. Most of their boyfriends are keen to join, and feel genuinely disgruntled to be barred from such a vital and inherently *interesting* organisation (their word).

The young women at Goldsmith's told me that hardly a month goes by without an enquiry from some student somewhere about setting up an Institute at another college or university. King's College in London has one, as do universities in Newcastle, Reading, Brighton and Middlesex. More are in the pipeline.

Part of the attraction for impecunious student members must be the practical benefit of making and baking things yourself, and belonging – in this new age of austerity – to an organisation so wholeheartedly committed to environmental awareness and sustainable living. Making do and mending has become fashionable again, even necessary, and self-reliance is an achievable ideal. That's why older WI members are being welcomed into schools to teach pupils knitting, or into clinics where they can talk about childcare and creating a family life to apprehensive young mothers who have no experience of either. The WI Movement was founded to combat the isolation of Canada's backwoods, and Britain's scattered, forgotten villages;

now it serves just as well in bringing together lonely city dwellers to create warm and loyal communities of active, responsible women.

Perhaps nothing's really changed at all.

On 1 January 2010, the Movement launched its new logo. Out went the old familiar tree of life, its badge for thirty years; in came a neat, uncluttered 'WI', with the strapline 'Inspiring Women'. The words 'Women's Institute' are no longer used in full. And the NFWI is big business now: related enterprises have taken over the running of the old WI markets, publishing, and selling Institute-related merchandise; there's a WI Moodle – an 'online learning environment' with training and features for members – and constant press releases about new campaigns, new Institutes, new opportunities, new initiatives.

All this is inevitable, and the WI has to adapt and go with the (frenetic) flow. But it would be desperately sad, and such a waste of its heritage, if the WI ever became too clean and shiny. Homogeneity is not what it's all about. When it was founded, essentially as a networking tool, its value was in drawing different, even unlikely, people together: women who might not ordinarily have met, and who gave each other strength and confidence. It empowered them. The impact of the organisation – 'the most important body formed during the twentieth century'[8] – was organic and broad-based. Too many young WIs, or metropolitan WIs, or even student WIs, without integration with more 'normal' WIs, will defeat the object.

For good or ill, it's a fact that even now there's a particularly keen spirit of allegiance in any organisation exclusively for women. There's still an air of sanctuary in women meeting together without men, a loosening of the shoulders and a slightly heady feeling of being off duty. That should be enough for the WI. It is crucial that members physically meet with one another, and are not just blogging or tweeting or posting things online. Personal contact with friends and communities is an essential part of any functioning society. We need it. The Facebook generation might find they need it more and more. So the WI is as necessary now as it ever was.

It is clear that at certain periods in its history the WI appears to have lost its way. No doubt there are problems ahead. But it was never in danger of collapsing, and it won't for a very long time because at its core, working quietly and behind the scenes, are the women for whom and by whom it was created. Grace Hadow's supportive 'sisters' are still meeting together in villages and towns across the country to make the world a better place.

A few summers ago, a number of WI members in Gloucestershire heard about an event coming up in Cheltenham, and decided to take part. It was a protest march happening the next weekend, about the closure of small local hospitals. Gill Thomas was County Chairman at the time, and when someone from Birdlip and Brimpsfield phoned to ask if she would join them, she agreed – though slightly reluctantly. She worked hard enough for the WI during the week; it seemed a bit much to have to give up a precious free Saturday too.

Gill is too young to have enjoyed the golden age of protest marches in the 1960s and 1970s: this would be her first. When the twenty-odd WI members turned up at the rallying point that Saturday morning, they were mortified to realise they didn't have anything to wave. Thousands of people were there, and the trades unions had the most beautiful, dignified banners. Others had sheets with painted slogans on them, or carefully lettered placards. All Gill and her friends had was a couple of printed signs from the NFWI pasted onto some corrugated plastic. Not even a stick to mount them on: they had to hold them up awkwardly, while they shuffled – you couldn't call it marching – through the suburbs of the town.

Gill felt embarrassed. Here she was, with an insignificant-looking group of women of a certain age trying to make their heartfelt protest heard, but completely overwhelmed by louder voices, greater numbers and clearer messages. One of her companions had an idea. Why not start singing? Fine – but what on earth would be appropriate? With uncertain voices, and no confidence, a few of them started 'Jerusalem'. Gill joined in, and soon the whole contingent was singing Parry's anthem, the signature tune of the WI – and with conviction.

Then, a remarkable thing happened. As the march progressed towards the centre of Cheltenham, those standing next to the WI women began to sing along, and those standing next to *them*, and so on – until everyone, as far as the eye could see, was singing 'Jerusalem'.

Women have a voice, and whenever they speak together, they are heard. The WI had taught Gill that in theory; now she *knew* it.

Notes

1 The Beginnings

1 Janet Lee's daughter quoting an early critic of the Canadian WI. Ambrose, *For Home and Country*, 28.

2 The indomitable Mrs Rigby did not become a member of the Women's Institute until after this assault on Mr Churchill (see Chapter 2), but as she would be the first to assert: once a WI member, always a WI member.

3 The farmhouse in which Adelaide was born, known as the Adelaide Hunter Hoodless Homestead, is now a museum dedicated to her memory and run by the Federated Women's Institutes of Canada.

4 MacDonald, 'The Angel in the House', 23.

5 *Ontario WI Story*, 16.

6 These are the official dates, listed by the Canadian state government; in fact WI activities appear to have begun in Whitby and Kemble a year or even two before they came into administrative existence, according to historian Linda Ambrose.

7 Courtney, *Countrywomen in Council*, 123.

8 Davies, *Grain of Mustard Seed*, 24–5.

9 *Times*, 1 July 1897, 6.

10 Hammond, *Village Labourer*, 62–3.

11 The satirical periodical *Punch* was especially keen on the subject, accompanying its discussions from the 1850s onwards with suitably unflattering cartoons of surplus women.

12 Pratt, *Organisation of Agriculture*, 250.

13   *Times*, 24 May 1911, 5.

14   Ibid.

2 Taking Root

1   Minute Book of the Llanfairpwll Women's Institute, 1915–16. Department of Manuscripts and Archives, University of Bangor (ref. Bangor 11503).

2   *Home and Country*, January 1927.

3   British Columbia Department of Agriculture, *Women's Institute Quarterly*, vol. 1, no. 3 (April 1916), 106. Quoted in Stamper, 'Voluntary Action', 1.

4   I am indebted to Professor Linda Ambrose, Madge Watt's biographer, for details of Madge's life.

5   Robins, 'A New View of Country Life', 588.

6   Fieldhouse, *A History of Modern British Adult Education*, 26.

7   NFWI Archive 5FW1/H/5.

8   Quoted in Davies, *Grain of Mustard Seed*, 49.

9   *Home and Country*, January 1949.

10 *North Wales Chronicle*, 18 June 1915.

11 Minute Book of the Llanfair P9 Women's Institute, 1915–16.

12 NFWI Archive 5FWI/B/2/1/29.

13 Quoted in Robertson Scott, *Story of the Women's Institute Movement*, 37.

14 Ibid., 31.

15 *Home and Country*, January 1949.

16 From an article by H. Duncan Hall on 'Women's Institutes and the Workers' Educational Association' (*Home and Country*, June 1922); quoted in Stamper, 'Breaking Down Social Barriers', 19.

17 NFWI Archive 5FWI/H/5 (Mary B. Strachan's reminiscences).

18 5FWI/H/20 (from *Journal of the Board of Agriculture*, vol. XXV, no. 7 (Oct. 1918)).

19 Deneke, *Grace Hadow*, 54–5.

20 *The Landswoman*, January 1918.

21 *Times*, 11 March 1918, 5.

22 NFWI Archive 5FWI/H/5 (Mary B. Strachan's reminiscences).

23 The uniform was a short-lived feature of the WI; see Chapter 5 for a description of its limited charms.

24 Watt and Lloyd, *The First Women's Institute School*, 107–8.

25 Alice Williams founded Deudraeth WI in Wales in 1916, when she was already well known as a dramatist, a tireless worker for the welfare of wounded soldiers, and a stalwart of the Lyceum Club for women in the arts and professions (much along the lines of London gentlemen's clubs but less exclusive and more homely). She was also an ardent contributor, under the Bardic name of Alys Meirion, to eisteddfods far and wide.

3 The Women Carry On

1 Matthew 7: 16.

2 Report of the AGM, October 1917, quoted in Stamper, 'Countrywomen in Action', 1.

3 Courtney, *Countrywomen in Council*, 49.

4 Louisa ('Lil') Wilkins, *née* Jebb (d. 1929), was a remarkable woman: the first to study Agriculture at Cambridge, a professional bailiff, intrepid traveller, champion of the Small Holdings Movement, writer and consultant on agricultural and horticultural education, a wife and mother. Her sister Eglantyne Jebb was a founder of the Save the Children Fund.

5 *The Landswoman*, April 1918. This was not the only one of Janet Begbie's poems to be published, but she was neither as prolific nor (perhaps undeservedly) as well known as her husband Harold (1871–1929), a farmer turned journalist, writer and poet.

6 *The Landswoman*, November 1918.

7 *Home and Country*, October 1941 (remembering 1917).

8 *The Landswoman*, September 1918.

9 Ibid.

10 Walton, *A Quarter of a Century of Women's Institutes in East Sussex*, 5 (quoting Caroline Huddart).

11 *The Landswoman*, February 1918.

12 Ibid., September 1918.

13 NFWI Archive 5FWI/H/30.

14 Ibid., 5FWI/B/2/1/29.

15 *Journal of the Board of Agriculture*, vol. XXV, no. 7 (October 1918).

16 NFWI, *Speaking Out: A Public Affairs Handbook* (updated annually), quoted in Stamper, 'Countrywomen in Action', 4.

17 Quoted in ibid.

18 Women's Library, London Metropolitan University, GB/106/7/AHW/H1.

19 *The Landswoman*, June 1918.

20 Robins, 'A New View of Country Life', 585.

4 Golden Eagle

1 Lady Denman's friend Neville Lytton, quoted in Huxley, *Lady Denman*, 132. I have relied heavily throughout this chapter on Gervas Huxley's sensitive biography. It's the only full study of Trudie Denman's life to have been published.

2 Butler, *The Cecils*, 28.

3 Huxley, *Lady Denman*, 25.

4 *Punch* (Melbourne, Australia), 23 November 1911.

5 Huxley, *Lady Denman*, 43–4.

6 The film was shot by the silent-movie pioneer Raymond Longford, and is preserved at the National Film and Sound Archive of Australia (title no. 9382).

7 *Leader* (Melbourne), 16 May 1914.

8 Huxley, *Lady Denman*, 70.

9 Ibid.

10 *Home and Country*, July 1924.

11 Nancy Tennant, quoted in Dudgeon, *Village Voices*, 99.

12 NFWI Archive 5/FWI/H/34.

13 *Home and Country*, November 1928.

14 Ibid., June 1923.

15 Gertrude Anson, quoted in Stamper, 'The 1920s NFWI Organiser', 1.

16 *Home and Country*, June 1946, on the occasion of Trudie's resignation from the NFWI.

17 Ibid.

5 Marthas, Marys, Pigeons and Crows

1   Grace Hadow quoted in *Home and Country*, July 1926.

2   Dudgeon, *Village Voices*, 19.

3   *Home and Country*, February 1924.

4   NFWI Archive 5FWI/H/23.

5   Ibid., 5FWI/H/10.

6   According to a report in *The Times*, 25 September 1925, 15.

7   *Home and Country*, November 1928.

8   Ibid., April 1933.

9   Ibid., December 1928.

10   Ibid., September 1935.

11   'Boo-Hoo' ('You've got me crying for you') was one of Guy Lombardo and the Royal Canadians' most famous hits. Lombardo was nicknamed 'the King of Corn', and the lyrics of 'Boo-Hoo' are almost completely meaningless. 'Red Sails in the Sunset' (slightly more romantic) was also recorded by Lombardo; its popularity endured much longer than that of 'Boo-Hoo'.

12   Stamper, 'Countrywomen in Action', 3.

13   NFWI Archive 5FWI/H/5.

14   Goodenough, *Jam and Jerusalem*, 18.

15   *Home and Country*, January 1935.

16   Ibid., February 1925.

17   Ibid., August 1936.

18   East Sussex County Record Office 100/3/1; *Home and Country*, January 1931.

19   *Home and Country*, September 1928.

20   NFWI Archive 5FWI/H/30.

21   NFWI Head Office Records, File 104.

22   NFWI Archive 5FWI/A/3/75.

23   *The Landswoman*, September 1918.

24   NFWI Archive 5FWI/H/5.

25   Ibid., 5FWI/A/3/75.

26   Delafield, *Diary of a Provincial Lady*, 190–2.

6 Change the World in an Afternoon

1 *Western Morning News and Mercury*, 1927; quoted in Andrews, *The Acceptable Face of Feminism*, 22.

2 Stamper, 'The 1920s NFWI Organiser', 1.

3 *Folklore*, vol. 45, no. 2 (June 1934), 192.

4 *Women's Institute Programmes* (NFWI), June 1937.

5 *Home and Country*, May 1937.

6 Ibid., July 1937.

7 Hampton, *Joyce and Ginnie*, 45.

8 *Home and Country*, June 1928.

9 A 1925 advertisement, reproduced in Robertson Scott, *Story of the Women's Institute Movement*.

10 *Home and Country*, April 1932.

11 I am indebted to Lynne Thompson for the story of Nurse Walton.

12 East Sussex County Record Office, 47/2/3.

13 NFWI Archive 5FWI/H/4.

14 Ibid.

15 *Times*, 20 May 1936, 17.

16 *Times.*, 23 May 1931, 9.

17 Gilbert Murray quoted in *Home and Country*, June 1932.

18 From the 1940s until now, however, the relationship between the WI and the ACWW has been close and supportive. Dorothy Drage of Criccieth dreamt up the idea of members donating at least a penny a year – 'pennies for friendship' – for welfare projects abroad, and WIs across the UK have welcomed foreign members to their meetings and their homes. They are similarly welcomed on their own travels abroad, and everyone spreads the word of women's cooperation and empowerment.

7 Mum's Army

1 McCall, *Women's Institutes*, 31.

2 *Home and Country*, August 1939.

3 Ibid., November 1934.

4 Ibid., April 1936.

5 The WVS became the Women's Royal Voluntary Service in 1966

in recognition of its sterling work for those needing help in communities all over the country. The WI was originally assured that it had been formed for the duration of the war only. Despite a few initial hiccups, the two organisations have worked perfectly well side by side since the war.

6   On the National Executive before the war, Hilda Chamberlain was one of the most urgent spokeswomen for peace and the power of empathy between nations.

7   *Home and Country*, November 1938.

8   *Times*, 1 January 1940, 9.

9   Ibid., 8 October 1941, 2.

10 Dudgeon, *Village Voices*, 80.

11 Ibid.

12 BBC broadcast given on 6 June 1941, quoted in Dudgeon, *Village Voices*, 93.

13 I am indebted to Lynne Thompson for sight of the Crofton logbook.

14 *Dorset Federation of Women's Institutes War Record Book 1939–1945*, Dorset History Centre, W 19/1.

15 Quoted in Walton, *A Quarter of a Century*, 33–4.

16 NFWI Archive 5FWI/A/3/075.

17 *Home and Country*, March 1941.

18 Ibid., September 1942.

19 Ibid., January 1939.

20 Quoted in Ridley, *Genome*, 292–3.

21 NFWI Evacuation Survey, December 1939.

22 NFWI, *Town Children through Country Eyes*, 20–1.

23 Bondfield, *Our Towns*, xi.

24 The proceedings of the AGM are recorded in *Home and Country*, July 1943.

25 *Home and Country*, October 1940.

26 Quoted by the NFWI's delegate at the conference; see Dudgeon, *Village Voices*, 96.

27 *Times*, 8 August 1942, 5.

28 Ruth Audis papers, private collection.

29   *Home and Country*, July 1942.

30   I'm indebted to Rose Graham for this Suffolk reminiscence.

31   Trudie Denman's resignation speech, quoted in Huxley, *Lady Denman*, 182.

8 Halibut Hall and the Revolutions

1   *Home and Country*, November 1947.

2   Ibid., November 1957. A later recipe features 'snail syrup', made by shelling 12 snails, submerging them (still alive) in some sugar, and then hanging them up in a muslin bag so the delicious syrup can drip through (contributed by Jersey WI to *The Times* on 23 July 1981).

3   This wonderful logbook is still in the care of Bacton and District WI, and I'm most grateful to the members of the Institute, and to Rose Graham and her husband in particular, for making it accessible to me and giving me permission to quote from it.

4   Imperial War Museum EPH 4229. Acccession no. 67/55.

5   *Home and Country*, February 1945.

6   Ibid., June 1944.

7   Hon. Mrs Betty Asquith, writing in *Home and Country*, December 1950.

8   NFWI Archive 5FWI B/2/1/36.

9   Ruth Audis papers, private collection. This very engaging account was brought to my attention by Jack Richards and lent to me by the late Mrs Audis's daughter Marion Mullins.

9 How to Be Happy though Educated

1   *Home and Country*, July 1926.

2   Published as *Headington Quarry and Shotover*, ed. A. Coppock, by Oxford University Press in 1933.

3   *Times*, 22 August 1925, 11.

4   *Home and Country*, November 1944.

5   Reproduced in *Home and Country*, July 1934.

6   Livingstone wrote an article for *Home and Country*, based on his speech, published in December 1943.

7   Lady Brunner's speech is transcribed in Anne Stamper's excellent
     history of Denman College: *Rooms Off the Corridor*, 246–8.

8   *Home and Country*, December 1943.

9   Quoted in Stamper, *Rooms Off the Corridor*, 73.

10   McCall, *Looking Back*, 96.

11   The late Claire Emery, remembered by Mrs R. Root.

12   McCall, *Looking Back*, 92–3.

13   Ibid., 97.

14   It was only a brief aberration on the part of Rachel's daughters,
     one of whom went on to join her mother at the WI and became
     an electrical engineer. Both girls have been to Denman on an
     advanced driving course, and one of Rachel's granddaughters
     accompanied her on a history course. Even her husband has been,
     to learn dry-stone walling. I'm grateful to Rachel for her time and
     generosity in providing material for this chapter.

10 Not According to Schedule

1   Chairman Mrs Sylvia Gray in her valedictory speech, quoted in
     Home and Country, July 1974.

2   'Deidre Thimble' is a pseudonym.

3   This cartoon is framed at NFWI headquarters in London; its
     source is unacknowledged.

4   From the papers of Mrs Peggy Willatts, kindly lent by her son
     Roger Willatts and her niece Miss Rosalind M. Willatts.

5   Ibid.

6   Ibid.

7   From the collection of Rachel Root; the journalist's newspaper is
     unattributed.

8   *Home and Country*, February 1981.

9   From the collection of Rachel Root.

10   See Garner, *Extra Ordinary Women*, 81.

11   Quoted in Carey, *Bows of Burning Gold*, 128.

12   NFWI Archive 5FWI/A/3/91.

13   *Home and Country*, July 1971.

14   Opinions derived from correspondence published in *Home and*

Country, and from member questionnaires conducted (or seen) by the author.

15 NFWI Archive 5FWI/A/28.

16 Ibid.

17 Ibid.

18 *Home and Country*, July 1967.

19 NFWI Archive 5FWI/B/2/1/104.

20 Ibid., 5FWI/B/2/1/154.

11 Bloody Marvellous

1 Headline in the *Daily Mail*, 29 July 2008.

2 *Home and Country*, July 1999.

3 *New Statesman*, 19 June 2000.

4 *Home and Country*, February 2004.

5 *Women's Institutes: their part in the reconstruction of rural life* (1916); quoted in Stamper, 'Countrywomen in Action', 3.

6 Quoted in the *Daily Mail*, 29 July 2008.

7 Ibid.

8 Robertson Scott, *Story of the Women's Institute Movement*, v.

Select Bibliography

Ambrose, Linda. *For Home and Country: The Centennial History of the Women's Institutes in Ontario* (Guelph: Federated Women's Institutes of Ontario, 1996)

Andrews, Maggie. *The Acceptable Face of Feminism: The Women's Institute as a Social Movement* (London: Lawrence & Wishart, 1997)

Blair, Tony. *A Journey* (London: Hutchinson, 2010)

Bondfield, Margaret et al. *Our Towns: A Close-Up. A Study made in 1939–42 with certain recommendations by the Hygiene Committee of the Women's Group on Public Welfare* (London: Oxford University Press, 1943)

Butler, Ewan. *The Cecils* (London: Muller, 1964)

Campbell, Alastair and Stott, Richard. *The Blair Years* (London: Arrow, 2008)

Carey, Helen. *Bows of Burning Gold: Celebrating 90 Years of the Women's Institute* (Skipton: Alfresco Books, 2005)

Courtney, Janet. *Countrywomen in Council: The English and Scottish Women's Institutes* (London: Oxford University Press, 1933)

Cowan, B. et al. *The History of Shottlegate & District Women's Institute* (Alfreton: Shottlegate & District WI, 2000)

Davies, Constance. *A Grain of Mustard Seed* (Denbigh: Gee, 1989)

Delafield, E. M. *Diary of a Provincial Lady* (London: Virago, 1984)

Deneke, Helena. *Grace Hadow* (London: Oxford University Press, 1946)

Doughan, David and Gordon, Peter. *Women's Clubs and Associations in Britain* (London: Routledge, 2006)

Drage, Dorothy. *Pennies for Friendship* (Caernarvon: Evans, 1961)

Dudgeon, Neil. *Village Voices: A Portrait of Change in England's Green and Pleasant Land* (London: WI Books, 1989)

Fieldhouse, Roger et al. *A History of Modern British Adult Education* (Leicester: National Organisation for Adult Continuing Education, 1996)

Garner, Gwen. *Extra Ordinary Women: A History of the Women's Institutes* (London: WI Books, 1995)

Goodenough, Simon. *Jam and Jerusalem* (London: Collins/NFWI, 1977)

Hammond, J. and B. *The Village Labourer 1760–1832* (London: Longmans, Green, 1911)

Hampton, Janie. *Joyce and Ginnie: The Letters of Joyce Grenfell and Virginia Graham* (London: Hodder & Stoughton, 1997)

—— *Joyce Grenfell* (London: John Murray, 2002)

Hesketh, Phoebe. *My Aunt Edith*. (London: Peter Davies, 1966)

Hinton, James. *Women, Social Leadership and the Second World War: Continuities of Class* (Oxford: Oxford University Press, 2002)

Home and Country (London: NFWI, 1919–2006)

Howes, Ruth. *Adelaide Hoodless: Woman with a Vision* (Ottawa: Runge Press, 1965)

Huxley, Gervas. *Lady Denman* (London: Chatto & Windus, 1961)

Kitchen, Penny. *For Home and Country: War, Peace and Rural Life as Seen through the Pages of the WI Magazine 1919–1959* (London: Ebury/NFWI, 1990)

The Landswoman (Blackheath, 1918–20)

Lloyd-Morgan, Ceridwen. 'Alys Meirion [Alice Williams] of Castell Deudraeth' (Dolgellau: *Cychgawn Cymdeithas Hanes a Chofnodion Sir Feirionnydd (Journal of the Merioneth Historical and Record Society)*, vol. XV, part IV, 2009)

MacDonald, Cheryl. *Adelaide Hoodless, Domestic Crusader* (Toronto: Dundurn Press, 1986)

—— 'The Angel in the House' (Winnipeg: *The Beaver*, vol. 66, no. 4, 1986)

McCall, Cicely. *Women's Institutes* (London: Collins, 1943)

—— *Looking Back from the Nineties* (Norwich: Gliddon, 1994)

Ontario WI Story: In Commemoration of the 75th Anniversary of the Founding of the Women's Institutes of Ontario (Guelph: Federated Women's Institutes of Ontario, 1972)

Price, Lance. *The Spin-Doctor's Diary* (London: Hodder & Stoughton, 2005)

Pratt, Edwin. *The Organisation of Agriculture* (London: John Murray, 1904)

Prochaska, Frank. *Women and Philanthropy in Nineteenth-century England* (Oxford: Clarendon Press, 1980)

Ridley, Matt. *Genome: The Autobiography of a Species in 23 Chapters* (London: Fourth Estate, 1999)

Robertson Scott, J. W. *The Story of the Women's Institute Movement* (Idbury: Village Press, 1925)

Robins, Elizabeth. 'A New View of Country Life' (London: *Nineteenth Century*, no. 505, March 1919)

Robinson, Jane. *Parrot Pie for Breakfast: An Anthology of Women Pioneers* (Oxford: Oxford University Press, 1999)

—— *Bluestockings: The Remarkable Story of the First Women to Fight for an Education* (London: Viking/Penguin, 2009)

Speaking Out: A Public Affairs Handbook (London: NFWI, published annually)

Stamper, Anne. *Rooms off the Corridor: Education in the WI and 50 years of Denman College 1948–1998* (London: NFWI, 1998)

—— 'Voluntary Action of a Membership Organisation – Countrywomen Organise Their Own Education' (paper given at a Voluntary Action History Society seminar held at the London School of Economics, 21 March 2000)

—— 'Countrywomen in Action – Voluntary Action in the National Federation of Women's Institutes 1917–1965' (paper given at the international conference '400 Years of Charity – a Conference on the History of Voluntary Action' held at Liverpool University, 11 September 2001)

—— 'Breaking Down Social Barriers' (unpublished, 2005)

—— 'The 1920s NFWI Organiser' (unpublished, 2005)

Stewart, Tricia. *Calendar Girl: In Which a Lady of Rylestone Reveals All* (London: Sidgwick & Jackson, 2001)

Thompson, Lynne. *The Promotion of Agricultural Education for Adults: The Lancashire Federation of Women's Institutes, 1919–45* (Cambridge: Cambridge University Press, Rural History series, vol. 10, 1999)

Town Children through Country Eyes: A Survey on Evacuation 1940 (Dorking: NFWI, 1940)

Walton, Marjorie. *A Quarter of a Century of Women's Institutes in East Sussex* (Hove: Combridges, 1947)

Watt, Mrs Alfred and Lloyd, N. *The First Women's Institute School* (Sussex: Executive Committee of the Sussex Federation of Women's Institutes, c. 1918)

WI Life (London: WI Enterprises, 2007–)

Williams, A. Susan. *Ladies of Influence. Women of the Elite in Interwar Britain* (London: Allen Lane, 2000)

Wilson, R. M. *Wife – Mother – Voter: Her Vote. What Will She Do with It?* (London: Hodder & Stoughton, 1918)

List of Illustrations

Drawings from Bacton and District WI's 'Operation Produce Logbook': Courtesy of Bacton and District WI

WI activities: *Home & Country*, April 1927, 1929, August 1933, October 1935, October 1937, December 1945; *Village Voices*, edited by Piers Dudgeon, WI Books, 1989

Denman College: Author supplied

Sam: *Home & Country*, January 1950

'Baker's Half-Dozen': Terry Logan/Rex Features

WI members at Westminster: National Federation of Women's Institutes

Shoreditch Sisters: National Federation of Women's Institutes

Acknowledgements

I have always thought it extravagant to claim that 'without [so-and-so] this book would not have been possible', but in the case of *A Force to Be Reckoned With* nothing else will do. Anne Stamper is the Women's Institute's Honorary Archivist. She was largely responsible for saving the organisation's records from a slow and mouldy death in a damp Oxfordshire garage, and ensuring their transfer to the Women's Library at London Metropolitan University, there to be stored, catalogued and made accessible to researchers like me. She is passionate about communicating the history of the WI, and as generous as she is knowledgeable. I'm hugely grateful to her. She was the first person I contacted when the idea of this book arose, and the first to read the manuscript. She corrected my blunders with patience and good grace; if any have slipped through the net it's entirely my fault.

Helen Carey, a former Chairman of the National Federation of Women's Institutes and something of a Renaissance woman, has been similarly helpful. She has an intimate knowledge of the workings of the WI, and embodies all that's most admirable about the Movement. NFWI General Secretary Jana Osborne has been unstinting in her support of the project, even though I am in no way connected with the WI. I'm indebted to her for permission to quote from *Home and Country*, the WI's house magazine. I am grateful to the current Chair Ruth Bond, to Karin Hickey and to all those staff members at NFWI HQ who have fielded enquiries and shared information so willingly over the past couple of years.

I must thank everyone connected with the WI at county and local level for helping me discover obscure records and forgotten stories, and all who responded to my request for personal experiences. There are too many to mention by name, but every contribution was valuable. Particular thanks must go to Beryl Bamforth, Taylor Bentley, Catherine Blaxhall, Sir Hugo Brunner, Jennifer Capper, Christine Clancy, Elaine Clarke, Mrs B. Cowan, Jess Cripps, Lady Anne-Louise Dalrymple-Hamilton, Sally Green, Diana Hackett, Emily Holbrook, Joyce Holmes, Catherine Jones, Susan Moore, Clare Mulley, Marion Mullins, Tracy Radcliffe, Jack Richards, Rachel Root, Tricia Stewart, Gill Thomas, Jan Walker and members of the Alderney WI Book Club, Margaret Watkins, Rosalind Willatts and Roger Willatts.

For pointing me in profitable directions I'm grateful to Heather Bartlett, Gyles Brandreth, Diana Evans, Anne Balfour Fraser, Janie Hampton, Ceridwen Lloyd-Morgan, Neal Maidment and Lance Price. Rose Graham told me about Bacton and District WI's 'Operation Produce' logbook, and generously invited me to see it, together with the Institute's canning machine, at her home. She also sent me a copy of the entire document. Lynne Thompson of the University of Exeter and Professor Linda Ambrose of Laurentian University in Ontario advised, encouraged, and lent me their expertise; Professor Mary Valentine, College of the Canyons, California – a rare American member of the WI – shared with me the fruits of years of research without a moment's hesitation. Her help has been invaluable. Anne Griffiths showed me around the WI's *Designs for Life* display at the Diamond Light Source in Oxfordshire (on a visit kindly arranged by Silvana Damerell), explaining its genesis and significance with understandable pride.

I have bothered so many people at County Record Offices, libraries and archives around the country. It might be invidious to single any out, but I'll do it anyway: the staff at the Women's Library, London Metropolitan University; the Bodleian Library's Upper Reserve; Dorset History Centre; and Alan Jeffreys and Sean Rehling at the Imperial War Museum.

On a personal level, I'd like to thank my agent Véronique Baxter at David Higham Associates and my editor Lennie Goodings for their confidence and enthusiasm; Ed James for his Wattock expertise (and forbearance); Richard James for his soothing cheerfulness; and Bruce for more than I could ever ask.

Index